ON THE PREVENTION OF WAR

ON
THE PREVENTION OF
WAR

by

JOHN STRACHEY

LONDON
MACMILLAN & CO LTD
1962

PRINTED IN GREAT BRITAIN
BY W. & J. MACKAY & CO LTD, CHATHAM

CONTENTS

AUTHOR'S NOTE

This is the third volume of a study of the principles of democratic socialism. Any such study which ignored the menace of nuclear war would be incomplete, to say the least of it. The first and second volumes were entitled *Contemporary Capitalism* and *The End of Empire* respectively.

PREFACE

TWENTY-FIVE years ago the decisive issues were economic. Either our highly-developed, industrialized societies would surmount their economic problems or they would fall into decay. Today the threat of nuclear war is the decisive issue. A failure to surmount this new crisis would lead not to decay but to summary destruction. So much will perhaps be readily agreed.

But the prevention of war, as distinct from its occasional avoidance or postponement, is a far more difficult matter than is even now realized. Many people, it is true, are tireless in reiterating that with the development of nuclear arms, peace has become indispensable. But those who most actively appreciate this truth are apt to overlook the fact that war is one of the most deeply rooted of all human institutions. They do not seem to realize that in asking mankind to do without war they are making a wholly unprecedented demand. On the other hand, those of a more realistic temperament—as they consider themselves—, who have noted the historical record, are apt to ignore the indisputable fact that to settle disputes between nation-states by the time-honoured method of war has become impossibly destructive. No one can blame mankind for failing, initially at least, to face the dilemma upon the horns of which the progress of physical science has impaled us. But the fact is that for our existing world of fully sovereign states war remains inevitable, but has become intolerable.

There is thus an urgent need for more comprehensive and more realistic studies of the nature of war in general, and of nuclear war in particular, than have yet been undertaken. To think that peace can be achieved without diagnostic studies of war, sustained by many workers and over many years, is as wishful as to suppose that cancer can be overcome without achieving an ever-increasing comprehension of the morbid condition of the affected tissue.

This is the explanation of the disscusion of current military doctrine in Part One of this volume. Captain Liddell Hart in his recent volume of essays *Deterrent or Defence?* (Stevens and Sons, 1960) has justly repudiated the hackneyed Roman maxim— 'if you wish for peace, prepare for war'. (What the Romans meant was, 'if you wish for victory, prepare for war'.) He re-writes the proverb, 'if you wish for peace *understand* war'. And this is profoundly true. It is only as and when we begin to understand the nature of war, in its military, political, economic and psychological aspects alike, that we shall be able to transcend it.

No doubt it will be thought presumptuous for a civilian like myself to discuss military doctrines and their consequences, as in Part One I do. I have only two lines of defence. The one, and much the slighter, is that my political fortunes have compelled me to study questions of defence, first as a British Secretary of State for War, and then as one of the defence spokesmen of the British Parliamentary Opposition, over the past twelve years. My second line of defence is that the particular issues here discussed are essentially those of nuclear warfare. As to those problems at least, my reply to those who say: 'What does *he* think he knows about it?' is simply: 'What indeed? But then, what do the Admirals, Generals, Air Marshals or anyone else know about it either?' In the terrible field of nuclear war, no one has either experience or tradition to guide him. We are all in the same boat: and the boat is on fire.

Journeys to the United States of America in order to discuss these issues with American defence experts were made possible by a grant from the Rockefeller Foundation (made through the Institute for Strategic Studies).

My indebtedness to individuals for help over this book is almost too great for me to record adequately. In this country, Mr David Astor, Professor P. M. S. Blackett, Mr Alastair Buchan, Mr Hedley Bull, the Rt. Hon. P. Gordon-Walker,

Mr Denis Healey, Mr Michael Howard, Mr Andrew Shonfield, Professor Arnold Toynbee, Mr A. D. Wilson, the Rt. Hon. K. Younger, and Mr Wayland Young have all read the book, either in whole or in part, and have made important corrections and suggestions.

In the United States, my indebtedness to the published works of such civilian defence experts as Professor Bernard Brodie, Mr Donald Brennan, Mr Morton H. Halperin, Mr Herman Kahn, Professor Oskar Morgenstern, Professor Thomas Schelling, Mr Henry Rowen, and Mr Albert Wohlstetter is acknowledged in the text and will be obvious to all informed readers. But in addition I have had the opportunity of discussions with these writers and with many others, including a series of seminars on Part One of the text arranged by Professor Robert Bowie at the Harvard University Center for International Affairs.

John Strachey

London, May 1962

The Stability of the Balance

I

Would the Survivors Envy the Dead?

Five Initial Ideas

THE invention of nuclear weapons has made general war
unacceptable. The word 'unacceptable' is used in the military sense: in the sense in which, for example, a commander
uses it if he decides that a particular attack cannot be undertaken because it will entail 'unacceptable' casualties.

To say that full-scale war has become unacceptable in this
sense implies that there is a sense in which it was acceptable
before the invention of nuclear devices. And this is so. However
horrible was pre-nuclear war, however deep were the wounds
which it inflicted upon the body of human society, nevertheless
it was practised. Pre-nuclear war proved to be (just) compatible
with the maintenance and development of civilization, and in
this sense it was, in fact, accepted.

The first contention of these pages is, then, that war in which
nuclear weapons are used to their full capacity is likely to prove
incompatible with the maintenance of civilization, and perhaps even with human life itself. Yet no other reliable method
of settling international disputes has been evolved. It is in this
sense that war has become intolerable while remaining inevitable. It will be submitted that this is our situation, until and
unless a basic revision of the role of force in the relation between
states is achieved. And this in turn may be found to involve a
revision of the way in which world society is constituted. First

of all, however, it is necessary to examine our original contention closely. For we may depend upon it that man will only remake the relationships of the nation-states into which the nearly 3,000 million inhabitants of the globe are at present articulated if he has to. If it proves even barely possible to survive as we are, we shall do so. Is it, then, certain that general or 'total' war, having become nuclear, is unacceptable because incompatible with human development and, possibly, even with human survival?

No one knows from experience what the character and consequences of full-scale nuclear war would be. Such an event has never taken place. The two nuclear devices, of a very early type, which were dropped on Hiroshima and Nagasaki in the closing days of the Second World War give only a faint and misleading impression of the consequences to be expected from the use of considerable numbers of multi-megaton, thermonuclear weapons. A good deal of evidence exists, however, which suggests that even the more extreme predictions of catastrophe might not prove exaggerated.

In order, however, to establish that the present organization of human society must be changed, as a condition of survival, something more than the finality of nuclear war must be shown. We must also show that there is a danger of such war. For the urgency of taking unprecedented steps in order to prevent it would not be great if we felt that its occurrence was in any case very unlikely. And this consoling view is, in fact, held by some of the informed thinkers who have devoted their attention to the subject. Marshal of the Royal Air Force Sir John Slessor, for example, has often made declarations in the following sense: 'With the advent of thermonuclear abundance total war has abolished itself' (*Survival*, January 1960—the monthly journal of the Institute for Strategic Studies). Evidence will be advanced to show that this immensely attractive view cannot, unfortunately, be relied upon. Sir John Slessor and many other experts who take this view are, it will be regretfully submitted, both too optimistic and too fatalistic. We shall be forced to the conclusion that on the contrary war, in becoming nuclear, has not abolished itself. War can only be abolished by means of our own purposive reaction to its threat. All that nuclear weapons in themselves can do is not to abolish war, but to abolish us. Hence the necessity for such enquiries as this, difficult, doubtful, and complex as they must be.

The degree of danger of the outbreak of full-scale nuclear war is often thought of in terms of the likelihood or the reverse of the outbreak of that particular war which we chiefly apprehend today (1962). This would be a nuclear war between those nation-states which are grouped round the United States of America and the Soviet Union respectively. As to the likelihood of that, the one thing which can be said without fear of contradiction is that the degree of danger of such a nuclear war will vary widely both in fact and still more in public estimation, even while this book is being written. In our apprehension and our ignorance we shall sway painfully between believing that such a war is imminent and predictable and supposing that now all is well, since the statesmen of 'East' and 'West' have achieved this or that measure of accommodation.

We shall consider the methods by which the danger of this particular war can be minimized. But the whole purpose and method of this book will have been misunderstood unless it is realized that something more difficult than the staving off, or even prevention, of one particular foreseeable war is at issue. In the nuclear age what has to be prevented is not this or that war but nuclear war itself.[1] Chapter 1 will attempt to evaluate the evidence as to the probable character and consequences of a full-scale nuclear war. The immediately following chapters will attempt to evaluate the probability of such wars[1] occurring if we make no basic changes in the character of world society.

Five initial ideas will, then, be submitted to the reader in the early chapters.

First, that nuclear war has become unacceptable as a method of settling disputes between sovereign nations.

Second, that this is because of a mounting volume of evidence

[1] The question of whether 'limited war', whether wholly or partially non-nuclear, can take place and remain limited will be discussed in Chapter 6.

that its consequences must involve, at the least, heavy social regression and, at the worst, extinction.

Third, that the risk of nuclear war's breaking out, while impossible to calculate, is not, unfortunately, insignificant.

Fourth, that it is imperative to make the most determined efforts to stave off the outbreak of nuclear war, even while the world remains articulated, as it is today, into sovereign nation-states; that there are political and also military policies which may make all the difference in this respect and which, therefore, it would be criminal folly to neglect: for their adoption may be decisive in gaining the time which the world must have.

Fifth, that nevertheless the prevention of nuclear war, which is a condition of our survival, will require a profound modification in our conceptions of the use of force between sovereign states, and that this in turn will imply far-reaching changes in the organization of the world.

Can Human Society Survive Nuclear War?

First, then, is it really true that full-scale nuclear war would be an unacceptable catastrophe? Our presuppositions, conscious and unconscious, as to what nuclear war would be like are neither unanimous nor necessarily self-consistent. On the one hand, it is doubtful how much the vast majority of the peoples of the world, or even of the peoples of the advanced, educated societies, have even yet realized the nature of what now hangs over them. On the other hand, a comparatively small, but highly articulate, minority, confined to a great extent, apparently, to the Western states, is so acutely conscious of the menace of nuclear war as to regard it as positively wicked even to examine the view that the use of nuclear weapons might not be the end of all things. Nevertheless it is necessary to ask whether or not there exist informed schools of thought which maintain that civilization in general, or their own societies in particular, might be expected to survive the use of nuclear weapons, even in full-scale, unlimited, war. There are such groups, and it will be useful to examine their views. For if after considering them we nevertheless maintain our original proposition that full-scale war, by becoming nuclear, has become unacceptable, it will then be unnecessary to examine the views of those who do not even attempt to maintain the more reassuring conclusion.

The Russian View

The body of informed opinion, it is useful to recall, which has in the past most forthrightly denied that even unlimited nuclear war would mean the destruction of their own society, has been the Soviet authorities. This question became, during the nineteen-fifties, a matter of controversy at the highest levels in Russia, and was decided—though only temporarily—in favour of the complacent view. (The reader may be surprised to find that in these pages Russian military doctrine is on several occasions discussed before taking up the discussion of our own Western doctrines. This is not because any special degree of belligerency is being ascribed to the Russians. In my opinion they are inherently neither more nor less militant than the rest of us. But it may be useful to remind the reader at the outset that the Russians do have military doctrines, and that sometimes, as in the case of the possibility of the survival of their own society in nuclear war, they are of the same character as those held by a school of thought in the West which is often accused of being 'warmongers'. I am, no doubt, partly provoked to adopt this order of exposition by the steady flow of communist-inspired propaganda which arrogates to communist societies exclusively the title of 'peace-loving states'.)

Towards the end of his brief period of power, in the early months of 1954, Mr Malenkov had said that a new war would lead to the 'destruction of world civilization'. Malenkov's view was, however, effectively challenged by his immediate subordinates in the Russian Government, and by April 1954 he had been forced to revise it. He then announced that a third world war would lead inevitably to the collapse of the *capitalist* social system. How much this 'deviation', as it was pronounced at the time to be, contributed to Malenkov's fall I do not pretend to be able to guess. Be that as it may, the official Soviet view, obligatory upon those who spoke on this subject, then became for some years that, while a full-scale nuclear war would obliterate the capitalist countries, the Soviet Union would survive, albeit suffering, it might be, serious damage.

Stated dogmatically, this assertion of relative Soviet invulnerability had no evidential value. It appears to have been based upon the view that the atoms, too, are class conscious. This is implausible. Their fissions and fusions may be expected to vaporize capitalist and worker, the just and the unjust, with impartiality. It might be rationally argued, however, that behind this Soviet assertion of relative invulnerability there lay special characteristics of Soviet society, either by way of military preparations, civil defence, or geographical or even social factors, which made Russia especially resistant to nuclear attacks. We shall postpone consideration of these factors until subsequent chapters, since they are relevant to the question of the balance of power at present maintained between the two alliances rather than to the question of the consequences of nuclear war. Suffice it here to say that although Russian military preparations in this field are undoubtedly thorough, as in every field, there is almost certainly nothing which she has done or can do to give her the sort of inherent invulnerability which her leaders at that time appeared to claim for her. (And this began, even at the time, to be implicitly admitted in the Soviet discussion of the doctrine of a 'pre-emptive strike', see p. 40 below, by means of which the scale of attack upon her might be reduced.) As to Russia's large size and her relatively low density of population, these factors undoubtedly mean that more and larger nuclear weapons would be needed to extinguish her organized social life than would be the case in smaller and more densely inhabited countries. But they mean no more than that. Again Russia's special social and economic system, it might be argued, would give her a high degree of social cohesion. But there again it is difficult to imagine that this factor could do more than increase the weight of the nuclear attack which would be necessary to destroy organized social life in Russia.[1]

[1] All this should be read without prejudice to the question of exactly how

In any case, the doctrine of special Russian invulnerability has not been maintained. Mr Khruschev, who superseded Mr Malenkov in the seat of power, appeared in 1960 to come round to the doctrine that nuclear war might, at any rate, destroy human society as a whole, not merely capitalist society. For example, in April 1960 he said, in Paris, 'Imagine what will happen when bombs begin to explode over our cities. Those bombs will not distinguish between communists and non-communists. . . . No, everything alive can be wiped out in the conflagration of nuclear explosions.' Again, in Austria in July 1960 he compared the human condition to that of the animals in Noah's Ark.

In some ways we on this planet are like the inhabitants of Noah's Ark. . . . If on this earth we are not able to live as living things were able to live in Noah's Ark, and if we start a war to settle disputes between states—some dislike socialism, some dislike capitalism—we shall destroy our Noah's Ark, the earth.[1]

These speeches are of high and hopeful interest. It would be wrong, however, to conclude from this that Mr Khruschev is admitting that the Soviet Union would certainly be destroyed in a nuclear war. He is merely admitting that she is not, certainly, invulnerable. Indeed, it is probable that both he and all Soviet authorities would still stoutly maintain that Soviet society, given the preparations which they are making, would stand a good chance of survival. And they might well be able to advance facts and figures to support this view. As, however, they do not (so far as I am aware) publish any material on this point, it will be necessary to pass to a consideration of another highly informed body of opinion which has expressed the view

---

vulnerable Russia in fact was to the particular level of attack which America could have launched upon her up to 1954. It seems as if Russia today (1962) feels at one and the same time much more the equal of America in nuclear power than she did, but that she is also much more *concerned* about the consequences of nuclear war. The chapters which follow will suggest that this would be a rational development of Russian attitudes.

[1] It is perhaps significant that both these speeches were delivered outside Russia. But the Noah's Ark speech was, according to Mr Edward Crankshaw, reported in the Russian press.

that *their* society at least might survive a full-scale nuclear war. For in this case quantitative estimates have been made.

The American View

These are the American defence thinkers, a highly articulate body of men.[1]

Some of these experts have expressed the view that the United States might survive, as an organized society, even a full-scale nuclear attack—at any rate, if she made sufficient preparations. They have done so primarily no doubt because they have genuinely reached this conclusion. But they have emphasized this contention, I think, in order to combat the impression that it was futile to make preparations against such an attack, and more generally, like their Soviet counterparts, to guard against the spread of a defeatist psychology amongst the American public. Hence their estimates of the consequences of full-scale nuclear war are unlikely to err upon the side of overestimating its fatal character. On the contrary, in citing their views we are citing the authorities least likely to confirm our original proposition that nuclear war is incompatible with the continuance of human civilization. If even their evidence in fact supports the proposition it will hardly be necessary to look further. In a word we are here adopting what might be called a 'Grand Jury' procedure.

It will be recalled that in this legal procedure (which has now been abolished in the United Kingdom, but is still used in the United States) the case for the prosecution is alone heard. For it is felt that the jury should have the opportunity to throw out the case even on that basis. In the same way we are here quoting exclusively the calculations of experts intent on showing that organized society might survive a nuclear war. If

[1] I refer not so much to officers of the three American Services or to officials of the Defense Department, but to the now considerable number of men who are employed, usually indirectly, by the Government or the Services, through the universities, or through special institutions such as 'The Rand Corporation', which is financed by a contract with the U.S. Air Force, to think and write about defence problems. There are also such men employed or associated with the major American corporations engaged upon defence work; others hold independent university appointments.

WOULD THE SURVIVORS ENVY THE DEAD?   11

therefore the reader comes to the conclusion that even *their* evidence proves that nuclear war is, in fact, incompatible with the maintenance of human society, there will be no need to cite the evidence of other scientists, and of laymen, who are intent to prove the unacceptability of nuclear war, and therefore paint a still more horrific picture of its consequences.

We may cite first the quiet, unsensational words of Professor Bernard Brodie of the Rand Corporation, taken from his authoritative work *Strategy in the Missile Age* (Princeton University Press, 1959):

Perhaps the most elementary, the most truistic, and yet the most important point one can make is that the kind of sudden and overwhelming calamity that one is talking about today in any reference to an all-out or total war would be an utterly different and immeasurably worse phenomenon from war as we have known it in the past. Also, and equally important, the chances of its occurring are finite and perhaps even substantial, the more so as we ignore them. One almost blushes to have to make such seemingly trite statements; but we are daily bombarded with indications, in the words and acts of high officials among others, that the points have simply not sunk home.

Professor Oskar Morgenstern (*The Question of National Defense*, Random House Inc., 1959), of Princeton University, a defence expert associated especially with the U.S. Naval authorities, writes more particularly:

We try to imagine sometimes, as well as we can, what the thermonuclear destruction would mean. But even writers of fiction have failed to give us a deep impression of the nature and extent of this catastrophe. Perhaps even they cannot truly visualize what it would mean to the survivors to see fifty, eighty, or a hundred million people killed within a few days or hours and tens of millions grievously ill, living without hope in hovels amidst poisonous radioactive debris.

We are at present focusing attention on the physical holocaust that a large thermonuclear, atomic war would surely bring to the United States. We recoil from that picture of death and destruction so unbelievably great. Our mind refuses to tell us that life after this war would be possible, or if possible, worth living. This may very well be so.

It must be repeated that these American writers are neither 'Left Wing' nor pacifist propagandists. On the contrary, they are dedicated champions of raising American defence preparations to a substantially higher level. In fact, Professor Morgenstern immediately follows the above passage with an impassioned description of the slavery to which, he considers, the American people would be reduced if they were either conquered by, or if they surrendered to, the communist governments.

He ends these passages with a temperate and humane reflection that neither the catastrophe of nuclear war nor the catastrophe of surrender need occur:

Neither should happen. Somewhere between these end points lie peace and understanding. That is what we strive for. Imperfectly. Inadequately. But perhaps with some hope.

These passages raise at once the question of whether surrender is not preferable to the risk of nuclear war. Surrender would presumably consist in one or other of the alliances which today dominate the world situation informing its opponent in advance that it would no longer resist by force the imposition of that opponent's will upon itself or upon the world. This question of whether or not it would be logical and rational, in view of the character of nuclear war, for either America (and her allies) to surrender to Russia, or for Russia (and her allies) to surrender to America, will be considered in Chapter 9. Here it may be sufficient to observe that the chance of either Russia or America taking this course is, to judge from common observation, minimal. Therefore we cannot in any case short-circuit our enquiry simply by advocating this course, unless indeed we are more interested in what we may happen to think ought to be done than in what can possibly be done.

Again these quotations from Russian and American authorities (and those which follow immediately) may cause the British reader to wonder why the discussion is carried on in terms of the possibility of the survival of American or Russian organized society. The reason is that while it is possible to hold the view that these societies might survive a full-scale thermonuclear attack, it is very generally agreed that there is no such possibility in the case of medium-sized, densely-populated societies such as Britain, West Germany, the Low Countries or France. Thus the British reader had better be faced at the outset with the fact that such societies as these, in the context of full-scale thermonuclear war (though in no other contexts) must be considered essentially as provinces of what is conveniently (if inaccurately) called 'the West'. (Britain, for example, is in this context a rich, important, highly developed and strong province: but a province.) Logically, therefore, our estimates and evidence as to whether organized society could survive a full-scale thermonuclear exchange should be given in terms of the communist and non-communist worlds as wholes. But no such evidence or estimates are available. So we must cite the evidence with regard to America. Moreover, all we need do is to add some proportion (perhaps as much again?) to the hypothetical levels of attack, of damage, and of casualties considered below in order to include Western Europe with America within the estimates. It should be noted that these levels of attack are hypothetical in the sense that they do not prejudge the question of whether either Russia or America could (in 1962) effectively deliver this weight of nuclear weapons upon its adversaries. But they are levels which their expert compilers regard as 'plausible'. Moreover, the point is of secondary importance, for even if neither contestant could effectively deliver these loads today, there is little room for doubt that they will be able to do so sooner rather than later. With these considerations in mind we may turn to further evidence from the American defence experts.

A quantitative estimate of the consequences of nuclear war is attempted in one of the studies of the Rand Corporation. *A Report on a Study of Non-Military Defense* (what is usually called 'Civil Defence') was issued in 1958, under the editorship of Mr Herman Kahn. This report reached the conclusion that the United States Government should consider undertaking an extremely extensive programme of shelter-building and other Civil Defence measures. It was argued that it might be possible by these means to preserve organized social life, and to rebuild a tolerable society even in the event of full-scale nuclear war. We may therefore be confident that the effects of nuclear attack were not overestimated, nor the possibilities of minimizing them underestimated.

Naturally the consequences of a nuclear attack would vary with the number and size of the nuclear weapons successfully delivered, with the amount of warning received, and with the degree of protection provided. In brief, the Rand report concludes as follows. Two 'plausible' levels of attack are assumed. In the first of these only the fifty largest American cities are destroyed (plus all Strategic Air Command bases). This scale of attack assumes the successful delivery of '1,500 megatons of fission products'; that is to say, assuming a ratio of 50 per cent fission to fusion products either 300 ten-megaton bombs or 3,000 one-megaton bombs, or in practice no doubt a combination of weapons of different sizes. On this scale of attack, and assuming no considerable Civil Defence measures, and further assuming a warning time for cities of between thirty and sixty minutes, the report calculates that 90 millions out of the 180 million inhabitants of the United States would be killed.

The second level of attack is assumed to destroy the 150 largest American cities. With no further Civil Defence measures such an attack is calculated to kill 160 million of the 180 million inhabitants of the United States. On the other hand, the report calculates that a relatively modest programme of fall-out shelters and evacuation would reduce the deaths to 70 million from the lower level of attack, and to 85 million on the higher level of attack. An extremely extensive programme of deep, blast-proof shelters ('plus arrangements for rapid entry') is calculated to reduce the number of deaths to 25 million for the higher level of attack.[1]

Several sections of the report then follow which throw a good deal of light upon what these experts suppose would be the

---

[1] It is thought that if 'strategic evacuation of all American cities' could be arranged, in addition to the full shelter-building programme, the deaths might be reduced to 5½ million.

conditions into which the survivors, in whatever number, would emerge. It is first of all necessary to note that they would have to remain in their shelters for some ninety days in order to avoid the intense short-term, and relatively local, 'fall-out', or radiation, which would otherwise prove deadly in many cases. It is therefore necessary to propose the stocking of the proposed shelters with food, water, sanitary facilities, etc. etc., for this period. When the survivors emerged they would encounter the long-term, and world-wide, radiation which would have been caused by the nuclear explosions not only of the enemy's attack but also by the nuclear explosions caused by their own forces' attacks upon the enemy. This radiation would be far less intense, but it would continue, though at a diminishing rate, for the rest of their lives.

Since the publication of this report, Mr Kahn has published a major work entitled *On Thermonuclear War* (Princeton University Press). In addition to amplifying much of the material given cursorily in the report, he considers the character of 'the post-attack environment'. He asks the question: 'Would the survivors envy the dead?' He writes:

It is in some sense true that one can never recuperate from a thermonuclear war. The world will be permanently (i.e. for perhaps 10,000 years) more hostile to human life as a result of such a war. Therefore, if the question 'Can we restore the pre-war conditions of life?' is asked, the answer must be 'No!'

It is true that Mr Kahn considers that if the measures which he advocates are adopted it need not prove to be the case that 'the survivors will envy the dead'. Nevertheless, the greater part of his readers may consider the fact that he has been impelled to ask such a question to be of more significance than the answer which he gives to it.[1]

[1] Compare Xenophon's account of the receipt of the news of the battle of Aegospotami by the Athenians: 'At Athens the disaster was announced by the arrival of the *Paralus* (this ship, Prof. Toynbee informs us, was the fastest sailer of the Athenian fleet) and a wail spread from the Piraeus through the long wall into the city as the news spread from mouth to mouth. That night no one slept. Besides mourning the dead they mourned far more bitterly for themselves. . . .' (*Xenophon*, Hellenica, Book II, Chapter 2.)

However, let us follow the calculation of the Kahn report upon this question of the degree to which the world would be permanently more 'hostile to human life' after a major thermonuclear war. The report calculates the amount and effects of the long-term radiation upon the basis of the delivery of 20,000 megatons of fission products. On the other hand, the report is based upon the successful institution, in the post-attack environment, of a number of complex and difficult measures for minimizing the effect of this radiation, involving such things as 'rationing' the amount of time any individual is allowed to expose himself. This means that the amount of time anyone could work, or be, in the open air would, in some places at least, have to be limited. Upon this basis the report finds that the effect of the long-term fall-out could be reduced to 1/100 of the level at which it would otherwise be. Granted the effective operation of these measures, the survivors would still be confronted with a rise in the incidence of bone cancer in themselves due to their increased intake of Strontium 90, and to genetic effects upon their children. The report estimates that the permanent effect of the former, and of other permanent ill effects of this increased degree of exposure to radiation, would be no more than a shortening in the average expectation of life by seven years. The genetic effects, the report estimates, might be to increase the chance of producing a stillborn, short-lived, or seriously defective child from 8 per cent as at present[1] to perhaps 12 per cent.

The report then turns to the problem which would be faced by the survivors in restoring both the agricultural and the industrial sectors of the economy. It concludes that these should prove feasible tasks, at any rate if adequate stockpiling and sheltering of key elements in both sectors of the economy had been undertaken.

[1] This is, presumably, a world figure, including the infant mortality rates of underdeveloped countries which may run up to something like 50 per cent. Thus long-term fall-out might be expected to cause a much more dramatic rise in the rates of developed countries such as Britain and America, where the existing rate is far lower.

Let us now make a few comments on the above estimates of both the short- and the long-term effects of nuclear war, made by those who claim that their own society at least might survive.

The first thing which strikes the layman faced with these calculations is that no allowance has been made for (a) pestilence and (b) mental derangement from shock amongst the survivors when they emerge after ninety days from their shelters, should such shelters be built and should they reach them in time. After all, they would, on these calculations, encounter at once many millions of corpses which it would have been impossible to touch for three months. Would it not be reasonable to suppose, not merely for this reason, but because of a general breakdown in the elaborate sanitary arrangements of urban society, that major outbreaks of pestilence would quickly and greatly reduce the number of the survivors and much enfeeble the remainder? Second, are we to assume a perfect rationality amongst the survivors? Might not the shock of such events be expected to drive a great number to every kind of irrational conduct, ranging all the way from lunacy itself to the constitution of armed bands bent on survival by means of preying upon their fellows, or, on the other hand, to contemplative despair and withdrawal from all mundane effort? Some, though not all, historical experience seems to suggest that this would be so. These seem to have been the psychological consequences of the break-up of the Roman *Imperium* at the onset of the Dark Ages. (On the other hand, they do not seem to have been the psychological consequences of the Black Death, see note at the end of this chapter.)

'The Earthquake is Not Satisfied at Once'

There is, however, little need closely to contest the views of either those Russians or Americans who contend that *their* societies at any rate would survive a major thermonuclear war. The possibility would no doubt depend upon such simple factors as how many and how large weapons were delivered upon each; upon the direction of the wind; upon whether or not the war could be cut short; or yet again on what self-protective measures had been taken. It would also depend, no doubt, on what had happened to the rest of the world. If, for example, the old European countries of high development had been blotted out, *en passant*, as is only too probable, successful reconstruction would be much more difficult. Again would India, China, the South American and the Australian secondary centres of development be intact (except for the long-term genetic consequences which all must suffer), and able to render succour, or would they have gone too?

This raises the controversial question of whether a nuclear war need necessarily be fought to a finish between the original belligerents with a high probability of the spread of its lethal consequences to the rest of the world. It is much too early in this narrative to take up this question. In general Mr Kahn's report and book have been quoted, not in order to attempt either to refute or endorse his particular conclusions, but primarily because his is much the best and most factual account of the consequences of nuclear war of which I am aware.

However, there is a further consideration which is, in my opinion, decisive in assessing the consequences of general nuclear war. No one can dogmatize as to whether a *particular* organized human society could survive a *particular* nuclear war. But then this is not the issue with which this book is concerned. The contention upon which its argument rests is that nuclear war is unacceptable, since it has become incompatible with the existence of civilized, organized human societies. But it is fully consonant with that contention that a particular society might survive a particular nuclear war. For if war, in its new nuclear dimension, survived also as the only known means of settling the disputes of sovereign nation-states, then nuclear war would recur, for the same reasons that war has always recurred in the past. And who can contend that the fabric of human society could hold together against the recurrence, every few decades, of nuclear war, with consequences such as we have just considered?

Yet what reason is there to suppose that, unless far-reaching changes are sooner or later made in the way that the human race is articulated throughout the globe, war will not recur as it always has done hitherto? Since the dawn of civilization there has seldom or never been a year when war, of some sort or another, was not being waged somewhere in the world. The periodicity of major wars has been more irregular; but there has seldom been more than a few decades between them.[1] Does anyone suppose that civilization, or perhaps even human life, could withstand the continuance of such a pattern in the nuclear age?

Historical experience is again relevant. The historians tell us that it is usually an oversimplification to suppose that this or that civilization was destroyed by some one catastrophic war. More usually society survived for a time the catastrophe which we now remember, and began the attempt at recuperation. But then new and consequential catastrophes overwhelmed it. Thus the major Islamic culture of the Baghdad Caliphate, then the highest point of human development west of China, was not snuffed out at one stroke by Mongol conquest in 1258. True the irrigation head works were broken. But they could be and were being repaired until successive waves of conquest descended upon the survivors, and in the end they lost heart and will. The same story seems to have been true of the great civilizations of Northern India, of the civilization of the once-irrigated part of Ceylon, and in many other instances. Experience seems to indicate that, not one, but a series of reiterated shocks has usually proved fatal to organized societies. Moreover, if the conditions generating the shocks are left unmodified, their reiteration may be expected to occur. It was no doubt this pattern of events which the poet Wordsworth had in mind when in the context of his experiences of the French Revolution he wrote the ominous line:

The earthquake is not satisfied at once.

[1] See p. 309 below for the possibility that even in a world organized as at present war in the nuclear age would be at least less frequent than hitherto simply because of the far greater dread of it. This is a real possibility, but who will deny that even infrequently recurring nuclear wars would be fatal to civilization?

The prognosis would therefore be profoundly unfavourable for the survival of contemporary societies even if, with their remarkable recuperative powers (see note below), they survived a particular full-scale nuclear war. If the conditions which have always hitherto bred wars are left unchanged, such temporary survival, however heroic, would be likely to be in vain. Thus it is difficult to avoid the conclusion that what is ultimately necessary for our survival is not merely the prevention of that nuclear war between the communist and non-communist coalitions which today impends, but the abolition of nuclear war itself.[1]

Note to Chapter i

It must be recognized that historical examples can be quoted which support the view of those who contend that large and well-prepared societies, though probably not the smaller, more densely populated societies of Western Europe, might survive a *particular* nuclear war. I repeat that we may recognize this quite readily, for this admission does little even to qualify the conviction that organized human society as a whole could not survive the recurrence of nuclear war at anything approaching the frequency with which major wars have always occurred in the past.

This said, it is useful to recall the remarkable, and apparently growing, powers of recuperation which human societies have exhibited both in past epochs and, more particularly, in the twentieth century. One may suppose that the great epidemics of bubonic plague, known as the Black Death, which scourged the later years of the Middle Ages were catastrophes of a comparable order of magnitude to a fair-sized nuclear war. In England, for example, the great outbreak of 1348 and 1349 is

---

[1] It is possible, however, to hold the view that there might be circumstances in which it was of the utmost importance for one or more of the belligerents to survive a particular nuclear war. Briefly this would be so if we continued to show too little concern, imagination and compassion to prevent another general war. For then the shock of such a war, fought with nuclear weapons, might be enough to rouse the survivors to establish a stable world society: that is, if there were such survivors.

said to have killed anything between one-third and three-quarters of the population. So this would be a disaster similar in scale to a nuclear war which killed between 60 and 135 millions of the 180 million inhabitants of present-day America. Yet English medieval society was not destroyed. Indeed, the chief effect recorded by the historians is the interesting one that the class balance between serf and lord was disturbed by the shortage of labour. (The Peasants' Revolt was occasioned by the repressive measures designed to redress that balance.) It may be said that the simple economy and society of the Middle Ages were less vulnerable to catastrophe than are our complex nation-states of the twentieth century. And this might prove to be the case. On the other hand, we possess incomparably better possibilities for social reconstruction than did the men of the fourteenth century. Nor has the twentieth century lacked experience of war-created catastrophes which, though not of a thermonuclear order of magnitude, are yet instructive.

We may cite three examples: Germany, Russia, and Japan. In the Second World War each of these societies was physically devastated, and had severe casualties inflicted upon its population. It is estimated that Russia, for example, suffered anywhere between 12 and 24 million deaths and in addition had something like 40 per cent of her production facilities destroyed. Germany is thought to have suffered some 4 million fatal casualties, while Japan had her major cities most thoroughly devastated. Yet in 1962, a bare seventeen years after these catastrophes, each of these three communities is unquestionably more prosperous, more productive and better organized than ever before. (Incidentally this seems to indicate that these remarkable powers of recuperation are independent of the social and economic systems of the societies concerned, see p. 303 below.)

Indeed, it has been argued that up till the invention of nuclear weapons the powers of recuperation of highly developed societies were growing much faster than their powers of destroying each other in war. This, no doubt, was partly because twentieth-century non-nuclear wars were, for some reason, markedly shorter than was usual in the case of earlier wars. But even allowing for this factor it seems undeniable that the two twentieth-century world wars did much less lasting damage to European civilization than, for instance, was done by some of the earlier wars of the non-nuclear epoch. The most striking comparison is afforded by German rates of recovery. Germany, in the sixteenth century one of the more advanced areas of civilization, took two and a half centuries to recover from the slow, but thorough, devastation of the Thirty Years War. The six years of the Second World War destroyed perhaps as much of her physical facilities, of her cities, of her means of production, communications and the like. Her 4 million fatal casualties, although they were, no doubt, a much lower casualty rate than that suffered in the Thirty Years War, were still no small loss. And in addition, Germany in 1945 was partitioned not merely into two states, but between the two world alliances or systems. Yet, in 1962, only seventeen years after the catastrophe, Western Germany has reached a higher level of prosperity than ever before. We tend to forget, in our dismay at the multiplied powers of destruction with which science has provided us, that she also, up to the invention of nuclear weapons, provided us with powers of reconstruction multiplied at least to the same power. But now nuclear weapons have apparently upset the balance between destruction and reconstruction. Civilization is now at the mercy of war to a far greater extent even than was the case when the creeping devastations and re-devastations of the armies of the Thirty or the Hundred Years Wars set back the rise of European civilization for generations. Even a single thermonuclear war would put the existence of organized human society into question. A series of such wars must surely end it.

2

What is the Risk of Nuclear War?

WE must now turn to the third of our original five propositions. It was that the risk of the outbreak of nuclear war,
while unknown, was not insignificant. This issue must be
considered, for if the risk were insignificant then the horror
and devastation which, as we have seen, such a war must cause,
would be no great matter. Moreover, we shall find that one
school of thought does in fact suppose that there is now little
risk of nuclear war, essentially because of its technical characteristics. On the other hand another school of thought believes,
on the contrary, that the risk is relatively considerable and may
grow, unless great care, intelligence and foresight, are devoted to
the matter by both sides. A comparison of these views will
inevitably lead us into the thorny paths of contemporary military controversy.

The Condemned Cell

On the basis of this comparison the book will make a series of
suggestions in the fields of defence preparations, disarmament
and international relations. It may well be that many readers
will consider these suggestions to be painfully inadequate. If
the consequences of nuclear war are indeed as black as they are
painted, and the risk of its outbreak considerable, ought we not
to demand immediate and all-embracing measures to deal
with its deadly threat? Either unilateral disarmament or the

immediate establishment of a world government, are often demanded by those who have suddenly realized the peril in which they stand. Such readers will have little patience with, for example, the measures for improving the stability of the military situation which are proposed in Part One.

It will be argued, however, that such an attitude is as mistaken as it is natural. True, nothing that is to be suggested in Part One can do more than procure us a stay of execution by nuclear war. But on the other hand, how much that is! The inhabitant of the condemned cell is ill-advised to despise a reprieve, even though only a full pardon will make him free again. In the same way, it would be particularly rash for us to spurn measures designed to increase the stability of the balance of power because it is undeniable that far more than these will be necessary to release us from that world-wide condemned cell which the human race today inhabits. Successive chapters of Part One will therefore contain a sustained remonstration with those sincere and passionate lovers of peace who see nothing but empty logic-chopping, or even prevarication, in the current discussions of the military 'postures' (as they are often called) of the two great alliances. Nevertheless the succeeding Parts of the book will seek at least to open up the discussion of those far more profound issues which must be faced before anything approaching a solution of the dilemma of mankind in the nuclear age can be achieved.

The Balance

Let us first enquire what it is that has so far prevented the outbreak of nuclear war. After all, nuclear war between the alliances of communist and non-communist states has not broken out. Something has staved it off for nearly two decades. Nor are such periods of peace between sovereign states or alliances unusual. In attempting to assess the likelihood or the reverse of nuclear war, we should enquire, then, why historical experience indicates not only that nation-states appear to have innate tendencies to go to war with each other, but also why they sometimes experience periods of peace.

It will be found that one at least of the ways in which such periods of peace have been maintained is by the establishment of what used to be called 'a balance of power', and is now, in the nuclear age, often and significantly called a 'balance of terror'. It will be further found that the present period of peace (in the sense of freedom from major nuclear war) has almost certainly depended upon the existence of such a balance.[1] A balance of power, or of terror, may exist either between two particular sovereign states or, as at present, between alliances of such states.

It has been usual in liberal circles to inveigh against the iniquities of basing a nation's policy upon this concept. If this arraignment were confined to pointing out that a balance of power between states or alliances has never yet, and probably never will, prevent the periodic recurrence of war, it would be justified. Historical evidence shows that such a balance invariably breaks down in the end. Then war recurs. But the object of all the efforts which have been made throughout modern history to establish and maintain such balances of power has not been to abolish war. It has been, partly, to postpone, to stave off, war. But it has also been to ensure, if possible, that one's own nation-state is not at a disadvantage when war recurs. Nevertheless it may have been hasty to disparage even such limited objectives as these, at any rate before any other and more effective method of preventing the outbreak of war had been discovered. Even in the nuclear age it may still be suicidal to abandon such a policy until and unless a more effective method of preserving the peace has been discovered.

In any case, the purpose of this chapter is not to suggest what ought to be, but to describe what is. And it cannot be denied that the world of the early nineteen-sixties is dominated by the fact of a balance of power, or terror, between two mighty alliances, with a substantial third section of the world

---

[1] The balance has taken curious and varied forms. In the early post-Second World War years it was, perhaps, a balance of American preponderance in nuclear weapons over against a Russian preponderance in conventional weapons, for example.

uneasily uncommitted to either camp. It is this world situation which must be appreciated in order to estimate the likelihood of unlikelihood of the outbreak of nuclear war. We shall postpone our consideration of the political factors which either help to maintain, or threaten to subvert, the present balance, although they are, in the long run, the more important. Just because of that the intentions of the leading nations of the alliances deserve separate chapters. And then we must take up the more general question of the inherent characteristics of the relations of sovereign nation-states.

The Military Factors

In this and the next chapters the military factors affecting the balance will be briefly described. For though less fundamental they are of special importance in the case of states equipped, for the first time in history, with nuclear weapons and thus capable of mutual annihilation. The following description of the 1962 military situation is not primarily intended as a contribution to the military doctrines of the non-communist or 'Western' coalition. For perhaps the single assertion which can be made with confidence in this connexion is that by the time these words are being read, technology will have altered the terms of the military equation in one way or another. Nevertheless the problem of maintaining the balance, and so surviving long enough to do something more fundamental, cannot today be discussed without reference to the military situation of the two alliances. The traditional, purely political, approach to the subject has become inadequate, unless it is informed by an appreciation of the military equation.

The main change which the advent of nuclear weapons has made in the traditional balance of power situation is indicated in the change of name, i.e. from 'balance of power' to 'balance of terror'. Beyond doubt the potential contestants are now much more frightened of each other than ever before. The question is, does this increased dread make war more or less likely? In other words does it increase or decrease, other things being equal, the stability of the balance?

The Optimistic View

There are two widely divergent schools of thought on this issue. We may, for short, call one school the British, or older, school, the other the American and Russian, or newer, school. The British view, which to a considerable extent was also fairly generally accepted outside Britain during the nineteen-fifties, was that the mutual terror which nuclear weapons inspired had markedly increased the stability of the balance, and so had greatly helped to stave off the outbreak of a third world war. We have already noted a statement of this view at its most sanguine, that of Sir John Slessor, made in the early months of 1960, to the effect that with the advent of thermonuclear abundance upon both sides, total war had abolished itself. But the fullest statement of this position was probably made by Professor Blackett in his book *Atomic Weapons and East West Relations*, published in 1956 by the Cambridge University Press. Professor Blackett wrote:

> It is becoming generally recognized that the danger of an all-out major East-West war breaking out is now quite small. This is certainly due in great part to the possession by both sides of atomic and hydrogen bombs, and consequently of their power of inflicting vast destruction on each other.

This estimate is reiterated in several passages of the book. And the conclusion is drawn that the British defence effort in particular, and the Western defence effort in general, should provide a minimum of resources in the nuclear field and should concentrate upon the provision of strong conventional forces. Professor Blackett wrote:

> Today strategical atomic weapons have not only cancelled themselves out and so made all-out total war exceedingly unlikely but have finally abolished the possibility of victory by air power alone against a great power.
>
> I think we should act as if atomic and hydrogen bombs have abolished total war and concentrate our efforts on working out *how few atomic bombs* and their carriers are required to keep it abolished. In the next few years I see the problem not as how many atomic bombs we can afford but as how few we need. For every

hundred million pounds spent on offensive and defensive preparations for global war, which almost certainly will not happen, is so
much less for limited and colonial wars, which well may.

The concept is often called the doctrine of 'minimum deterrence'. It will be seen that Professor Blackett was thinking
primarily in terms of the numbers and size of the nuclear
weapons held by each side. He was also thinking mainly in
terms of 'air power', i.e. of the delivery of the weapons by
means of manned bombers. Moreover, he goes on to base his
conclusion that nuclear war is most unlikely, as long as the
West maintains even a minimum of nuclear deterrent power, on
two further considerations. First he considers that any physical
defence of a nation's cities and population is unattainable. And
he reaches the at first sight paradoxical conclusion that this
impossibility of a physical defence, in the sense of the actual
warding off of an attack which has already been despatched, is
one of the reasons why the risk of nuclear war is so small. For a
potential aggressor will be *deterred* by the knowledge that he
too cannot prevent the return blow.

In all this Professor Blackett was merely expressing with
precision what most people, and not only in Britain, assumed
to be the situation in the nineteen-fifties. For example, Mr
Richard Rovere, an American commentator, put this reassuring consensus into vivid words. He wrote:[1]

'If the Russians had ten thousand war-heads and a missile for
each, and we had ten hydrogen bombs and ten obsolete bombers
. . . aggression would still be a folly that would appeal only to an
insane adventurer.'

In the nineteen-fifties such eminent and diverse authorities as
Sir Winston Churchill, General Gallois, General Gavin, Mr
Henry Kissinger, Mr George Kennan, Mr Dean Acheson and
many others were expressing similar views.

It can be imagined how difficult it was, and to some extent
still is, to controvert a view at once so authoritatively supported

[1] Quoted by Mr Albert Wohlstetter: 'The Delicate Balance of Terror', in
Foreign Affairs, January 1959.

and so comforting as this. For if all this was, and remains, true, then there is no need for the West to worry about the size and quality of its deterrent force, nor to spend vast sums of money upon it. If the power of even a small and not necessarily up-to-date nuclear striking force is so great that only a lunatic would incur the risk of having it launched in retribution upon him, then it is obviously folly to maintain a striking force four or five times as powerful. Moreover, in that case, the risk of nuclear war will be very small for the balance of mutual terror will have great inherent stability. It will be independent of the particular magnitudes of power possessed by either side, at any rate so long as both are above a low minimum. If we could depend upon it that this doctrine was correct, we should have to worry much less about the whole subject of nuclear war.

The Pessimistic View

But can we depend upon it? The reader will find that I myself believe that this doctrine *can be made* valid, but only upon condition that certain careful, elaborate and expensive military measures are taken, and maintained. Until and unless this is done the whole immensely reassuring and attractive doctrine of 'minimum deterrence' is, it is to be feared, open to serious criticism. In its original, unqualified form it has received such criticism and is now, in the nineteen-sixties, less generally held. It has been assailed above all by the military experts of both the United States and the Soviet Union. We must, of course, discount, to whatever extent we may think necessary, their particular 'interest' in the matter. These experts are, naturally, intent that their respective nation-states should be secure, come what may. Therefore they are bound to be critical of a doctrine which suggests that a comparatively modest effort in the nuclear field is all that is necessary. They are bound to incline to 'alarmist' views which suggest that great attention, and great resources, should be devoted to maintaining and developing the power of their respective nuclear deterrent forces. And this they do. However, let us hear what they have to say.

In the first place it is important to realize two comparatively recent developments. One is that few people will now (1962) be inclined to reckon the power of a country's nuclear deterrent force according to the size of its stock of nuclear weapons. The capacity to deliver these weapons is now considered much more important. For it is not difficult to possess a more than adequate stock of weapons. Their means of delivery, their capacity to penetrate the enemy's defences and, *in particular*, their degree of invulnerability to a previous attack by *his* nuclear striking force, are what are held to matter. The second development is that few people now suppose that either side would strike initially at its opponent's cities. An aggressor would be compelled to strike, with all his might, at the originating points (airfields, rocket sites or whatever) of his opponent.[1] For his whole hope of avoiding devastating retaliation would be to destroy, at one blow, his opponent's capacity to strike back. This is called 'counter-force strategy'.

This doctrine of 'counter-force strategy', as it is called, is clearly dependent upon the view that it may be technically possible for an aggressor, using the methods of surprise attack, to knock out almost all his opponent's capacity to retaliate. Blackett denied this technical possibility (op. cit., pp. 60-61). He considered that each side had too many bases, too well defended, too dispersed or too concealed, for there to be any question of a sudden surprise 'first strike' knocking the nuclear weapons, as it were, clean out of the hands of one or other side so leaving that side at the mercy of its opponent.

Mr Albert Wohlstetter, an American defence expert, in his well-known article in *Foreign Affairs* (January 1959) entitled 'The Delicate Balance of Terror' was perhaps the first to present, in detail, a carefully argued counterview. Wohlstetter argued that Professor Blackett and the whole school of thought which he represented were in error largely because of the

---

[1] The consolation to be derived from this fact for us, the inhabitants of these cities, is unfortunately less than might be supposed. For 'the shorts and overs' (to use the language of World War II bombing technique) of missiles thus aimed at airfields and rocket sites might with their primary fall-out kill a great many of us quite effectively.

discovery of how to make H-bombs of enormous power yet small enough to be carried on the nose of an intercontinental ballistic missile. (Professor Blackett had written in 1956 that this development 'seemed very unlikely', op. cit., p. 53.) This ominous development has taken place. Clearly, if no other, and possibly compensating, changes had been made in the terms of the equation of mutual deterrence, this would gravely affect the situation. For it might be possible for a power possessing a sufficient number of intercontinental ballistic missiles (I.C.B.M.s as they are called) simultaneously to deliver, with a warning time measured in minutes, one or more H-bombs upon all the airfields and rocket sites of its opponents, and so destroy his power of retaliation.

In practice, however, experience seems to indicate that this particular development is only one of several highly significant technical developments, *essentially in the means of delivery*, which are modifying the terms of the equation of deterrence, and so affecting, some in one direction, some in the other, the stability of the balance. Mr Wohlstetter seems, in restrospect, to have made too much of Professor Blackett's failure to foresee this particular development. (On the other hand, we should take warning from it and abstain from any dogmatism on the likely course of future technical development. For if a Nobel prizewinning physicist of the first rank, such as Professor Blackett, can prove wrong, what chance would a layman have of avoiding far greater errors?) What, it will transpire, seems to have happened is that a whole series of technical developments have first undermined the basis of the above reassuring view as to the inherent stability of the balance, but have also indicated to us ways in which it should be possible to restore and maintain that stability upon a relatively secure basis.

In the early nineteen-sixties, it is hard for the layman at least to controvert the views of the military experts (on both sides) who assert that it will be by means of careful, difficult and expensive measures alone that (short of agreed arms control or disarmament) a stable balance can be maintained. Let us notice at once what these measures might be.

Invulnerability : the overriding priority

The exponents of the reassuring view of 'minimum deterrence' had, partly, based their doctrine of the inherent stability of the balance upon the permanent supremacy of the offensive over the defensive. Blackett further wrote, for instance (op. cit.) :

> Reliance will presumably be increasingly laid—and by both sides—upon the stability resulting from the superiority of offence over defence, rather than the superiority of the offensive power of one side over that of the other. There is, of course, a possible difficulty about any policy which essentially relies on the supremacy of offensive atomic weapons over defensive possibilities. For there is always the conceptual possibility that the balance of destructive offensive power might be upset by a break through in defence technology. It is an odd situation where a drastic improvement of defence might have highly unsettling effects. However, the technical possibilities of such a break-through seem remote.

The exponents of the pessimistic view are not, however, primarily worried about a hypothetical 'break-through' in defensive technique. What they argue is that the very supremacy of the offensive may lead, not to stability, but to the exact reverse. This may be so if the objective of a potential aggressor should be, not the cities, but the airfields and rocket sites of his opponent. For if the offensive is supreme, and to the extent that he appreciates that all these airfields and rocket sites are vulnerable to his attack, he can be sure of destroying his rival without fear of retaliation. Still worse, he may come to feel that his *only* security lies in delivering such an attack. For until and unless he does so he has the terrible knowledge that his enemy might make such an attack upon *him*, and so destroy *him*, with impunity. Such a situation, in which both sides knew that they could destroy the other with impunity by striking first, and only by striking first, would clearly be a situation of maximum *instability*.

Such a situation would resemble, as was noted by both Blackett and Wohlstetter (agreeing at least on this), nothing so much as the stock situation of the 'Western' in which survival depends upon who is 'quickest on the draw'. Blackett, after arguing that such a situation of maximum instability is technically impossible, continues:

> However, suppose that I am wrong and that such an operation is a technically possible one for both sides. Then we get the psychological situation of a duel. The one who strikes first wins: the one who fails to strike first is destroyed. In order not to be destroyed, the West would have to strike first—that is the West would have to wage what would amount to preventive war.

He adds that it is 'an article of faith' in the West that the waging of a preventive war 'cannot be done'. In these passages Blackett seems to imply that because a particular view of the technical possibilities has exceedingly unpleasant connotations for the West, it must be false. This hardly seems to be good logic. Perhaps what he really has in mind is that it was foolish of the defence thinkers of the West to work out such a doctrine and so put it into the heads of the Russians (which may have been what happened, see p. 41 below). But if this technical possibility really exists the Russians would surely have seen it for themselves sooner or later. It is surely impossible to ignore the existence of this terrible possibility of extreme instability if there is any danger of its coming into existence and, above all, if ways and means exist, however elaborate and expensive, of averting it.

Wohlstetter defines the above situation of maximum instability as follows:

> Suppose both the United States and the Soviet Union had the power to destroy each other's retaliatory forces and society, given the opportunity to administer the opening blow. The situation would then be something like the old-fashioned Western gun duel. It would be extraordinarily risky for one side *not* to attempt to destroy the other, or to delay doing so, since it not only can emerge unscathed by striking first but this is the sole way it can reasonably hope to emerge at all. Evidently such a situation is extremely unstable.

Moreover, many military experts, both in the United States and the Soviet Union, believed towards the end of the nineteen-fifties, that this horrible situation of maximum instability was in fact tending to arise. Fortunately for our peace of mind they now suppose that measures to prevent it are fully practicable and that some at least of these measures have begun to be taken. At the end of the nineteen-fifties, it is true, such authorities as Professor Bernard Brodie, Professor Morgenstern and many others took the view that the American capacity, which is what, naturally enough, they were principally concerned about, to retaliate to a Russian 'first strike' aimed at America's airfields and rocket sites was in danger of being compromised. They believed that the trend of technical development was such that sooner rather than later it would be possible for an aggressor to be fairly sure of knocking out all, or almost all, of their fixed and largely unprotected airfields and rocket sites. They accordingly proposed a series of far-reaching measures, designed to alter this situation. The objective of these measures was to make American (and Western) capacity to retaliate invulnerable to surprise, first strike, attack.

There is then a flat contradiction between this pessimistic view and the sanguine view described above. The pessimistic view asserted that the balance is always potentially unstable unless we make continual efforts to maintain its stability and that any marked difference or 'a-symmetry', as it is called, between the strengths of the two sides, will be highly dangerous. Such a dangerous difference in strength would not be so much in the number of nuclear missiles possessed—above a certain level this may not be decisively important—as in *the capacity to deliver them*, both in the sense of being able to penetrate the enemy's defences and, above all, in the above sense of being vulnerable or invulnerable to a surprise blow at that capacity to deliver.

3
Russian and Western Nuclear Doctrines

WITH intense reluctance we shall be forced, then, to conclude that the danger of nuclear war cannot be written
off as inconsiderable. If we wish to evaluate the degree of risk
which in fact exists we had better begin by noting the current
military doctrines held by the Russian and Western military
authorities respectively.

Russian Military Doctrine

We may first turn to Soviet military doctrine. Again we do so,
not in order to accuse the Soviet Government of any special
degree of militancy. On the contrary it will emerge that, while
Soviet military thinkers have undeniably toyed with some of the
most perilous doctrines of nuclear warfare, yet there is now
(1962) evidence that the Soviet Government itself at no time
adopted these views as a basis of its actual defence policy.
(Moreover we shall see that the extreme views were probably
borrowed from a certain school of thought in the West.)
Nevertheless it may be useful again to approach the matter
from the Soviet side in order to exhibit the fact that the Russian
authorities, while probably no more 'defence minded' than
their Western counterparts, are certainly no less so either. For
unless we recall this fact we may become bemused, as many well-
intentioned persons have been bemused, by the ceaseless flood
of communist-inspired propaganda which represents the Russian

Government in the role of M. Picasso's dove of peace. We shall see that in fact the Russian authorities in general, and the Russian defence planners in particular, have, apparently, had much the same preoccupations, made some of the same mistakes, suffered many of the same anxieties, and come to many of the same conclusions, as those of the West.

The evolution of Soviet military doctrine in regard to nuclear war is a curious story. In 1942, immediately after the German armies had been checked at the gates, first of Moscow and then of Stalingrad, Stalin laid down his 'principles of war', as they used to be called in the older military textbooks. What these 'principles' amounted to was that the outcome of a war depended, not on this or that military factor in the narrow sense, nor on the brilliance of this or that general, nor on the possession of this or that new weapon but on the general character and stamina of society as a whole. A sound, healthy, united society would, again in the long run, produce the good generals, the good arms and the high morale which would win the war.

No doubt this was both good sense, as well as being good Marxism with its strong emphasis upon the social character of war. And Stalin proceeded to formulate the military principles which he considered decisive in what he called 'the permanently operating factors'. They were:

The stability of the rear, the morale of the army, the quantity and quality of divisions, the armament and quality of divisions, the armament of the army, the organisational ability of the army commanders.

There was nothing very new in all that. Clausewitz would not have dissented. But such was the character of Soviet society that these 'permanently operating factors' became a dogma in Russian military theory which no one was allowed to question for the remaining years of Stalin's life. This would not have mattered but for the advent of nuclear weapons. But once this revolution in military technique had taken place, Stalin's permanently operating factors became more and more misleading. In particular, they forbade all serious consideration of the possible consequences of a surprise attack. And it was, in form at any rate, on this issue of a surprise attack, rather than on the issue of nuclear weapons as such, that the controversy came to a head in 1953, the year of Stalin's death.

The subject of a surprise attack was a forbidden one so long as the old dictator lived. It could not be raised without discussing the painful fact that Stalin's armies had been catastrophically surprised by the conventional, non-nuclear, laboriously mounted, attack of one hundred German divisions in 1941. Partly for this reason no one in the Russian military press was allowed as much as to suggest that surprise, even with nuclear weapons, might be a danger. Moreover, this was in fact only one aspect of a Russian military doctrine, which during these years denigrated, in public at any rate, the importance of nuclear weapons in general. They were said to be the characteristic resort of imperialists who could never trust their own people to fight for them. They might do damage but they could never decide a war. Wars would be decided in the future as in the past by mass armies operating over the continents and over the years.

It was natural for the Russians to propagate these views during the early years of the nuclear age. For at first they had no nuclear weapons of their own, and up till perhaps 1955 they were markedly inferior in the nuclear field. But it is clear from two facts that, whoever else the Russian Government misled in the matter, it did not mislead itself. First the most energetic and brilliantly successful efforts were made to acquire nuclear war-heads and, secondly, equally energetic and successful efforts were made to develop what turned out in the end to be the most effective method of delivering them, namely intercontinental ballistic missiles, or rockets. For, no doubt, even Stalin himself believed that, whatever the importance of 'surprise attack' might be, Russia had to have nuclear weapons if she was to remain a super-power in the nuclear age. A few years after Stalin's death in 1953, these efforts had borne fruit and Russia became possessed of a rapidly-growing nuclear capacity. And sure enough, as and when Russia approached a parity of nuclear power, her military doctrine was changed also. The possibly decisive importance of surprise in general, and of nuclear surprise in particular, was recognized.

There was never any hesitation, I repeat, about the Russians' acquisition of the actual nuclear weapons. In this respect their antiquated doctrine seems to have had no effect at all. It may, however, have affected their actions in one way. The Russians were slow to create a fleet of inter-continental strategic bombers to carry their nuclear bombs. They remain to this day (1962) greatly inferior to America in this field. It does seem as if false doctrine slowed down, at any rate, a recognition of the potentially decisive effect of strategic bombing with nuclear weapons.

But this mistake, if it was a mistake, has not mattered to the Russians in the long run. For, as all the world now knows, during these very years, while in words they were minimizing the importance of nuclear weapons, and neglecting their strategic air force, they were concentrating on the development of ballistic rockets. And in the quality of these they may now lead the world.

Nevertheless the evolution of Russian military doctrine is important, since it throws light on Russian fears and intentions in respect of the use of nuclear weapons. The change in doctrine was made, it seems, with more difficulty and friction than the actual development of the new weapons. The change began in 1953 when several writers in the authoritative and official military journal *Military Thought* (the circulation of which is restricted to officers of field rank) began saying in their articles that while 'of course' the only finally decisive things were the 'permanently operating factors' yet surprise might be pretty important too. They were reproved by more conservative senior officers, but the semi-heresy kept cropping up and the controversy went on all through 1954. It went on, however, in terms of the question of *surprise* in general, rather than of the power of nuclear weapons in particular, though these were increasingly mentioned. And then in the spring of 1955 *Military Thought* published an article by Tank Marshal Rotmistrov which the editors had held up for some time. No wonder they had held up publication for the article began with a flat statement that

The experience of history has shown that the skilful employment of surprise brings true success not only in battles and operations but also in war.

This was followed by historical examples in which surprise had paid high dividends in conventional war. Then followed a specific recognition that nuclear weapons could be decisive.

Surprise attack, employing atomic and hydrogen weapons and other modern means of conflict, now takes on new forms and is capable of leading to significantly greater results than in the past war. It must be plainly said that, when atomic and hydrogen weapons are employed, surprise is one of the decisive conditions for the attainment of success not only in battles and operations, but in war as a whole.

The Doctrine of the Pre-emptive Strike

The American writer Mr H. S. Dinerstein, from whose book *War and the Soviet Union* (Atlantic Books, 1959) this account of the evolution of Soviet doctrine is largely drawn, goes on to assert that the Russians have drawn an ominous conclusion from their belated recognition that nuclear weapons could prove decisive. He asserts that they have adopted what is called the doctrine of 'the pre-emptive strike'. This theory asserts that the only way, or at least much the most effective way, of warding off a surprise nuclear attack is to strike first oneself, and so if possible knock the enemy's weapon out of his hands before he fires it. It should be unnecessary to emphasize how perilous a place the world would become if either or both of the contestants adopted this theory.

Mr Dinerstein writes that Marshal Rotmistrov's article went on to say that the American, and generally Western, imperialists do plan to make a surprise nuclear attack upon the Soviet Union. How then should they be countered? 'The Soviet Union', Marshal Rotmistrov wrote, 'should always be ready for

O.P.W.–D

pre-emptive action against the aggressor's schemes.' The Marshal continued:

> The duty of the Soviet armed forces is not to permit an enemy surprise attack on our country and, in the event of an attempt to accomplish one, not only to repel the attack successfully, but also to deal the enemy counterblows, or even pre-emptive (uprezhdaiuschchie) surprise blows, of terrible destructive force. For this the Soviet army and navy possess everything necessary.

Dinerstein agrees that Rotmistrov is not here advocating preventive war in the old sense. Rotmistrov says this himself:

> The aspiration to seize and hold the strategic initiative should not be understood as an intention to begin a preventive war against the enemies of the U.S.S.R. who are preparing to attack us.

The doctrine of the 'pre-emptive strike' presupposes that the threatened country, in this case Russia, somehow knows for certain that it is just about to be attacked. Then it must 'get its blow in first'. Dinerstein goes so far as to write (p. 188, op. cit.) that 'readiness to strike a pre-emptive blow' became early in 1955 a principal aim of Soviet military policy. He submits as evidence of this two editorial statements in the March and May 1955 issues of *Military Thought* immediately following Rotmistrov's article. They read:

> We cannot ignore the lessons of history and we must always be ready for pre-emptive actions against the perfidy of the aggressors.

and

> The task is the purposeful elaboration of all aspects of this question, especially the elaboration of ways and means to prevent an enemy surprise attack and to deal the opponents pre-emptive blows on every scale—strategic, operational, and tactical.

Dinerstein also cites a good many other Soviet pronouncements on the issue, which point in the same general direction, but which less definitely commit themselves to pre-emption. As against this the Soviet Government has, naturally enough, always publicly denied that it favours the doctrine of pre-emptive attack.

Subsequent developments have made it plain, moreover, that Dinerstein was not justified in his positive assertion that the Russians had adopted this fatal doctrine of 'the pre-emptive strike'. Whatever their military thinkers may have written, the actual military policy of the Soviet Government, it is now (1962) clear, has in fact been much closer to the doctrine of minimum deterrence than to that of the pre-emptive strike. The actual, existing, Russian strategic deterrent has, that is to say, turned out to be far more suitable, both in size and character, for a 'second strike' (see below) deterrent role than for a first, or pre-emptive, strike. What may have happened is that the Russian military thinkers, like Rotmistrov, when they rather suddenly discovered the vast power of nuclear weapons [1] and the immense difficulty of preventing their successful delivery, rushed from one extreme to the other. Forced by Stalin's dogmatism to pretend for years that nuclear weapons were not so very important; that wars would be long; that wars would be decided in the end in the old way by mass armies, they may have become slightly intoxicated when they were allowed to realize that nuclear weapons could destroy every major city in either Russia or America in a few hours, and that there was no effective way of preventing their delivery. Hence they suddenly enunciated the pre-emptive strike doctrine.

But where did that doctrine come from? There is little doubt that it had been developed in the circles of the American Strategic Air Force. Professor Bernard Brodie in *Strategy in the Missile Age* writes (p. 188):

One school of thought has argued that the American system of defence must be based upon the concept of anticipatory or 'pre-emptive' attack, that is an attack provoked by an imminent and certain enemy attack. One wag has described this as the principle of 'I won't hit first unless you do'. The pertinent question is what is the probability that such fine calculations can be made to work in practice?

[1] Or perhaps when they were rather suddenly allowed to state publicly what that power was. Very likely they had themselves appreciated that power much earlier, or even all along.

Even more revelatory perhaps than this particular passage, Professor Brodie's book as a whole bears unmistakable evidence of a severe struggle between such wise minds as his own with a certain school of thought in the Strategic Air Force which had adopted the doctrine of the pre-emptive strike. The adoption of such a doctrine on the part of S.A.C. was deeply foolish if only because, as Professor Brodie and Professor Blackett agree, the United States Government was most un-likely to allow them to implement it. Thus the adoption of the doctrine of the pre-emptive strike by S.A.C. tended to result in the preparation of a force enormously strong for this sort of 'first-strike' action, but, perhaps, dangerously weak for carry-ing out the actual policy of the American Government, namely the maintenance of a strong, relatively invulnerable, deterrent force, capable of surviving an enemy's first strike, and then inflicting intolerable retaliation upon him on 'second strike'. This profoundly inappropriate military 'posture' is only now being corrected: and that largely by the development of the Polaris-carrying submarine on the part of the U.S. Navy, and Minuteman by the U.S. Air Force.

In fact there has been a long drawn-out struggle within the American defence world as to which military 'posture', as it is called, to adopt. We shall describe this struggle in more detail below. For it is impossible to overestimate the importance of this question of 'posture', i.e. of the *kind* of military preparations which states and alliances make in the nuclear age. If, for example, they prepare forces only capable of a first or pre-emptive strike, then naturally their potential opponents will conclude that this is what they intend to do. For in these matters deeds speak, by an order of magnitude, more loudly than words. If both sides prepare only such 'first strike' forces, then we get what Professor Brodie well calls 'a situation of intolerable mutual menace'. Fortunately, I repeat, there is evidence that better councils are prevailing in American defence circles and that relatively invulnerable forces, capable of second strike retaliation, are being pepared.

The validity of the distinction between characteristically

first and second strike forces is sometimes denied on the grounds that second strike, or relatively invulnerable, forces are also capable of first strike. But this fact does not invalidate the distinction, which rests upon the all-important consideration that characteristically first strike, or relatively vulnerable, forces are not capable of second strike, for they would have been destroyed in an enemy's first strike. Thus defence planners, on both sides, are bound to pay the most careful attention to the *kind* of strategic deterrent which their opponent has prepared. If he has left his strategic deterrent force vulnerable, but potent, it is a signal that whatever he may say, he is thinking of striking first. If he has gone to the enormous trouble and expense of making his force as invulnerable as possible, he must be thinking primarily in terms of a retaliatory second strike. For, at the same expense, he could have procured a much larger vulnerable force. The reality, indeed the supreme importance, of this distinction between relatively vulnerable forces, good for nothing but first strike, and relatively invulnerable forces capable of second retaliatory strike, will become apparent as the argument proceeds.

On the Russian side also cumulative evidence is now available that the Soviet Government has not adopted the desperate theory of pre-emption. We may resume our story of the development of Russian military doctrine. By 1960 Mr Khruschev, it is true, had become a most ardent convert to the overwhelming importance of nuclear weapons. This was shown, most clearly of all perhaps, in his speech to the Supreme Soviet on 14th and 15th January, 1960. Mr Khruschev announced, it will be recalled, that the combined strength of the Russian armed forces (Army, Navy and Air Force) would be reduced by 1,200,000 men to a total of 2,425,000 men. No one should underestimate the size of this proposed reduction. It would have gone some way towards abandoning the traditional Russian military concept of a mass standing army 'in being'. However, Mr Khruschev went on to explain that he was making this reduction in conventional forces entirely because they were being 'replaced' by nuclear forces. His words were:

Soviet scientists, engineers and workers have made it possible to equip our army with armaments never known to man—atomic, hydrogen, rocket and other modern weapons—the Party, the Government, the entire Soviet people warmly thank the scientists, engineers, technicians and workers, whose knowledge and labour have brought about great successes in developing atomic and hydrogen weapons, rocketry and all the other things that have made it possible to raise the defence potential of our country to such a high level. . . . The Soviet Union has stockpiled the necessary quantities of atomic and hydrogen weapons—our state possesses powerful rocketry. With the present development of military techniques, military aviation and the navy have lost their former importance. These arms are not reduced but replaced. Military aviation is almost entirely being replaced by rockets. Now we have sharply cut down and will, it seems, reduce still further or even entirely the production of bombers and other obsolete equipment. In the navy the submarine fleet gains in importance whereas surface ships can no longer play the role they played in the past. Our armed forces have been to a considerable degree regeared to rocket and nuclear weapons. . . . The Soviet Army today possesses such military techniques and such firepower as no army has ever had before.

No one could have announced the conversion of Russian military doctrine to the decisive importance of nuclear weapons in more emphatic terms. There seemed no doubt that the Russians had at length abandoned their obstinately held belief that vast land armies, fighting long wars, are by themselves the decisive arm. They seemed to have 'gone nuclear' in a big way; they seemed to be reorganizing the 'size and shape' of their armed forces in a process similar to that undertaken by, for example, the British Government in the late nineteen-fifties.

Nothing in all this, however, proved that Mr Khruschev was a convert to Marshal Rotmistrov's doctrine of the necessity of the pre-emptive strike. And indeed Mr Khruschev went on to state clearly that he adhered to the alternative view that a country such as Russia, even if struck first and by surprise, could retain enough nuclear power on second, retaliatory strike, to deter anyone but a madman. His words are so important that they should be quoted in full:

A question puts itself forward, however: if it is not ruled out that some capitalist States can overtake us in modern armaments, cannot they take the treacherous step of attacking us first, in order to exploit the factor of surprise attack with such terrible weapons as nuclear rockets, and thereby secure advantages to win the war? No. The present means of warfare do not give such advantages to any side.

It is possible to attack first. It wouldn't require many brains to do this. It would rather require recklessness: and we are, of course, fully aware that some of our potential opponents are rather prone to that.

We see many instances of advocates of the 'policy of strength' breathing fire now in one country, now in another—even though it would seem that Hitler's 'laurels' should have a cooling effect on them. Their reasoning, however, is apparently so fuzzy that they have forgotten those sharp lessons of history.

Supposing, however, that some State, or group of States, succeeds in preparing and carrying out a surprise attack on a Power possessing nuclear and rocket weapons?

Even if we accept for a minute that it would succeed in delivering a surprise blow—would the attacking side be able to put out of action at once all the stocks of nuclear weapons, all the rocket installations on the territory of the power attacked? Of course not! A State subjected to a surprise attack—provided of course it is a big state—will always be able to give the aggressor a worthy rebuff.

We are aware that our country is ringed with foreign military bases. That is why we locate our rockets in such a way as to ensure a double and even treble margin of safety. We have a vast territory and we are able to disperse our rockets and camouflage them well. We are developing such a system that if some means of retaliation were knocked out, we could always fall back on others and strike the enemy from reserve installations.

In view of this it is not possible to agree with Dinerstein that the Soviet Government has officially adhered to the doctrine of the pre-emptive strike. On the contrary they have now (since Dinerstein wrote) officially repudiated it as unnecessary to Russia's safety. It is, of course, possible to say that Mr Khruschev was here talking for public consumption only: that privately he adhered to the view of Rotmistrov and the editors of *Military Thought*. The decisive test of that is however provided by the character of Russian military preparations. Are they preparing an *exclusively first-strike* force incapable of surviving a pre-emptive, counter-force American attack? Or are they preparing a genuinely deterrent, retaliatory, second strike nuclear force?

What the Russians Actually Did

By the beginning of 1962 it had become apparent that what the Russians had in fact prepared was a strategic nuclear force which was, in respect of both its size and character, better suited to the second strike, retaliatory role than to a pre-emptive, first strike, counter-force, role. This reassuring conclusion emerges from the drastic revision of the estimates of Russian nuclear strength which have been made and published by the American authorities. It is now evident that in the late nineteen-fifties many defence experts greatly exaggerated the probable rate at which Russian nuclear capacity for a pre-emptive first strike, or indeed for any other purpose, would grow. Not un-naturally misled by resounding Russian statements (of which that just quoted from Mr Khruschev is merely one example) of their determination to go all out in nuclearization, and still more misled no doubt by the overwhelming proof provided by her space programme of Russia's capacity to produce the largest and best long-distance rockets in the world, these experts estimated that by 1962 the Russians would have 200 I.C.B.M.s or four times as many as America would have at the same period. Again, as early as 1956 Russia was thought to be capable of making twenty-five long-range intercontinental bombers a month, so that by 1962 she might well have come to possess some 1,500, or nearly as many as the 1,700 which Mr McNamara, the American Secretary of Defense, announced on November 12th 1961 to be possessed by America.

In the event these same American Defense experts now (1962) estimate that Russia in fact possesses only fifty I.C.B.M.s, or about the same number as America, and only 150 intercontinental bombers or less than one tenth the American strength. (In addition America possesses, according to Mr McNamara, some eighty largely invulnerable Polaris missiles, plus 80–100 highly vulnerable Thor and Jupiter intermediate range missiles,

200 still more vulnerable carrier-borne aircraft and nearly 1,999 supersonic fighters all capable (because of America's possession of advanced bases in Europe and Asia) of delivering nuclear weapons on to Russian territory.

What reason is there, it may be asked, to put more reliance on these new estimates of Russia's relatively low nuclear strength than should have been placed upon the earlier and higher estimates? There is this reason. Defence Departments and fighting services nearly always tend to overstate the strength of potential opponents in order to stimulate their own Governments to pay for increases in their own strength. I think therefore that we may depend upon it that only the most convincing evidence would have caused the American Defense authorities (including the Air staff, though not S.A.C.) to accept and publish the new estimates. In a word 1962 has arrived and instead of an alarming Russian strategic nuclear predominance being revealed, America is seen to possess a predominance which may well be alarming to the Russians!

Here, then, is important evidence to show that the Russians, for whatever reasons, have in fact prepared a comparatively small, characteristically retaliatory, second strike force instead of the large and at any rate potentially first strike, pre-emptive force which they almost certainly could have created (though no doubt at very heavy cost to their economy). We may say that the actual Russian strategic nuclear force is characteristically second strike because it is relatively invulnerable, though the invulnerability has been obtained in a different way to any open to the West. The Russian I.C.B.M.s, and to some extent their bomber bases also, are protected by the wall of secrecy which a communist society alone can give to such installations. (The Americans make no attempt at all to conceal the location of their I.C.B.M. and S.A.C. bases, for in our type of society such an attempt would be hopeless.) Moreover, as we shall find, the Russians have shown themselves intensely sensitive to anything such as American U2 or satellite reconaissance or to test ban inspections, which might compromise the secret of the location of their bases (see p. 171 below).

All this is evidence that what the Russians have done is to prepare a relatively small strategic nuclear deterrent, as invulnerable as they can make it, essentially in accordance with the doctrine of minimum deterrence, as qualified by the necessity of invulnerability.

Indeed, at the cost of some anticipation of future chapters we should note here a possible explanation of the extreme militancy which Mr Khruschev showed in the autumn of 1961, when he resumed testing, began letting off 50-megaton weapons and announced the cancellation of the aforementioned reduction of the Russian armed forces from 3.6 million to 2.4 million men. May it not have been that Mr Khruschev, and the Russian, defence planners generally, somewhat suddenly came to the conclusion that they had put much too much reliance upon the theory of minimum deterrence? After all the Russians, for whatever reasons, had provoked greatly increased tension by precipitating and then pressing the long-drawn-out Berlin Crisis of 1958 to 196?. This had, naturally, led to an increase in the American defence budget to 47 billion dollars, spent partly on an acceleration of the invulnerable (largely Polaris and Minuteman) part of the strategic deterrent and partly on the provision of additional conventional forces in Germany. It had also led to (largely nugatory) efforts to increase the conventional forces of Germany, France, Britain and the other N.A.T.O. allies. Although the Russians certainly had only themselves to blame for this (not very extensive) Western re-armament they may have been frightened by it. At any rate it is not easy to find any other plausible explanation for their ostentatious belligerency in late 1961. Letting off a 50-megaton bomb was almost certainly not a very reasonable thing to do from a strictly military point of view; but it was a shrewd enough move if the intention was to make the world believe that the Russian strategic nuclear deterrent was a good deal stronger than was actually the case. Paradoxical as it may seem this spasm of Russian militancy may have been caused by a sudden feeling of weakness.

These recent developments suggest that the Russians, in

practice, have been nearer to the theory of minimum deterrence than to that of the pre-emptive strike. Their actions are not, on that account, entirely reassuring for the future however. Having discovered the limitations and weaknesses of minimum deterrence they may now be inclined to swing over to the other extreme. Moreover, as we shall find in Part Two, when we come to discuss the possibilities of disarmament, the present Russian nuclear posture, though by no means so menacing as it is evidently intended to seem, is a particularly difficult one to reconcile with the requirements of a test ban treaty, or indeed with most other possibilities of disarmament.

How then should we sum up the doctrine of the pre-emptive strike? Who can doubt that if both sides had permanently and wholeheartedly adopted this doctrine there would have been little chance of avoiding the early outbreak of full scale nuclear war? Whatever protestations either side may make as to the difference between policies of preventive war and of pre-emptive strike, who can doubt that their result would be the same? For of course the fatal fallacy in the theory of the pre-emptive strike is the assumption that one side can ever be *sure* that it is just about to be attacked. How on earth can the Russian or, *mutatis mutandis*, the American Government *know* that the other is just about to press the buttons on its rocket sites? The truth is that nations have frequently been sure that they were not going to be attacked when they were, and certain that they would be attacked when they were not. The Russians, I repeat, would not believe that they were going to be attacked in 1941 even when Hitler mobilized one hundred divisions on their frontier! And the American Government did not believe it was going to be attacked even when it decoded the Japanese operations order for Pearl Harbour. But just because both of the super-powers have been through those traumatic experiences of surprise attack, either or both might well 'know', at the next moment of tension (or the next, or the next) that they were going to be attacked, when they were not. Either or both might determine that a pre-emptive strike was their only hope of survival. Each might determine to pre-empt the other's supposed pre-emption. We should be back in the hopeless situation when survival depended on who had 'the fastest gun'. The guns would be fired as readily as in a 'Western'.

Fortunately the evidence does not compel us to conclude that in the present instance either Government has adopted the doctrine of the pre-emptive strike. It would probably be truer to say that both Governments have considered it seriously. And this is a grave enough conclusion. Moreover, it is not much use pointing out the fatal character of the doctrine unless we can suggest measures which will prevent its adoption from seeming inevitable to the contestants. It may be presumed that the 'gun-toting' characters of the nineteenth century American West did not (in real life as distinct from the films) at all enjoy having to depend for their survival on the possession of 'the fastest gun'. On the contrary they were driven to be quick on the draw by their mutual terror. If a situation of the above type of maximum instability were to be allowed to develop, both Governments might be driven, however much against their wills, in this fatal direction.

Vulnerability again

Thus it is no use blaming either the Russian soldiers or the American airmen for having had these thoughts. We must return to a consideration of the factor in the military balance which has induced these thoughts in their minds. And of course that factor is the vulnerability, or supposed vulnerability, of their respective nuclear forces to surprise, pre-emptive, first strike attack. We must say advisedly 'or supposed vulnerability' because what matters in this case is not only the facts, but also the states of mind of the respective authorities who control the switches which, if thrown, would kill them, and us. It is not enough for Mr Khruschev on the one hand or Sir John Slessor or Professor Blackett on the other to argue that as a matter of fact the delivery systems of the West and of Russia are mutually invulnerable in practice at the present time. We fervently hope that they are right. They make what sounds to the layman an attractive case that a potential pre-emptor could never be *sure* of knocking out a high enough proportion of his opponent's points of delivery. Sir John Slessor, in particular, has repeatedly asserted that the calculations which are often made as to the relatively modest number of megaton weapons which would have to be launched in order to knock out any given number of airfields and rocket sites, allowing for the known, mean radial error of each missile, for the known proportion of misfires, etc. etc. is mere 'slide-rule strategy', unrelated to the realities of actual warfare. It may be so. On the other hand this view seems to conflict with another of Sir John Slessor's *dicta*, namely that no rule derived from the experience of pre-nuclear war has any application to nuclear war. Certainly an exchange of I.C.B.M.s aimed at each other's launching points would seem to be a form of warfare much more susceptible to quantitative, mathematical prediction, than any form of warfare which the world has hitherto known. We can only hope that enough un-certainty still adheres to it to add a restraining influence to the other influences which may be brought to bear to restrain a potential pre-emptor.

Of these potential restraining influences, the degree of in-vulnerability which can be given, by one means or another, to the means of delivery of both sides is, surely, by far the most important. We may demonstrate this by realizing that if 100 per cent invulnerability for the nuclear striking power of both sides could be achieved, the whole advantage of pre-emption would be gone. Such 100 per cent invulnerability is no doubt in practice unattainable. But a degree of invulnerability sufficient to deter a would-be pre-emptor appears to be fully attainable, whether or not it has yet been fully attained. The question is what *degree* of invulnerability is (*a*) practicable and (*b*) in existence, on either side at present (1962). The layman is not called upon to attempt any estimate of the degree of invulner-ability of the existing Russian or American delivery systems. Moreover, the situation is certain to have changed, probably several times, before these words are read. Here again the optimistic and the pessimistic schools of thought are widely at variance. The optimists believed that the delivery systems of both sides are, already in practice, invulnerable enough, at any rate, to deter any but the most reckless of pre-emptors. The pessimists in the West thought that unless we took great care we might drift into a position of tempting vulnerability in respect of Russia. And some Russian military opinions, as we have seen, feared that Russia was, in the nineteen-fifties at least, open to a crippling and perhaps decisive blow unless she struck first. What cannot be ignored is the fact that the haunting, and in tension potentially lethal, fear that their own installations are vulnerable has arisen in the minds of both sides. To put it at its lowest, a doubt exists as to the invulnerability of present delivery systems to a surprise, pre-emptive first strike. *It is surely evident that so long as that doubt exists no task compares in urgency with that of making the rival delivery systems mutually invulnerable?*

Nevertheless, this conclusion is still not accepted by all the advocates of the optimistic, or 'minimum deterrence', school of thought. Professor Blackett for example has written a considered rejoinder to his critics entitled 'Critique of Some Contemporary Defence Thinking' (*Encounter*, April 1961). In it he consistently minimizes the importance of devoting our efforts to increasing invulnerability because, he maintains, the respective deterrents have been, in practice, sufficiently invulnerable all along. (For example he denies that the advent of Polaris Submarine has improved the stability of the balance.) It is difficult to accept Professor Blackett's conclusions. No doubt the exact degree of vulnerability which the respective deterrent forces have had, have, or are likely to have, is debatable. But, I repeat, if there is even a doubt in the minds of either side— as undeniably there is—of their invulnerability, surely it is imperative to increase invulnerability by every possible means, if only in order to calm the minds and nerves of those on whom (on both sides) the awful responsibilities of nuclear warfare are laid?[1]

[1] Professor Blackett's article as a whole gives the impression that in contrast to most Western writers, the danger which he chiefly apprehends is of an American surprise attack on Russia and not vice versa. It is no doubt useful that someone in the West should emphasize this view: for,

Naturally, we can only attend to our own system. We must leave it, with some confidence, to the Russian Government to attend to theirs. However, it is on balance actually in our interests (because in the interests of stability) that the Russians also should perfect the invulnerability of their nuclear forces. Hence it will be all to the good if the widespread Western discussion of the matter leads them to do so. It is not, however, my intention to enter here into a technical discussion of how the Western delivery systems can be made invulnerable. I am unqualified to do so and technique is changing so fast that a continuing series of measures will surely be necessary.[1] What is possible for the layman is to emphasize the extreme importance of the *principle* of invulnerability, however achieved.

Summary and Conclusions

What, then, must be our conclusion as to the degree of risk of the outbreak of nuclear war which the world is currently (1962) facing? With deep regret we shall be forced to the conclusion that the extreme mutual dread which the consequences of nuclear war now undoubtedly arouse in the minds of both the Russian and American Governments is not a guarantee that there will be no such war. Nuclear abundance, on both sides, has come but in itself it cannot be relied upon to abolish full-scale nuclear war. On the contrary, the greater that mutual dread becomes, the *more* likely, in certain circumstances, one or other side might be to strike first, in panic lest it itself be struck. These circumstances, in which mutual dread would become a factor of instability instead of stability, are those in which one or both sides have allowed their deterrent forces to become vulnerable to a surprise first strike attack.

But if we cannot, for these reasons, subscribe to Sir John Slessor's or Professor Blackett's comforting view yet we need not go to the other and despairing extreme of supposing that either

---

as we have seen, it is, naturally enough, widely held in Russia, and it would be naïve of us to suppose that it could be dispelled by protestations.

[1] We shall note some of the techniques suggested for achieving a higher degree of invulnerability in the next chapter.

or both sides have actually adopted the fatal theory of the pre-
emptive strike. On the contrary we shall find that some technical developments are making it easier to secure the indispensable objective of mutually invulnerable nuclear striking forces
and that measures to that end are being undertaken.

In Part One we are discussing only the military and technical
factors in the stability of the balance of power, or terror, between the two world alliances. But of course major political
considerations profoundly affect the issue. We shall come to
them. Nevertheless, let me register one firm conclusion. The
stability of the existing balance of power is an objective of great
importance. For although such a balance cannot, in the long
run, save us from the recurrence of nuclear war, yet there is no
observable alternative method of staving off the catastrophe.[1]
Thus to maintain the stability of the balance seems the one
way of giving ourselves the decades which we shall certainly
need in order to find our way out of the dilemma of the nuclear
age. Our dilemma I repeat is that war, while remaining inevitable so long as the world is organized as it is, has become intolerable. If then, the interim, or short run, necessity of promoting
the stability of the balance by all practicable means is agreed,
the importance of military doctrines, capacities, or 'postures'
as they are now sometimes called, which may maximize or
minimize that stability, should be apparent. The next chapter
will examine the military aspects of the balance from another
point of view. It will examine that doctrine of *deterrence* which
prevails today in the Western and Eastern camps alike.

[1] In Part Two the possibilities of disarmament are discussed. On the
whole the conclusion is reached that those steps in disarmament which would
themselves contribute to the stability of the balance, at a lower level of
armaments, are the most hopeful.

4

Deterrence

From Defence to Deterrence

THE defence efforts of modern states are now habitually commended to their respective publics in terms of the provision of what is called 'a deterrent'. We are asked, that is to say, to spare somewhere between 5 and 15 per cent of our national incomes in order to provide armed forces which, we are told, will deter potential enemies either from attacking us with nuclear weapons or, perhaps, from doing other things which we may consider prejudicial to our interests. (The distinction, as we shall see immediately, is an important one.)

This sort of explanation of the need to provide armaments is peculiar to the nuclear age. No governments talked like that before 1939. In those days governments asked for money with which to provide armaments in order 'to defend the Country'. By this they meant, in some cases sincerely enough, armaments which could physically ward off a potential armed attack. Naturally, all governments in fact had the necessity of striking back, if war came, in their minds. And some governments, such as Hitler's, were obviously concerned, under a thin pretence of 'defending the fatherland', with striking first and so securing this or that national objective by means of war. Nevertheless in the pre-nuclear period governments habitually presented their expenditure on armaments as designed to defend the country in the primary, literal sense of physically warding off an attack: and some governments really meant what they said

O.P.W.–E

(cf. the much criticized 'Maginot-mindedness' of the French Government, which envisaged a war almost exclusively defensive in the strict, physical, tactical sense).

The reason why no government in the nuclear age commends its expenditure on armaments to its people in this reassuring manner is of course that defence, in the strict physical, tactical, sense, against nuclear attack, does not appear to be possible. It is true that methods by which a very high proportion, or even all, of the manned bombing aircraft of an attacking force might be shot down are now thought to exist. But the very means, namely rockets carrying nuclear war heads, which may serve this defensive purpose provide also an alternative and more deadly means of attack. Large rockets can, as we all know, be shot from continent to continent carrying thermonuclear warheads in the megaton range. And, in 1962, no means of avoiding their arrival has been devised. Some means of intercepting such rockets may be devised in the future. (We shall note the possible consequences of such an invention in the next chapter.) But, so far, after the first fifteen years of the nuclear age, it is generally conceded that there is no practicable means of defence, in the old warding-off sense, against nuclear attack. If therefore a government is to explain to its people the need for providing nuclear armaments it must do so in terms not of defence but of deterrence. (Unless, indeed, it is willing to say that it intends to use its nuclear arms for purposes of aggression: and no government is likely to be willing to say that.)

Those who in the West are against the provision of nuclear arms (either by their own nation or, in some cases, by the American-led alliance as a whole) are accustomed to point to the above facts of the technical situation and to say that the impossibility of defence, in the narrow sense, makes the provision of armaments futile. They usually go on to deny the possibility of deterrence also, with a variety of arguments which we shall discuss. And indeed we shall find that deterrence is by no means a simple concept. We shall find that, unless we think the matter out most carefully, the preparations which we are being asked to make in this field may become irrelevant or ineffective for their declared purposes. In particular we shall find that deterrence is not all of a piece: that there are several kinds of deterrence and that different kinds of preparations are necessary if we wish to possess ourselves of each of them. We shall also find that deterrence is by no means an all-or-nothing concept. A nation may possess a certain amount of deterrent power but not more. The relevant questions to ask will turn out to be: first, how much deterrence, and of what kinds, do you think you need? and second, how much, and what kinds of deterrence do you think you have got?

But it may be useful to say plainly and at the outset that whatever the difficulties, both theoretical and practical, of the concept, there is no alternative to deterrence but surrender. It may be said that surrender is not unthinkable. I agree: indeed we shall think about it in Chapter 9. Here, we are making the single point that, today, if we come to the conclusion that we are unwilling to provide any form of deterrence against the unwelcome actions of potential opponents, then we must be content to abide by the will of those opponents. It may be argued that it is morally right, that it is prudent, or that it is inevitable, to do this. Or, it may be argued that no one has anything but benevolent intentions towards either our own nation or the alliance of nations of which ours may be a member. These views will be considered. The fact remains that if we wish to retain any capacity to settle our own destiny without being obliged, if threatened, to obey the will of another nation or alliance, we must, in the nuclear age, retain some form of deterrence.

The fact that, for the present at least, defence in the narrow sense against nuclear attack is technically impossible is one of the important characteristics of the nuclear age. In this age, therefore, the power to deter, however exercised, remains, apart from aggression on our own part, the one way in which a nation, or an alliance, can assert a will to survive as self-determining societies. We must now examine the various ways in which it may be possible to deter potential opponents from actions unwelcome to us.

The First Kind of Deterrence

The preceding chapter on the risks of nuclear war in a balance of power situation was in fact a discussion of one of the kinds of deterrence which are possible in the nuclear age. The discussion turned on the possession of a capacity to deliver an unacceptable quantity of nuclear weapons upon an opponent who had already attacked one with his own nuclear weapons. It was agreed that if, but only if, a nation really did possess this kind of deterrence, it could be relatively secure against deliberate nuclear attack. The question at issue was: was it or was it not technically difficult to possess this kind of deterrence? For we noted that this kind of deterrence depended upon what was called 'second strike capacity'. We also saw that it used to be rather generally assumed that the possession of any reasonably efficient nuclear force automatically conferred on a nation, or alliance, this capacity. But it was now being argued that, on the contrary, a capacity for deterrence of this kind could only be retained by careful and elaborate measures designed to protect one's own nuclear striking force from the otherwise obliterating effects of an opponent's unexpected first strike.

We must now notice that some, usually lay, observers have gone to the other extreme, and are suggesting that, far from its being easy, it is now technically impossible to retain a second strike, or retaliatory capacity. They are usually persons who oppose the possession of nuclear weapons by their own country, or their own alliance. They wish, therefore, to argue (*a*) that it is 'unthinkable' that we should use these weapons first and (*b*) that it is impossible to use them second, since they will inevitably have been obliterated by our opponents' first strike. Therefore they conclude that nuclear weapons are useless and should be immediately scrapped. In assessing this argument, it is worth noting that neither of the main contenders appear to attach any weight to it. And in fact the argument does not appear to be technically sound. Without any attempt to evaluate them, we may list the measures which are currently proposed for making a strategic nuclear striking force relatively invulnerable to surprise attack, and so enabling it to retain that capacity to retaliate in kind on which this first sort of deterrence evidently depends.

Methods for Decreasing Vulnerability

When it first began to be realized that Russia if she possessed enough rockets might, by surprise attack, destroy a high proportion of the American Strategic Air Force on the ground, before it could take off, the first reaction of the American Air Force seems to have been simply to demand more bombers. This was a natural rather than an intelligent reaction. The provision of more bombers, if, but only if, they were dispersed at more bomber bases, would indeed impose upon the Russians the necessity of firing more rockets. But there was little reason to suppose that they could not provide themselves with the means to do so much faster than the Americans could build bombers and bomber bases.

The second reaction was to demand that the bombers, or a high proportion of them, should be kept ready to take off at a few minutes' notice, since it was estimated that about fifteen minutes' notice of the approach of I.C.B.M.s could be given by a first-rate warning system. This is called a 'ground alert'.

The third reaction was to demand that a proportion of the bombers should be kept continually flying with their nuclear missiles ready to go. This is called an 'airborne alert'.

These two reactions have both, in some degree, been adopted by S.A.C. The airborne alert is not so fantastic a proposal as it sounds. Professor Morgenstern (op. cit., p. 77) estimates that it would cost between $1 and $3 billion per year to keep 'something like 50 per cent of S.A.C. constantly airborne.' As it happens, this, Morgenstern notes, is just about the sum which Americans spend annually on pleasure boating. So it would be difficult to maintain that this measure, if it could provide a good deal of invulnerability, and so retain the first kind of deterrence, would be economically unacceptable. However, the assertion that this sum would keep as high a proportion as 50 per cent of the force airborne surely must be a large overestimate. Indeed it is difficult to see how maintenance problems could allow of anything approaching one-half of a strategic bomber force to be kept permanently in the air, whatever sum was spent upon the attempt. But even 15 per cent of such a force as S.A.C. kept permanently in the air would no doubt much increase invulnerability. Nevertheless, as Morgenstern himself agrees, the airborne alert bears all the marks of a stop-gap device. No one could suggest that this is a satisfactory permanent solution to the problem of invulnerability.

It may be supposed that the problem facing S.A.C. is rather that of the general re-design of the force for second strike rather than pre-emptive purposes. This may involve not only some degree of airborne alert but also such measures as changes in the flight patterns of the bombers when they are in the air, of the provision of different types of aircraft and of air-launched weapons of long range.

The fourth reaction was to demand the creation of American I.C.B.M.s. And this too is being done. But it is clear that the mere creation of a number of American I.C.B.M.s on known, highly vulnerable bases, does little more, in itself, than does the creation of more bomber bases, to retain the first kind of retaliatory deterrence. It does no more than increase the number of Russian aiming points and thus to raise their minimum requirement of I.C.B.M.s. In fact it is less efficacious than the provision of more bomber bases, since you cannot keep an I.C.B.M. airborne.

The fifth reaction has been to demand what is called the 'hardening' of both bomber and I.C.B.M. bases. 'Hardening' simply means to dig in and/or cover with concrete, the missiles and their launching equipment, and, so far as is practicable, to do the same thing with the bombers. Interestingly enough, this proposal for some time encountered, and to some extent still encounters, the obstinate opposition of the Air Force authorities. They feel that any more money which may be made available should always be spent on more bombers thus increasing their offensive power, rather than on concrete or on digging: that 'hardening' is a degrading sort of defensive

'Maginot-mindedness'. (It is of the nature of airmen to think like this.) The extreme irrationality of this view, if second strike retaliatory deterrent capacity is to be preserved, has, however, led to the airmen being overruled and some 'hardening' is taking place in America. In particular the second generation of land-based I.C.B.M.s, called Minutemen, can not only be fired at much shorter notice but are to be provided with hardened sites. (At one time it was proposed that these weapons should be fired from mobile sites: but there now seems to be doubt as to the practicability of this.)

It is clear however that there are real limits to the utility of hardening. All that it too can do (though this may be important) is to raise the number of I.C.B.M.s which the Russians (or *mutatis mutandis* the Americans) would have to fire (with a given degree of accuracy) on first strike in order to have a prospect of destroying all or almost all their opponents' installations. (Or alternatively hardening can force the aggressor to use larger, as well as more, war-heads.) For what 'hardening' does is to reduce the radius of the target which must be hit in order to knock out the base. No practicable amount of hardening can withstand a direct hit with a 10-megaton weapon. Moreover, forcing your potential opponent to increase the size and number of his missiles for first strike, 'counter force', purposes has the incidental disadvantage that you would lose, if he did strike, still more of your cities and their populations as a result of his 'shorts and overs'. Finally the hardening process is in one aspect a race between the degree of protection which can be given and the increasing accuracy of missiles. And it is thought that the factor of accuracy may be rising the more rapidly. Thus hardening is a by no means definitive answer to the problem.

The sixth reaction to the threat has been to demand that launching points should be made mobile. If this can be done a marked decrease in vulnerability will result. In the case of bombers it can be done, and is being done to some extent. But the inconvenience, and resulting loss of efficiency, caused by continually moving one or two bombers about at random, away from their maintenance facilities, and from everything that these incredibly complex monsters need to support them, is very great. In the case of missiles mobility is impossible for the older generation of liquid fuel missiles. But it is possible for the new generation of solid fuel missiles, such as Polaris and Minuteman, even if they are land-based. They can be moved about on land, by rail and by canal barge: however it appears that the disadvantages of this are greater than had been supposed. Finally they can be sent to sea and mounted on surface ships or submarines.

This brings us to the seventh reaction, which has been that of the United States Navy. The U.S.N. has produced the Polaris missile-firing, nuclear-powered submarine. In 1962 this 'weapon system' is being extolled as the solution of the problem of invulnerability. And certainly the possession of a fleet of nuclear-powered submarines, each carrying sixteen Polaris missiles, cruising for months at a time anywhere in the Seven Seas or beneath the Polar ice seems likely to confer upon the United States a far less vulnerable second strike, retaliatory force than she has lately possessed. Thus it should markedly restore and increase her deterrent power of the first, retaliatory kind.

A world in which both Russia and America possessed nuclear fleets of this sort as their main nuclear striking forces would probably be a much safer place, in which the balance of power had far greater inherent stability. For neither side would, for the time being at least, have any hope of destroying the other's nuclear capacity by a first strike. There would be little or no temptation to strike first. Counter-force strategy would be an impossibility. Both sides would know that they would be committing suicide, or rather reciprocal homicide, if they struck at each other. Thus there would be no necessity to be quick on the draw; there would be no premium on the fastest gun. Consequently there would be a marked decrease in 'accident proneness' on both sides. No one would be faced with the choice of rendering his country helpless or ending the world within 15 minutes.

America is in 1962 coming to possess a growing fleet of Polaris-carrying nuclear submarines. Russia is thought to be developing a similar fleet. But Polaris submarines will, surely, not turn out to be the only way, or perhaps even a permanent way, of securing a high degree of invulnerability. For example the Russians may prefer to rely on the unique degree to which they can hide their fixed rocket bases—though it is much to be hoped that they will not. (See p. 171 below.) Their type of society makes it possible to conceal the existence of even an I.C.B.M. base. (Hence the marked American desire to do air reconnaissance over Russia.) To what extent the Russians have succeeded in thus 'masking', to use the old gunner's term, their I.C.B.M. batteries is unknown to me, and perhaps to everyone else.

In any case it is inherently improbable that any one solution—Polaris submarines or another—will permanently solve the problem of invulnerability. But it may be reasonable to hope that a constantly developing variety of measures—if they are taken in time—will be able to confer a tolerably high degree of invulnerability on the main nuclear striking forces on each side. We may sum up the situation by saying that a fairly high degree of invulnerability, which, as we have seen, is a prerequisite of the first kind of deterrence, will not come of itself. But on the other hand it should prove possible to obtain it and maintain it by suitable, if elaborate, measures. It can be got—to a sufficient degree at least—if we realize its importance and take enough trouble to get it. And get it we must. For a neglect of this aspect of defence policy would, in my opinion, do more to render the balance unstable, and so to increase the risk of nuclear war, than any other single error.

The Second Kind of Deterrence

The second kind of deterrence is possessed by a country which feels able and willing effectively to threaten a potential opponent with nuclear attack on first strike, if that potential opponent commits acts which, while short of nuclear aggression against the first country, are nevertheless highly unwelcome. For example, when Russia threatened to bombard Britain with nuclear rockets unless Britain desisted from the Suez adventure in 1956, or again when Russia (equivocally) threatened the United States if the latter intervened in Cuba in 1960, she sought to exercise deterrent power of this second kind. Or again the late Mr John Foster Dulles' whole policy of 'massive retaliation at places and times of our own choosing,' against acts of aggression of a limited war type, was a general doctrine of deterrence of this second kind.

The instinctive view of many people in Britain is that neither Britain nor even the West as a whole ought to possess this second kind of deterrent power. It is felt that we ought in no circumstances to contemplate using nuclear weapons first, and that therefore we must abandon all atempts to deter other nations by these means from actions short of nuclear attack on ourselves.

There is no doubt that both the Western and the Russian attempt to use deterrent power of this second kind has often been reckless or foolish or both. One of the worst, because least convincing, of these attempts is made in paragraph 12 of the British White Paper on Defence for 1958. The doctrine is there enunciated that Britain will attack the Russian cities with nuclear weapons if Russia makes a large-scale attack upon Western Europe using conventional weapons only. The trouble with this sort of statement is not so much that it is immoral, nor even that it is rash; the trouble is that no one is in the least likely to believe it. For Britain, while she could today (1962) perhaps destroy a good many Russian cities on first strike, does not possess nearly enough means of delivering her nuclear weapons to give her any expectation of blotting out Russian retaliatory power. Britain, to use the technical term, has quite insufficient 'counter-force' power for that. Thus if Britain *initiated* a nuclear attack on the cities of Russia, by herself, she could be obliterated by the Russian retaliatory strike within a few hours.

If the threat enunciated in the British White Paper was really intended to be made on the part of the West as a whole it was

no doubt rather more convincing. Indeed in the early years of
the nineteen-fifties it was, probably, possible for the West as a
whole to make this kind of threat without facing unacceptable
Russian retaliation on second strike. In 1962 however it is
difficult to argue that the West would strike at the Russian
cities in response to any Russian move short of so general an
assault on the West that no doubt was left that Russia had
embarked on the immediate military conquest of the world. For
to do so might leave the West's cities open to the scale of
retaliation discussed in Chapter 1.

On the other hand it might be possible to argue that the
West as a whole could still threaten a 'counter-force' first strike
at the Russian launching sites as a response to some Russian
action (such as large-scale conventional invasion of Western
Europe), which, while short of a nuclear attack on America,
was felt by the West to be intolerable. In order to make such a
threat credible it would have to be at least possible that S.A.C.
might obliterate, on first strike, all, or almost all, the Russian
launching sites and bomber bases, so that Russian retaliation,
on second strike, would be reduced to 'an acceptable level'.
It is true that S.A.C. is an extremely formidable force, if
launched in this way, on first strike. For then something
approaching 100 per cent of the force could take off, instead of
the mere survivors of a Russian first strike. S.A.C. on first strike
is indeed an almost inconceivably powerful instrument of
devastation, even allowing for a fairly high degree of successful
interception by the Russian defences. Even the shorts and
overs of such a counter-force attack by S.A.C. might kill a high
proportion of the Russian population. Nevertheless whether or
not S.A.C. could be anything like sure of destroying an equally
high proportion of the Russian capacity to retaliate is another
matter. (We shall return to this issue on p. 100 below in the
context of the limits of limited war.)

Be that as it may, we must face the fact that *technically* this
second kind of deterrence is in some respect a much easier
thing to possess and to maintain than the first kind. For the first
kind depends on second strike capacity, which it is difficult to

preserve intact, while the second kind depends upon first strike capacity, which is that of the whole force.

It is probable that this second kind of deterrent power is nevertheless diminishing. For the West in particular it is partly a residual asset, dating from the time when the West had a monopoly, and then a predominance of nuclear power. As, first, the nuclear balance becomes more even and, second, each side takes steps to render its own deterrent power less and less vulnerable to the first strike of its opponent, it will diminish. This waning of the second kind of deterrence has far-reaching consequences for the West, which we shall discuss.

Let us first, however, consider the broad question of whether or not we ought to deplore or look forward to the complete disappearance of this second kind of deterrence. Its disappearance would be marked by an overt recognition by America that she would never use thermonuclear force except in retaliation for a thermonuclear attack upon herself. Before we voice an enthusiastic demand that either Britain or, more important, America shall make such a declaration, it may be well to realize what is involved. Once she had wholly divested herself, or had been divested, of this second kind of deterrent power, America would be unable to deter Russia, for instance, from convincingly informing the British (or the German, French or any other) Government that Britain would be obliterated unless Britain conformed to the wishes of the Russian Government in this or that respect. Even if much less (for us British!) than our own obliteration were at stake, America, and in present conditions therefore the West as a whole, would in this case be impotent to deter the Russian Government from many actions we might think highly objectionable. One can think of a dozen instances of some possible Russian action—the seizure of Denmark in order to open the Baltic, the occupation of the Middle East oilfields, support of a Chinese attempt to conquer India (or Japan) etc., etc., which, while very different from the bombardment of America, the Western Alliance might consider it essential to stop, lest Russian power became virtually invincible. Let us face the

fact that up to the present (1962) the method relied upon by the
West to deter the Russian Government from such actions has
been in the main nuclear deterrence of the second kind. As we
have just noted, both the American and the British Governments
have sought to maintain a standing threat to use their nuclear
weapons, on first strike, if Russia 'goes too far'. (Moreover, a
version of the doctrine is still (1962) the official 'line' preached
by the staffs at S.H.A.P.E., the headquarters of the N.A.T.O.
organization, see pp. 90–91 below.) Moreover, they possess
what appear to be remarkably inadequate alternative methods
of deterring the Russian Government from this type of action.

   The question is: is it right or wrong, either for us or for the
Russians, to depend upon deterrence of the second kind in this
way? In my opinion it is wrong for both sides to do so. From our
point of view it is wrong because it is increasingly unrealistic
and therefore increasingly dangerous. It will soon become
incredible both to ourselves and to our potential opponents that
we should in fact launch a full-scale thermonuclear war, in
the hope that our initial counter-force strike would completely
cripple Russian retaliatory capacity, except at extreme provocation. Therefore the Russian Government, if Western doctrine and preparations remain as they are, will increasingly feel
uninhibited from doing anything short of that extreme provocation. And the converse applies to Russia. The increasingly
frequent Russian threats to launch their rockets on particular
nations which are doing this or that which the Russians dislike
are not only irresponsible but also less and less credible. For
(as we shall see below, p. 100) it would be madness for Russia
to use nuclear force short of an all-out counter-force strike
designed to destroy S.A.C. And do we really believe that
Russia will do *that*, with all its possible consequences to herself,
because she disapproves of what is being done in the Congo or
in Cuba?

   To sum up, a position of rough nuclear equality tends progressively to weaken deterrence of the second kind. And this, in
the absence of other methods of deterrence, tends to enable both
sides to commit acts of aggression short of total attack, with

increasing impunity. This is not, however, to say that we can (on either side) dispense with the second kind of deterrence altogether. For there is a third kind of deterrence, which is of great potential importance but which is largely dependent upon the retention of at least some deterrent power of the second kind.

The Third Kind of Deterrence

The third kind of deterrence is deterrence by means short of all-out war. This third kind of deterrence is possessed by a nation which has the capacity *to reply in kind* to the unwelcome actions of other nations, short of full scale nuclear attack. This is the oldest form of deterrence. It existed and was practised in the pre-nuclear age, even when direct defence, by which an attack could be physically warded off, was still possible. One nation, that is to say, was often deterred from invading another, not only by the possibility that its own invasion would be repulsed, but also by the possibility that the defending country would then 'pass to the counter-attack', either by invading the aggressor, or by doing other unpleasant things to it. For example, the function of the British fleet was not only to beat off forces seeking to invade the island (as in the case of the Armada) but also to exert counter-pressure upon Continental enemies by means of blockade (as in the Napoleonic and the two World Wars). The question is, do the communist and non-communist alliances of today (*a*) need, and (*b*) possess, this third kind of deterrence?

Right through the nineteen-fifties the dominant school of military thought in the West either denied the need of this kind of deterrent power, or minimized it. This denial followed naturally enough upon a belief that we possessed a great deal of the second kind of deterrent power and were willing to use it. For if you feel able and willing to threaten your opponent with nuclear obliteration if he does not desist from unwelcome actions, there is clearly no need to be able to deter him by means of your armies and fleets. Thus alliances which believe that they have a heavy nuclear predominance will naturally be inclined to neglect the third kind of deterrence. Alliances which feel a marked nuclear inferiority will on the contrary tend to regard this third kind of deterrence as all important. We may recall for instance that the Russians up till about 1955 at any rate affected to regard nuclear arms as indecisive and to believe that wars would still be decided by mass armies. A more important question is this: is there a need for this third kind of deterrence when the nuclear forces on each side are in rough balance? This is an acutely debated question within the Western alliance in 1962.

On the one hand a still dominant, if waning, school of military thought declares that the West has only a very limited need for this sort of deterrence. Deterrence of the third kind must, be it observed, be exercised either with wholly non-nuclear, 'conventional' forces, or, at most, with small nuclear weapons employed on or near the battlefield. (We shall discuss this important secondary issue below.) Almost everyone would, it is true, concede that no doubt there is a need for small conventional forces, mainly to exert power in the large uncommitted world. But dominant military opinion at any rate at N.A.T.O. headquarters would strongly oppose dependence upon a conventional defence against, or counter-attack upon, any serious act of aggression on the part of the communist alliance. To prepare for and rely upon any such limited response would, they say, be actually to increase the likelihood of this type of aggression. For it would be a tacit admission that we should not respond by means of all-out nuclear retaliation. By maintaining adequate conventional forces we should, they declare, be weakening our deterrence of the second kind, which depends upon our opponents believing that we really would start throwing thermonuclear weapons if, for example, we suffered a fairly large attack with conventional weapons alone.

This argument holds only, be it observed, if we believe that we still possess a large amount of deterrence of the second kind. And in 1962 that takes a lot of believing. When we consider what might be the consequences to our enemies, to the world in general, and to ourselves in particular, of launching the West's full thermonuclear force, on first strike, it is remarkably difficult to believe that we would do it as a response to actions which did not unequivocally threaten our own survival. This, however, is an exceedingly grave conclusion. For if this is the real situation and if we fail to provide adequate deterrence of the third kind, it means that there are a hundred most unwelcome acts which our potential opponents can do to us with relative impunity. This is not a situation which can be met by bluff. If we really do not possess much deterrent power of the second kind it is not much good pretending that we do. That is the sort of bluff that will be called sooner rather than later.

On the whole therefore it would seem much better to acknowledge, both in words, and, far more important, by our actions, that our deterrent power of the second kind is inevitably waning, and to provide ourselves with an adequate degree of deterrent power of the third kind. This of course means, in practice, and above all, the equipment of N.A.T.O. with adequate ground forces which must be capable, in my opinion, of resistance to aggression using either purely conventional, or alternatively, small nuclear weapons. We shall discuss below the size and character of the problem which the provision of such forces presents. Existing N.A.T.O. doctrine, which discounts the importance of deterrent power of the third kind, and indeed considers its provision positively undesirable, if it suggests that we might respond to a considerable conventional aggression in Europe by conventional means alone, is, I repeat, largely a hang-over from the period of immense Western nuclear superiority. Up until about 1955 it may well have been true that American thermonuclear power, on first strike, was so predominant that it was credible to the Russians that S.A.C. would take off in response to any considerable Russian conventional aggression. For Russia would then, perhaps, have been able to do no more than relatively small damage to America in retaliation. I fear that the minds of those who lay down N.A.T.O. doctrine have not adjusted themselves to the present situation. That is the simple explanation of the illogical character of N.A.T.O. doctrine today (1962). We shall find (see p. 92 below) that a similar 'doctrinal lag' alone accounts for the marked tendency of the N.A.T.O. authorities to allow the conventional capability of its ground forces in Europe to atrophy and to rely exclusively upon small, or so called, tactical nuclear weapons.

We must not, however, go to the other extreme and suppose that conventional forces will be of any use without the maintenance of, rough, nuclear parity. For clearly an alliance with so strong a nuclear superiority as to give it the prospect of a completely successful counter-force strike could not be deterred by conventional forces however strong. It could always 'trump' them by threatening nuclear action. We shall see that the same 'trumping' might occur at the intermediate level of the smaller or shorter range nuclear weapons by an alliance which had a monopoly of these, even if it had no more than an equality at the thermonuclear level. In other words the third kind of deterrence can only exist on the presumption of rough nuclear parity above it. It is only if both sides are deterred by fear of the consequences from raising the stakes that the balance of power at the conventional level becomes important. But *on that presumption* the third kind of deterrence, above all at the conventional level, becomes exceedingly important. Woe betide the alliance which neglects it, for it will sooner or later find itself outclassed at the conventional level, and deterred by the consequences to itself of going up to the next level.

Interdependence of the Three Kinds of Deterrence

Each of the three kinds of deterrence are, then, interdependent. It is not much use having one of them without the other two. Even the second kind, although it is probably of decreasing significance relative to the others, should be preserved in residual form as long as possible, in order, precisely, to induce the potential contestants to keep their contests down to the lowest, or third, or conventional level. And this principle applies whether these contests are carried on by means of threat and counter-threat, or by means of actual, but limited, armed contests.

O.P.W.–F

These considerations bring us to the question of whether so
called 'limited wars' are or are not a possibility in contemporary
conditions, and with that to the whole question of the possible
characteristics of wars in the second half of the twentieth
century. But before discussing these questions let us sum up the
question of deterrence.

Some well-intentioned persons consider that the whole conception of deterrence is fallacious or worse. They are consequently particularly irritated by attempts such as the above to
distinguish between different kinds of deterrence. Such views, I
fear, rest upon a failure to distinguish between the actual and
the desirable. It is only too true that a peace resting upon
the mutual deterrence (i.e. latent threats) of two (or more)
alliances is inherently unstable. What we have been pointing
out is that this is, unfortunately, the character of the present
peace. For that matter this has been the character of most of
those periods of peace which the world has hitherto experienced. For mutual deterrence is merely the form taken by the
traditional balance of power situation in the nuclear age, when
the physical, 'warding-off' kind of defence has become technically impossible. Therefore when we arraign the concept of
deterrence and point out its manifest instabilities and dangers,
all that we are doing is to point out the instabilities and dangers
of a balance of power. And that is true rather than new. A
balance of power has never done more than postpone the recurrence of war. Undeniably that, in the nuclear age, is not
enough to preserve our existence. But it is also true that no other
policy as between sovereign states, or alliances of comparable
power, has done even so much. Hence it seems barren to
denounce these conceptions as iniquitous, until and unless we
have something better to put in their place.

5

Some Further Possible Characteristics
of Nuclear War

War Without Fighting

CLAUSEWITZ begins the seventh chapter of his third book with these words: 'The reader expects to hear of angles and lines, and finds, instead of these citizens of the scientific world, only people out of common life, such as he meets with every day in the street'. He goes on to make fun of the 'scientific' military textbooks of his day with their pretentious geometrical diagrams, their coloured squares representing *corps d'armée*, their swooping arrows and lines representing the wonderful 'strategic' moves of the generals; for they overlooked, he writes, the simple fact that wars are decided not by geometry, but by which of the opposing armies of human beings can longest bear the agony of battle.

The battles of the Napoleonic era, as Clausewitz describes them, were confrontations of close packed ranks of men who fired muskets and cannon into each other's faces, until one side or the other could bear it no longer and ran away. Moreover, throughout history, actual fighting, allowing for differences in weapons, has been much more akin to this characterization of it by Clausewitz, the great realist of war, than the more fanciful descriptions in the textbooks. (Certainly what glimpses I had of fighting in the Second World War were of this general character, the main difference being that the missiles which the

combatants threw at each other were of much longer range.)
With the coming of the nuclear age, however, Clausewitz's
descriptions seem at length to have become out of date. This
is not indeed because strategy has come into its own: nor
because men have become more heroic: it is simply because a
major nuclear war would be likely to be waged without anything which could normally be described as fighting at all.

War without fighting is a singular conception. But it is
difficult to see how a major interchange of nuclear weapons
would involve anything in the nature of combat. At what
might be called the despatching end there would be squads of
technicians. They would, it is true, be doing a good deal more
than pressing buttons. The rockets and their warheads, the
bombers and their bombs, the nuclear-powered submarines
and their missiles, are all immensely complicated things which
need relatively large numbers of highly skilled technicians to
keep them in order. But it would be strange to call this maintenance work fighting. The sailors under the polar ice cap in
their Polaris-carrying vessels, the bomber crews in the strato-
sphere, would be remote from and unconcerned with their
opposite numbers on the other side. And at the receiving end
there would be millions of corpses: little else. Moreover, it
might all be over in, perhaps an hour, perhaps a day, perhaps
a week. In such a war there would be little room for courage,
endurance, comradeship—for those military virtues, the
flickering light of which has at least relieved the blood and filth
of traditional warfare. All-out nuclear war would be a far
worse thing than even the bloodiest, stupidest Passchendaele or
Stalingrad: but it would be war without fighting.

Absolute War

Moreover, nuclear war would appear likely to be different in
several other fundamental respects from war as mankind has
hitherto known it. Clausewitz, in his initial chapter, entitled
'What is War?' lays down what amounts to his 'permanently
operating factors'. He does so with an insight which Stalin did
not approach. He begins by telling us that in the abstract, *in*

theory, war must always be what we now call 'total': it must be, that is to say, an unlimited, all-out, attempt to impose one nation's will upon another. It is this short initial passage of a few pages which no doubt earned Clausewitz his quite undeserved reputation of being an advocate of total war. Of course he was just the opposite—as indeed is revealed in the one phrase of his which everybody knows—that war is a continuation of policy by other means. For the implication is clear that what matters is the achievement of the objectives of policy, by whatever means. A given degree of violence may or may not be necessary, Clausewitz held, to that achievement. For, *in practice*, wars, he continues, have not been anything like 'absolute' (or total as we now say). For three 'modifications in the reality' have, as it were, adulterated the abstract totalness of war.

In the first place, Clausewitz writes 'War is never an isolated act . . . war does not spring up quite suddenly, it does not spread to the full in a moment'. This means that each side can gain experience of the other in the course of the war and discover, in the end, how to conclude a peace. In the second place 'war does not consist of a single instantaneous blow'. This means that neither side need put all its forces into the field at the outset. There will be time to mobilize the full national power and resources during the course of the war. 'It is also in the nature of these forces and their application that they cannot all be brought into activity at the same time. These forces are the armies actually on foot, the country with its superficial extent and its population, and the allies.' In the third place 'The result of war is never absolute . . . the conquered state often sees it only as a passing evil, which may be repaired in aftertimes by means of political combinations. How much this must modify the degree of tension, and the vigour of the efforts made, is evident in itself.'

It is a deeply disturbing reflection that none of Clausewitz's three 'modifying factors' apply to nuclear war. All-out nuclear war might well 'spring up quite suddenly and spread to the full in a moment'. It very likely would 'consist of a single instantaneous blow'. Its results would be only too likely to be 'absolute'.

In a word all those technical immaturities which (usually though not always) inhibited nations in the past from making total war to annihilation upon each other, have disappeared. The brakes have been taken off war.

There is no technical limit to the absolute or total character of nuclear war. Vast nations of hundreds of millions of inhabitants may now be able to exterminate each other in a few hours. The dread of a catastrophe so unprecedented hangs over the present generation of mankind. No doubt that dread is itself some safeguard against the catastrophe actually happening. It is already apparent that nations in the nuclear age draw back and temporize much more readily than formerly: that they accept insults, and overlook incidents, without referring to their 'honour', as they were once so fond of doing. This is a great gain: but we pay the price for it of knowing that, so long as the world is organized and armed as it is today, catastrophe of a new order of magnitude awaits one failure in restraint.

Three Sorts of War

Many people suppose that neither the American nor the Russian Government will ever now deliberately make war upon each other, for fear of the consequences to themselves. We have noted that this expectation depends upon the maintenance of an adequate degree of invulnerability in their deterrent forces. But granted that they both do maintain adequate invulnerability, we may legitimately hope that this expectation is well-founded. Certainly, the recent (1961) Russian reiteration, in the course of their controversy with the Chinese, that nuclear war would be likely to be 'ruinous' to both sides, is a very great step forward. (Poor Malenkov, in his Siberian power station, or wherever he is, must read all these statements somewhat ruefully. For this was exactly his thesis, for which amongst other things he was ruined. He was a premature convert to nuclear sanity!) Moreover, there is evidence that the 'lunatic fringe' of American airmen have also given up their dreams of being able to knock out Russia without fear of retaliation. Thus sheer dread of the instantaneous, automatized, horrors of nuclear war-without-fighting does appear to be making what may be called *deliberate* war a good deal less likely.

Unfortunately, however, this is a very different thing from making nuclear war in general impossible. For only a minority of the wars of past history have been deliberate in this sense. Indeed, it is probable that a majority of the wars of history have arisen from the mutual fears, suspicions, and misunderstandings of the Governments concerned, rather than from premeditated intent. We may call such wars as these *unintended* wars. Again, some wars have arisen, mainly at least, from particular accidents. We may call these *accidental* wars. Moreover, we shall have to face the unpleasant fact that in the opinion of most experts, nuclear weapons have seriously increased the danger of both unintended and accidental wars.

Accidental War

Let us first consider the possibilities of accidental nuclear war. That they are by no means negligible may be readily gathered from the works of the American defence experts. Professor Morgenstern has some particularly alarming passages in his book *The Question of National Defense* on this subject. He alleges that geese have been mistaken upon the radar screens for Russian bombers and S.A.C. alerted. Moreover, he considers that the situation will become (if nothing is done about it) much more dangerous still when missiles have become the main method of delivery. He alleges that 'showers of meteors' and other 'electrical phenomena' may be mistaken for I.C.B.M.s. There would then be only minutes or seconds left for verification and decision. Moreover, if the missiles are fired they cannot, like bombers, be recalled. Yet if they are not fired they may be (*if, but only if, we have been criminally negligent enough to leave them vulnerable*) all destroyed upon the ground.

These allegations are hotly denied by other defence experts as greatly exaggerated. The layman is unable to judge of the degree of risk but he can hardly escape the conclusion that two characteristics of nuclear weapons as they exist at present render them 'accident-prone'. On the one hand the warning

time which can be expected between the first signal of an attack
and the arrival of the weapons has already to be reckoned in
minutes and, in Morgenstern's phrase, 'approaches inexorably
to Zero'. Second, the two deterrent forces may be to an unknown
but appreciable degree mutually vulnerable to surprise first
strike attack.

It is difficult to see what can be done about the first of these
characteristics. Once again it is the second which can be modified. If only *both* sides possess themselves of invulnerable forces,
there will be no necessity for anyone to face the intolerable
decision of launching a nuclear war or running the risk of his
country's whole deterrent power being knocked out of its
hands. For once a country's main deterrent force is invulnerable the necessity for instant response disappears. Even if the
marks on the radar screen *are* Russian (American) missiles, and
not geese or meteors, there will be no need to despatch the
retaliatory force before they land. To do so will not save one's
own country, nor will it be necessary for retaliation. Above all
*the mere fact that full retaliation will always be possible, even after a
surprise first strike has landed, will be an immense reassurance to both sides
that such a first strike will not in fact be launched. The marks on the screen
will be much less likely to be missiles, and much more likely to be geese or
meteors. The whole vicious circle of pre-emption, the 'I must hit him first
before he hits me first' psychology, can be prevented from developing.*

Unintended War

Wars may break out in yet a third way, which is neither
deliberate nor *accidental*, in the senses given to those words above.
This is *unintended* war. War, that is to say, may occur neither
because Country A makes up its mind to attack Country B and
does so, nor because it relentlessly pursues some objective of
policy which is flatly contradictory to the security of Country B,
nor because of some unforeseen accident by which the one
country mistakenly supposes itself to be under attack, but
because of a series of unpremeditated events which produces in
one, or both, sides the belief that they are in acute danger, and
that their only safety lies in immediate attack.

Mr Herman Kahn (op. cit.) gives a vivid and romantic illustration of this danger. It is drawn, if not from history, then from mythology, those illustrative parables of the experience of the race. He calls it 'The Camlan problem'. He reminds us of the account of King Arthur's last battle in the *Morte Darthur*. At Camlan, it will be recalled, the armoured hosts of Arthur and his rebellious son Mordred were drawn up facing each other in array. But each side was appalled at the consequences which must ensue from a total struggle, and negotiations between Arthur and the rebels were begun. They were progressing well, peace and reconciliation seemed just about to be achieved, when one of the knights drew his sword to cut down an adder which had bitten him. The opposite ranks saw the sun flash upon the naked blade; they felt that they were just about to be charged; they drew, and the two hosts thundered down upon each other. In a few hours only Mordred, the fatally stricken Arthur, and two other knights were left alive.

The parallels for the nuclear age are only too easy to draw. We have noted the preoccupation of Russian military thought with the concept of the pre-emptive attack: we may recall in particular their assumption that the Russian authorities would always be aware of an American intention to strike. Is it not easy to imagine some American move, which, in a moment of tension, the Russians might interpret not otherwise than the Arthurian knights interpreted the drawing of the blade? (or conversely).

Kahn points out that unintended war, war, that is to say, which both sides wish to avoid but which comes upon them with seeming inevitability, born out of the dialectic of their military moves and counter-moves, is nothing new. The actual outbreak of World War I had this character. In this case the respective acts of mobilization were the analogues of the drawing of the blade. Austria mobilized to chastise Serbia, Russia mobilized to restrain Austria. But if Russia were allowed to complete her mobilization undisturbed (a two weeks' process) she would have gained an immense advantage over Germany, should she in fact mean to attack her as well as Austria.

We now know that she had no such intention. But the German General Staff did not know this and were convinced that they in turn had to mobilize in self-preservation. But if Germany mobilized, France would be at her mercy unless France mobilized also. For it was well known that the German war plan was for an all-out attack on France, not Russia. At the last moment the Kaiser enquired whether it might not be better to cancel all the war plans, leave France alone, and threaten, and if need be attack, Russia in order to prevent her restraining Austria, and so limit the war to Eastern Europe. He had to be told by the General Staff that whatever the diplomatic or political advantages of such a course might be, it was technically impossible. The railway network, the very train schedules, the whole immensely elaborate Army orders permitted a deployment westwards alone. If he attempted to head his armies eastwards against Russia, they would become a rabble.

The flash of the blade of the secondary Austrian knight, as he drew for the incidental purpose of chastising Serbia, was seen all round Europe. The hosts thundered down upon one another, and when all was over the old Europe was dead.

Unintended War the Main danger

There have been a good many *deliberate* wars in history, and some *accidental* wars, but no doubt *unintended* wars have been the most numerous. There is little doubt that it is this third category of war, intermediate between the other two, which is by far our greatest danger in the nuclear age. It may be over-optimistic to suppose that *deliberate* war can now be completely ruled out. But it can realistically be estimated that as the sheer, cold dread of nuclear consequences comes to be appreciated by government after government (as they were evidently appreciated by the Russian government some time in 1959 or 1960) deliberate nuclear war will become less likely, so long at any rate as both sides take the elementary, if expensive, precaution of keeping their deterrent forces invulnerable. If we may assume that they will do that, deliberate war would indeed become the act of a madman. To use a British colloquialism, when *that* particular penny has dropped down the mental slot-machines of the principal governments of both East and West, it is hard to believe that either side will deliberately institute nuclear war. (It is partly, I think, because they have concentrated too exclusively on this kind of war that Sir John Slessor and his school of thought have been able to reach the dangerously complacent conclusion that nuclear war has abolished itself.)

There remains, then, first, accidental war. The dangers of that, once they are realized at all, are often perhaps even exaggerated. The possibility of mistaking geese for bombers, meteors for missiles, the approach of waiting time to zero, the necessity of split-second decisions on which hang the fate of the world, are intensely dramatic and alarming. But in fact the actual degree of danger of this particular kind of war also largely turns upon the vulnerability or invulnerability of the deterrent forces. Professor Morgenstern sums up the matter as follows:

> *Accidental, large-scale war is a distinct possibility when one side has a highly vulnerable retaliatory force. The situation is correspondingly worse when both are so equipped. The dangers are particularly great when vulnerably placed missiles are used.*

But, for the reasons already given, if an adequate degree of invulnerability can be achieved and maintained, as it almost certainly can, given the necessary determination, the risk of genuinely accidental war can be reduced to a low level.

There remains the danger of unintended war, and this is surely the great danger. This kind of war cannot be sharply differentiated from the other two. It is a blurred category. On the one hand it shades off into deliberate war if one or more of the governments concerned pursue policies which, while they may hope that they will produce the surrender of their opponents instead of a war, are incompatible with the elementary security of other states. On the other hand it shades off into accidental war if some quite adventitious act of military preparation by one party is misinterpreted by the other as a preliminary to immediate first strike attack. Between these two there are a thousand possible situations which could set the feet of sincerely unwilling governments upon the fatal path. In this case invulnerable deterrent forces, while they will indirectly help, by calming the nerves of otherwise alarmed military authorities, are not a complete answer. As we shall see in the next chapter, governments might be led up a sort of escalator of violence until they found themselves at the final, thermonuclear, destination, even though they knew that the invulnerable deterrent force of their opponent awaited them there. But before leaving the subject of nuclear war itself, we should outline one more of its characteristics.

Symmetry and A-Symmetry

Since war is at present being averted by a balance of power, the stability of the balance is of the essence. Any sudden advantage gained by one side is dangerous. It will tend to tip the scales to the point at which either the weaker side feels that all is lost unless something drastic is done in redress, or to the point at which the stronger side feels that now it can strike with impunity and eliminate its rival once and for all. Such an advantage may be political: an uncommitted, important country may adhere to one alliance or the other. But it may also be technical. It is readily conceivable that the unilateral invention or development of a new 'weapons system', as such things are called, may give, temporarily, a marked relative advantage. Out of this consideration the conception or principle of the desirability of *symmetry* in armaments has arisen. The most responsible American Defence experts have not hesitated for example to write that it is to the advantage of America that Russian defence preparations should, in some respects at any rate, develop in parallel with those of America. Professor Morgenstern for example holds that it will promote the stability of the balance, and so promote a true American interest, if Russia should develop the invulnerability of her deterrent force at the same time as America. He writes:

In view of modern technology of speedy weapons delivery from any point on earth to any other, it is in the interest of the United States for Russia to have an invulnerable retaliatory force and vice versa.

For if America alone possessed an invulnerable deterrent, not only might she be tempted to strike—a hypothesis which Morgenstern would reject—but the Russians might panic at the thought that they alone were vulnerable and mount a pre-emptive strike, as their only salvation, in any period of acute tension.

The desirability of symmetry produces some paradoxical conclusions. For example there is nothing that informed opinion dreads more than the invention and development, by one side only, of a 100 per cent effective method of intercepting I.C.B.M.s (and of course manned bombers too). If either side achieved this without the other, or did it some years ahead of the other, the consequences of this in itself, and at first sight, purely *defensive* invention would be the destruction of the balance. For in this event not only its deterrent force but the whole of one country, or even the whole of one alliance, would become invulnerable to the other. The other therefore would be at its mercy, to be destroyed at will. The country which had failed to develop the defensive weapons system would have lost all three kinds of deterrence at one fell swoop. Thus, it can be imagined that the mere rumour that one or other of the contestants was making marked progress towards the development of such a watertight defence might be enough to throw the other into panic followed by pre-emptive action.

Fortunately the scientists suppose that the development of such a failure-proof defensive system, though not inconceivable, is remote. But then several developments, which seemed remote but very recently (see p. 31 above), have taken place. The layman can say little about such matters. But the example of the hypothetical 'anti-missile missile' as it is called may illustrate the deadly importance of the principle of symmetry. In the autumn of 1961 Russia claimed that she had developed such an anti-missile missile. But her claim did not much impress the world: nor has Russian conduct since that moment suggested that the claim was well-founded.

We now encounter the fact that the balance of power under which we live is a *moving* balance. Both sides are rapidly augmenting their power to wage nuclear war. The balance can only be maintained if they augment their power at approximately the same rates. And that is largely a function of the relative success or failure of the rival teams of scientists and technicians. All that either side can do is to press on as best it can with its own developments, lest its opponent get ahead. This is the traditional 'arms race', which we shall discuss below (Chapter 8). Here we may already note the strange new fact that some sophisticated American defence experts now worry not only about their own country's progress but also about whether their opponent is keeping up. They may actually desire that he should not fall behind in some important particular. They may (rightly) value the stability of the balance so highly that they will not welcome a tilt, even if that tilt is in their own favour, lest their opponent be driven to desperation.

Summary

Before, however, we can discuss the arms race (in Chapter 8) we must deal with another important aspect of war in our period, namely limited, and (probably) non-nuclear war. This we shall do in Chapters 6 and 7. In this chapter we have been concerned to outline some of the remaining characteristics of nuclear war as such. We have seen that it is a new and bizarre type of 'war-without-fighting', and all the more horrible for that. We have seen that it is absolute war without the 'modifying factors', which, Clausewitz noted, have usually hitherto cushioned and moderated the grapple of the nations. We have seen that the sheer dread of the thing, as it becomes appreciated by the main governments of the world, gives an increasing degree of protection against what we have called *deliberate* nuclear war. A deliberate attack, that is to say, by one country on another, in order to gain this or that supposed advantage, is becoming less likely. We may look forward to its becoming a remote contingency, on condition that the nuclear powers make their deterrent forces as invulnerable as possible, and keep them so.

But this reflection is less reassuring than it might be because of two other possible types of nuclear war, namely *accidental* war and *unintended* war. Of the two it was unintended war which we chiefly apprehended. Accidental war was not indeed impossible: but again with reasonable regard to invulnerability, it should be successfully avoided. It was the broad, vague category of unintended war: of war stumbled into by the dialectic of fallible, emotional men acting, and reacting, under great strain, to the chances and changes of a balance of power situation, which seemed the real danger. For that very dread which is proving a barrier to deliberate war might drive governments to strike out in panic for fear that, if they did not, they would be struck down in the dark. Finally, we noted that the balance of power under which we live was a moving balance: that both sides were competitively increasing their strength, and must do so lest they be outclassed. Stability could only be maintained if the strengths of the alliances grew in at least rough symmetry. And we noted the paradox that the invention of a wholly effective *defence* against nuclear attack, if such an invention were made, as it well might be, a-symmetrically, by one side well ahead of the other, was considered to be one of the worst dangers to which the almost all-important stability of the balance might be exposed.

6

Limited War

Limited War Possible

IT is denied by two schools of thought that there can be anything in the nature of small or limited wars in the nuclear
age. And this is curious. For in this strange new epoch, one of
the very few things that we can say with certainty is that small
or limited wars, which do not develop into world nuclear
holocausts, can occur. For in the first fifteen years of the
nuclear epoch a number of them have occurred.

The Korean war is no doubt the best-known example. The
Korean war demonstrated that a war may be fairly large,
involving several hundreds of thousands of men on each side,
including the forces of one at least of the super powers, and that
it may be prolonged—for three years in this case—and yet not
become general. But the war in Indo-China is another example.
So too, in rather a different way, are the second Arab-Israeli
war and the Suez operation. Moreover, it is important to
remember that a short, but fierce, limited war was being waged,
almost simultaneously with the Israeli and Anglo-French operations of 1956, by Russia in order to put down the Hungarian
rebellion. And then there have been the Malayan, Mau Mau and
Algerian wars: but these perhaps may be thought of as guerilla
operations, however prolonged and severe, rather than as wars.

In the face of this conclusive evidence, why is it often maintained that there can be no such things as limited wars, in the

nuclear age? The reason is, I think, that two very different schools of thought have wished to establish this clearly untenable proposition. On the one hand extreme proponents of the omnipotence of nuclear weapons—chiefly airmen, and in particular American airmen—have wished to deny, or at least belittle, the possibility of limited war. For they wished to see the national effort concentrated on the provision of nuclear striking power. In so doing they have had the support of much American opinion in general. For some American airmen the very term 'limited war' became at one time a term of derision. Many Americans of all kinds had been profoundly disturbed, shocked, and even humiliated by what seemed the disproportionate effort, in relation to the purely defensive results achieved, of the Korean war. The airmen, in particular, came near to the position that even a nuclear war would be better than another Korea. For they had by no means envisaged (in 1950–3) the consequences to themselves of an unlimited nuclear war, in which America would suffer, as well as inflict, nuclear bombardment.

At the other extreme of the gamut of opinion, pacifist, or near-pacifist, writers are accustomed to maintain the same position, in order to deny that any form of war can fall short of full world disaster. For they wish to be able to take up the position that nothing short of a policy of complete non-resistance will suffice to preserve the world. This state of mind is well illustrated in the distinguished example of Bertrand Russell. With a far too narrow logic, Bertrand Russell has swung from at least considering the possibility of a preventive war at the beginning of the nuclear age, when Russia had no nuclear weapons, to the advocacy of policies which must lead toward the surrender of the West today. Both extremes of opinion seem to share something of an all-or-nothing type of reaction to the problem. The views of neither school of thought have evidential value.

Importance of Non-Nuclear Arms

On the other hand the reader of the preceding chapters of this

book may well have gained the impression that nuclear arms
and nothing else are of importance today. If there is little doubt,
they may say, that the initial thermonuclear, intercontinental
bombardment would prove decisive, what function—other
than that of the role of military police in support of the civil
power—remains for non-nuclear, or 'conventional' (as they
are called) armed forces? Why keep up armies and navies
when everything will be decided above their heads in a few
hours? Even for the purpose of imposing our will upon a
recalcitrant minor power, will not the menace of nuclear bombardment be far more effective than conventional force? Will
not the greater force always contain within itself the lesser,
as it were?—'the dog we keep to deal with the cat will be able
to deal with the kittens.'

Curiously (and expensively) enough, however, experience
has already shown that this plausible view is quite false. A
nation or alliance which maintained large nuclear weapons
alone would put itself at an extreme disadvantage, as compared to a nation or alliance which maintained both such a
nuclear striking force *and* adequate conventional forces also. The
latter would almost certainly be able to have its way on all issues
of less than life-and-death importance. And over the years such a
series of secondary triumphs might well add up to world
hegemony. Hence the importance of armies, navies and for
that matter air forces, using non-nuclear, or *possibly* small
nuclear weapons (we shall consider this case carefully) remains
very great.

This paradoxical conclusion is explained by the fact that if
(but only if) there is a rough parity between the contestants in
thermonuclear power (and if their means of delivery are
relatively invulnerable) the deterrent forces will tend to cancel
out. Both sides, as we have seen will be extremely loath to
resort to their use, knowing that fatal retaliation awaits them.
Hence there will be a whole range of secondary, but important,
issues on which one side can insist on having its way, with
considerable assurance that it will not provoke all-out nuclear
retaliation. Alliance A can, for instance, use its conventional

forces to maintain, or subvert, governments in secondary states in some security that Alliance B will not unleash its thermonuclear forces because of that. But equally if Alliance B possesses adequate conventional forces it can use them to prevent the maintenance, or subversion, of the minor governments in question, without much fear that the answer will be thermonuclear.

It follows that any alliance which wishes to keep its end up all over the world will be rash indeed to deprive itself of conventional forces adequate to hold their own in exercises of force which may range all the way from police action in aid of the civil power to a war at least of Korean size and duration, and for all we know to a larger size still. We may confirm this statement by observing that, for example, Russia would have been in grave difficulties in Hungary in 1956 if she had possessed only thermonuclear forces. Not only would she have risked starting a thermonuclear exchange if she had blotted out Budapest with a 10-megaton bomb or rocket; such an act would have had the most dire consequences on her reputation; and finally it might have led, in the absence of Russian ground troops, to unmanageable guerilla warfare in the rest of Hungary.

Again, as the American government in the event concluded, it would have been both too risky, and probably ineffective, to have dropped H or A bombs on the jungle round Dien-Bien-Phu, in an attempt to preserve French colonial power in Indo-China. In this case America did not possess the will or perhaps even the ability, to commit the necessary ground troops. And so the local communists were able to reach a compromise settlement fairly favourable to themselves. The Korean example is also relevant, in the sense that the real choice turned out to be between letting the opposing alliance have its way or opposing it by conventional means. Finally, the Israeli-Anglo-French operation against Egypt is instructive. Here it is arguable that, if Britain and France had possessed the right kind of conventional forces, which could be deployed within days rather than months, they could have imposed their will on Nasser, at least temporarily. (In my opinion this would have been a disastrous kind of success, because it would have led merely to a long drawn-out guerilla war with the Arab world. But this has nothing to do with the military case.) In any case no one supposed it possible for Britain to use her, quite sufficient, nuclear power to coerce Egypt. And in the end even the slow motion conventional forces which the British and French in fact used would undoubtedly have been (disastrously) successful if, on this occasion, the Western alliance had not been hopelessly split, with its predominant power, America, aligned (rightly in my view) with Russia to restrain the British and French.

Such instances could be multiplied. But these may suffice to show the undeniable importance which conventional forces have had, to both sides, during the fifteen years of the nuclear epoch. Who can doubt that such examples will (unfortunately) occur again in the future?

N.A.T.O. and the European Special Case

There is one area of possible conflict between the communist and non-communist alliances of which it has been maintained with special vehemence that, here at least, there can be no such thing as limited war. In Europe, we are told, any war must rapidly expand to the full thermonuclear level. And yet, paradoxically, this is the one area in which the non-communist alliance stations (fairly) considerable conventional forces. What are they there for? For if it is true that *any* war in Europe must quickly 'spiral up' into the thermonuclear exchange, it is hard to see what difference the presence of twenty or thirty N.A.T.O. divisions on the ground would make.

N.A.T.O. theory and practice are evidently here at variance. And fortunately N.A.T.O. practice, *insofar as it is implemented*, is very much to be preferred to N.A.T.O. theory. For it is simply not true that any war in Europe *must* become thermonuclear. The only sense in which we could *know* that this would be so would be if we were really determined to make it true, by responding to any Russian, or satellite, use of violence by loosing S.A.C. on Russia.

It was, no doubt, during the period of American monopoly, and then preponderance, in thermonuclear power that this doctrine of the impossibility of limited war in Europe was promulgated. It was intended as a warning. During this period it may have been plausible. Today it is not. It is easy to imagine a dozen moves by the Communist forces in Europe which no one can really suppose would trigger off the thermonuclear exchange, *now that what is in question is an exchange.* Therefore, if N.A.T.O. possessed no conventional forces, or inadequate conventional forces, there are a dozen things which the non-communist alliance would have to suffer in impotence.

Nor would such Eastern moves necessarily remain unimportant. Before this book is read we may have (a second) experience of one of them, namely a renewed attempt to make the Western presence in Berlin impossible. Or violent intervention might occur in a dispute between the two Germanies. Or, more grave still, an attempt might be made to occupy Denmark in a few hours and so open the Baltic. Or, far more likely, the Russian move might be in connexion with some event which it is as impossible to foresee today as it was impossible to foresee the Hungarian uprising before 1956. We cannot know what the event might be, but we can know very well, unless we choose wilfully to blind our eyes, that any such medium-sized Russian move in Europe would, in the absence of adequate N.A.T.O. forces on the ground, confront the West with the almost unbearable dilemma of submission or of launching the thermonuclear exchange. Who can suppose that the decision of the American President (and it would be his decision alone) would be to start the thermonuclear exchange in such circumstances?[1] Therefore for N.A.T.O. to possess no forces on the ground, or merely token ground forces, would be a formula for piecemeal capitulation.

So much is, perhaps, gradually coming to be conceded, as the facts of thermonuclear parity begin to be appreciated. But it may still be said that if N.A.T.O. conventional forces barred

[1] The British Cabinet could, no doubt, send off the V Bomber force for what that was worth.

the way to such medium-sized moves as these, the resultant fighting would still be sure to spiral up into a thermonuclear exchange. Of course such a danger exists. The danger of the spread and intensification of even the most limited war is always grave. But once again how can we *know* that the worst must happen, unless we really mean that we ourselves are determined to make it happen? And that would mean that we were in fact determined to turn every war in Europe into a nuclear war. But if we have not made up our minds to start the spiral ourselves, why should there be anything peculiar about the soil of Europe which would make it impossible for a violent initiative to remain limited there, in the same way that the limited wars mentioned above have remained limited?

If, however, so much as this is conceded it becomes necessary drastically to revise existing N.A.T.O. theory and practice. If we have a real intention to stop a medium-sized Russian move on the ground by conventional forces, we must take far more seriously than hitherto the question of both the quantity and quality of the N.A.T.O. divisions. To take the question of quantity first. The N.A.T.O. Supreme Commander tells us that he requires thirty first-class well-equipped and mobile divisions. He has in fact some twenty by no means first-class or well-equipped divisions. Does anyone suppose that it is beyond the capacity of such rich, populous, and militarily experienced states as Britain, France, West Germany, and America, to mention the chief allies alone, to provide the extra ten divisions and to bring the whole thirty to a really high standard? Is it not perfectly clear that the failure is here one of *doctrine*? The N.A.T.O. governments have never yet appreciated what is the true function of their ground forces in Europe. They have talked vaguely of providing 'a trip wire', of 'psychological reassurance', phrases which revealed that they supposed that all that really matters is S.A.C. and its thermonuclear weapons in the background. They have never fully realized that the era of Western nuclear predominance is over: they have never faced the military necessities of the era of nuclear parity. They have talked manifest nonsense about the impossibility of matching 'the Eastern hordes' except by throwing nuclear weapons at them, ignoring the simple fact of arithmetic that Western Europe is more populous than Russia and that Russia is hardly likely to employ, say, Hungarian divisions in the West. No doubt they have talked like this partly because of the pain and expense of providing adequate ground forces adequately equipped; but it has also been because of a failure to think out what is the *function* of those ground forces.

Small Tactical or Battlefield Nuclear Weapons

And then a further complication has arisen to bedevil the attempt at clear thinking on the subject of limited war. When, during the nineteen-fifties, the N.A.T.O. commanders saw that the N.A.T.O. governments were not going to provide them with adequate ground forces, they sought, and thought that they had found, a way out. And this was to equip such ground forces as they had with new and relatively small types of nuclear weapons, which were contemporaneously being developed in America, for use, not in intercontinental bombardment, but on the battlefield or close behind it, as a new sort of artillery in support of ground forces. In this way, it was supposed, the lack of N.A.T.O. divisions could be compensated for.

This argument seemed logical so long as the same idea did not occur to the Russians. But that period proved short. As we have noted above (p. 44) Mr Khruschev is now (1962) enthusiastically engaged in, as he puts it, 'gearing' the whole Russian ground forces to the use of small, tactical, or battlefield, nuclear weapons—call them what you will. Directly that has happened the *differential* advantage hoped for by the N.A.T.O. commanders disappears. Large forces equipped with tactical nuclear weapons may be expected to predominate over small forces so equipped no less than large conventional forces predominate over small conventional forces. Arguments have now been produced to the effect that, anyhow, tactical nuclear weapons favour the defence against the attack. But these arguments are strongly contested by some military authorities. The layman may be pardoned for supposing that no one has any idea what their effect would be, since there is absolutely no experience of their use.

The introduction of tactical nuclear weapons to redress the balance between the ground forces in Europe was, then, a wholly unsuccessful move. But this is not to say that they could now be entirely abandoned. Once the Russians have possessed themselves of such weapons it is manifestly impossible to ask N.A.T.O. troops to face them with conventional weapons alone. One might as well ask them to throw away their automatic rifles and resume the pike. There remains the question of whether the Russians would have introduced tactical nuclear weapons if N.A.T.O. had not done so. Perhaps they would: if so little has been lost. But it is extremely dangerous to harbour the illusion that something has been *gained* by our adoption of these weapons: that we can in some mysterious way 'answer' a Russian attack (of whatever size), made with conventional weapons alone, by resorting to tactical nuclears. One can perhaps conceive of circumstances in which N.A.T.O. forces would be driven to do this. But they must realize that they would immediately be exposed to a Russian riposte in kind and that there is little reason to suppose that they would have acquired any *differential* advantage by shifting the contest up one step from the conventional to the tactical nuclear level. And yet the illusion that 'we must have tactical nuclears to compensate for the Russian masses' persists in N.A.T.O. circles. This is mere nostalgia for the period of Western nuclear predominance.

This illusion is particularly dangerous because it is leading to a situation in which the N.A.T.O. forces in Europe, partly because of the nature of their equipment and even more because of the nature of their *training*, will soon feel themselves unable to undertake more than a border skirmish *without* the use of tactical nuclear weapons. Lip service is paid at N.A.T.O. headquarters to the need for preserving the capacity to fight with conventional weapons alone. But conversation with officers of, at any rate, the British N.A.T.O. contingent makes it clear that the doctrine has spread that it would be impossible to

meet any considerable Russian move, even if undertaken with
conventional weapons alone, except by using tactical nuclears
from the outset. It is contended that troops cannot be asked to
have a dual capacity at any rate in the same theatre of war.

This disastrous doctrine ignores the obvious fact that it
presents the Russians with the opportunity to confront
N.A.T.O. with the same dilemma, albeit on a lower level, as,
we saw, would be afforded if N.A.T.O. possessed little or
nothing but heavy, strategic thermonuclear striking forces.
In this case, too, the Russians might use a few divisions in a
strictly conventional role [1] in support, to take an example at
random, of some European communist or pro-communist
or even neutralist party, or government, which had got into a
civil war with the opposite forces in its own country. (Or again
one can think of the coercion of a heretical communist government on the Yugoslav model.) N.A.T.O. might well be charged
by the vote of the United Nations Assembly to stop Russian
'intervention'. (We should be back in something analogous to
the Spanish situation of the nineteen-thirties.) What would be
the position of the N.A.T.O. governments if they were informed by their commanders that nothing could be done unless tactical nuclear weapons were used from the outset?

Escalation

N.A.T.O. *might* use tactical nuclear weapons in such a situation. There is nothing flatly incredible about it, as in the former
case of responding by the thermonuclear bombardment of
Russia. But let us observe what must happen if we did. In the
first place the inhabitants of the disputed state would be
sacrified. However *geographically* limited a war waged with
tactical nuclear weapons *might* remain, there would be nothing
limited about it for the inhabitants of the area in which it was
fought. (For of course the Russians would respond in kind—
they could not do less.) The inhabitants would be killed. Therefore it is easy to imagine passionate appeals from the country
in question to the United Nations Assembly asking that body

---

[1] I am using the term conventional to mean non-nuclear throughout.

to counter-instruct the N.A.T.O. governments *against* intervention, since Russian occupation was by far the lesser evil.

More serious still, the N.A.T.O. decision to use tactical nuclear weapons would have started the horribly dangerous process known in defence discussions as 'Escalation'. Escalation simply means putting your feet upon the fatal escalator that leads upwards, by a process of challenge and response, all the way from the local disturbance, through conventional limited war, through limited war using tactical nuclear weapons, to the thermonuclear exchange. For just as there is no law that every limited war will become unlimited, so also there is no assurance that one day one of them will not 'escalate' or 'spiral up' into a thermonuclear exchange. Indeed there is always serious danger that one will. For to set against the dread that every government which is not lost to reason must feel at the idea of blowing up a considerable part, at least, of the world, there is always a temptation to 'escalate'. It will always be extremely difficult for a government, which has just seen its own forces checkmated, and perhaps annihilated, by an opponent who has 'escalated' to the next stage up in weapons, to accept defeat. This would be far more difficult than to accept repulse, without clear-cut defeat, such as the communist alliance accepted in Korea for example, when that repulse was inflicted by using the same kind of weapons with which the original move was made.

For these reasons the present tendency of N.A.T.O. to discount, both in theory and more still in practice, the possibility of meeting anything but the smallest Russian moves in Europe on the conventional level is deeply to be deplored. It should be reversed at the earliest possible moment. That will mean, of course, the provision of at least the full thirty divisions required by the N.A.T.O. authorities.

The Thirty Divisions Target

Naturally to provide thirty really well-equipped and trained divisions will require a considerable effort. Providing the manpower is probably the smaller part of the problem. Britain for example would probably merely have to live up to her original pledge to provide four divisions (or their equivalent in brigade groups) without conscription. But there is one condition. That we give up the silly anachronism of scattering 'Imperial garrisons', for a largely non-existent Empire, about the world. What we want in that connexion is air-transportable brigade groups kept at a high state of readiness either in the United Kingdom or in Germany, and some, though by no means all, of the existing overseas bases for stockpiling.

France would have to cease to use practically her entire army for narrowly national purposes in Algeria, and provide, say, half-a-dozen of her already first-rate divisions. And so on. It is ridiculous to pretend that Western Europe cannot provide the thirty divisions required. To equip them superbly, and train them superbly (and nothing less will do), would undoubtedly be a costly matter. It might cost Britain £50-£100 million more on the Army estimates for example—out of a Defence Budget of £1,600 million. But again to say that it is impossible for such rich nations as these to do the job—nations which are spending in 1962 in most cases well under 10 per cent of their national incomes on defence—is plain prevarication. The truth is that the Western governments do not want to do the job because they have never understood the point of it. They have never appreciated the nature of the new period of nuclear parity which we have entered or the necessities it imposes upon them. And so out of our ignorance, stupidity, meanness and incomprehension, we are failing to provide those forces which can alone ensure that we shall not be faced with the intolerable dilemma of piecemeal surrender or world destruction. If we fail to provide these forces it is not difficult to suggest from historical experience what will happen. We shall choose first one, and then the other, of those intolerable alternatives. We shall allow our opponents to 'get away with it' on several occasions. And then at the last minute, when anything short of all will be not enough, we shall be driven to resist, since complete surrender will now be the only alternative. It has happened before.

Symmetry Again

At this point the full application of the principle of symmetry comes into view. This does not mean that it is necessary to match the Russian ground forces man for man. But we now see that nothing less than at least an approximate symmetry of power *at every level*, conventinnal, tactical, nuclear, thermonuclear. is indispensable to the stability of the balance. For if either side lets itself become markedly inferior, at any level, it will be faced with the dilemma of 'escalating' to the next level above or of surrender. And once the process of escalation has begun the danger of its continuing to the end is acute. This is not to say, however, that, once even the tactical nuclear level of conflict has been reached, a full thermonuclear exchange is 'inevitable'. How do we know? In this field no one has any experience to guide them. Therefore it seems foolish loudly to proclaim that total disaster is *certain* if the first tactical nuclear is detonated. If we convinced our opponents of that we might regret it one day. What we must convince our own governments and military authorities of is this: once we take the first, major step in escalation from the conventional level to the tactical nuclear level, we have immensely increased the danger of going all the way to the thermonuclear exchange. The one obvious, clear-cut halting place is at the conventional level. That is why it is criminal negligence on our part to fail to provide the necessary conventional forces to hold our own at that level.

The Limits of Limited War

Thus far we have defined the need for N.A.T.O. conventional capacity in terms of meeting some medium-sized Russian initiative—the seizing of a city, or a small country; armed intervention in a dispute between the two Germanies, support or subversion of 'their' or 'our' types of government in a border country, etc. But what, it will be asked, should our response be if Russia launched a general invasion of Western Europe with 'horse, foot and artillery' with the evident intention of occupying the whole continent? Is it contended that N.A.T.O. either could or should limit its response to such an onslaught to resistance by conventional arms?

Now such a Russian invasion might itself either use conventional arms alone or it might use tactical nuclear weapons. In the latter case N.A.T.O. would, of course, have to respond in kind by using our tactical nuclears. This is why we have to have them. Otherwise our forces would be quite helpless if the Russians decided to use theirs. But if the Russians confined themselves to conventional weapons, even in a full-scale invasion, should we or could we resist them by these means alone? Existing N.A.T.O. doctrine is extremely averse to our attempting to do so. It is argued that unless we now threaten to use, and sincerely intend to use, our tactical nuclears first, we shall fail to deter the Russians from such an onslaught. But in fact all we should do by such threats, if the Russians really had decided on a general invasion, would be to force them to use their tactical nuclears too. In other words, in this case also N.A.T.O. doctrine appears to be still living in the previous period of a Western monopoly, or near-monopoly, in nuclear power.

The second argument used to support existing N.A.T.O. doctrine is that it is in any case impossible for N.A.T.O. to resist Russian numbers by means of conventional weapons alone. This view is strongly contested by some eminent military authorities. Captain Liddell Hart, for example, has repeatedly made calculations designed to show that if N.A.T.O. would in fact provide the thirty first-rate divisions on the central front in Europe we should have a good chance of halting even a full Russian conventional invasion. Experience of the last war indicates, it seems, that the defence usually succeeded in holding unless the attack possessed more than a three to one superiority. (And instances are given where the defence succeeded at an inferiority of five or even ten to one.) It is further calculated that for logistic reasons the Russians could not deploy more than ninety divisions in a westerly direction; so, with thirty N.A.T.O. divisions, the ratio of three to one would be achieved. Finally, Captain Liddell Hart has made interesting calculations on what he terms the ratio of force to space. These calculations tend to show that the length of front which any given number of men can hold has been steadily increasing for the past 200 years, owing of course to the enormous growth of fire-power. And he considers that thirty divisions, highly equipped and mobile, would suffice to hold the Central European front.

It would be inappropriate for a layman to express a decided opinion on this controversy. Moreover, it is the less necessary to do so because it should, in my view, be frankly admitted that if the Russians launched a general invasion of Western Europe with ninety divisions we should have reached the very limits of limited war. For the fact is that in doing so they would have unequivocally announced their intention of dominating the world immediately and by military force. In that extreme event an American thermonuclear response becomes much more credible. The American President of the day would have the awful responsibility of permitting an almost certain Russian world hegemony, if he allowed all Western Europe to be con-quered, or of destroying Russia and killing perhaps 80 per cent or 90 per cent of her inhabitants (and of accepting the awful consequences of Russian retaliation). For there is no doubt about the ability of S.A.C. *in such circumstances*, when it was presented with the opportunity of first strike, to do this.

The truth is that it would be almost incredibly rash of the Russians to start a *general* war by means of an invasion of Western Europe with conventional arms. For by doing so they would hand the opportunity for a thermonuclear first strike to S.A.C. on a platter. And however much we may criticize its vulnerability for purposes of second strike retaliation, *as a first strike* force, undamaged and undiminished, S.A.C. is an almost inconceivably terrible instrument. Whether indeed the Presi-dent's military advisers would report to him that they were confident that S.A.C. could, even in these highly favourable circumstances, knock out all the Russian rocket sites and bomber bases, and so avoid retaliation on America, is another matter. But no doubt S.A.C. could greatly diminish such Russian retaliation and also utterly devastate Russia.

Therefore, unless the Russians have failed utterly to appreciate the nuclear equation as it exists today (and this does not now seem to be so, to judge from the recent Russian pronouncements quoted above) one of the least likely of all Russian moves would be a full-scale conventional invasion of Western Europe. If the Russians meant deliberately to set out upon the military conquest of the world (itself in my opinion a remote hypothesis) they would not dare to begin in any other way than by a counter-force strike upon S.A.C. To begin in any other way would be to lay themselves open to almost certain destruction.

In other words, America retains, we are appreciating, a good deal of the second sort of deterrence against, at any rate, a full invasion of Western Europe. It may be guessed that those who think chiefly in terms of such a full-scale Russian invasion, either using conventional or, still more, using tactical nuclear weapons, have not realized the nature of the thermonuclear balance. They have not appreciated the fact that for either side to expose itself to the other's first strike by beginning what would be unmistakably a general war at one of the lower levels, would be to court its own destruction. Ought we to conclude, then, that it is unnecessary for N.A.T.O. to make the very considerable, if quite feasible, effort necessary to provide conventional forces which should be able to hold a full-scale Russian invasion of Western Europe with, say, ninety divisions? Can N.A.T.O. content itself with providing conventional forces capable of dealing with medium-sized Russian actions? It is tempting to answer yes to such a question, in view of the double improbability of the contemplated situation arising. It is improbable that Russia will set out to conquer the world by military means, and it is improbable that if she did so she would dare to choose any opening move other than all-out counter-force action against S.A.C. But improbable events sometimes happen. And think of what would be at stake if this improbable event *did* happen. An American President would have to make what can only be described as the most awful decision which any man in human history has been called upon to make. If N.A.T.O. were manifestly incapable of holding the Russians on the ground, he would have to decide on whether to acquiesce in Russian, or Sino-Russian, world hegemony, or by loosing S.A.C. to destroy the lives of many hundreds of millions of human beings, including almost certainly many tens of millions of his own fellow-countrymen.

Is it not the duty of the N.A.T.O. states, including of course America herself, to leave open a third course of action, that of resisting such a Russian invasion by conventional forces which were large and well equipped enough to stand a good chance of success? After all, the difference in the number of first-rate divisions which N.A.T.O. must in any case maintain in order to meet secondary Russian moves, and the number needed to meet full-scale Russian invasion, is not overwhelmingly large. What is at issue here is rather the question of reserves. If secondary operations alone are to be contemplated at the conventional level, reserve forces are not particularly important. But, if the possibility of having to hold a major conventional attack by conventional means is even contemplated, the whole question of reserves, of both men and materials, resumes its traditional importance and the N.A.T.O. nations should provide them. However small the chance of a Russian conventional invasion may be, I for my part consider that it will be negligent if N.A.T.O. does not provide the forces necessary to meet it conventionally—even if to do so is in the nature of a re-insurance.

Nevertheless, it remains far more probable that Russia will continue to restrict herself to moves which are much below the level of an aggression which could credibly evoke a first strike by S.A.C. What does not seem to be understood by the N.A.T.O. authorities is that quite large acts of aggression come within this category. Is it credible that an American President would unleash S.A.C., with all the appalling consequences of such an act, including the extreme risk of the destruction of a good many American cities, with the loss of several tens of millions of American lives, for anything short of a Russian move on the scale of a general invasion of Western Europe? (Or of course a thermonuclear attack on Western Europe or

America herself—of moves that is to say which unmistakably showed that Russia intended to conquer the world by means of a general war.) I do not myself believe that in practice he would. In other words America retains deterrence of the second kind only against some act of Russian aggression which unmistakably indicated an immediate intention to conquer the world by military force. For all acts of aggression below that level, we cannot rely upon the deterrent power of S.A.C. Therefore why should Russia run so hideous a risk as to provoke even the possibility of the unloosing of S.A.C. upon her when there are a dozen secondary, but very important, gains which she can make with relative impunity, so long as N.A.T.O. fails to produce the forces necessary to bar her way at the lower levels? The fact is that such acts as the general invasion of, or thermonuclear attack upon, Western Europe mark the limits of limited war. For it is as foolish to say that all acts of aggression, however large, will remain limited as to say that every act of aggression must lead to general war. (Some of these considerations are set out more fully than is possible here by Professor Bernard Brodie in Chapter 9 of his *Strategy in the Missile Age*.)

Nuclear Chess

In order to summarize the conclusions of this chapter, it may be helpful to compare the military aspects of the present international situation to the game of chess. The Russians are now the world's greatest chess players; so the comparison must often occur to them. First, we may think of the two thermonuclear striking forces as the queens. At first sight they seem all important; and so they would be if there were not one on each side. But as it is they are balanced one against the other. In chess they are fairly often exchanged at a comparatively early stage in the game—'the queens were off the board by such and such a move', write the commentators. In nuclear chess they cannot (unfortunately) be exchanged, but, if they are kept invulnerable to each other, they do in fact to a very considerable extent cancel out.

O.P.W.–H

Second, the other major pieces of the chess set may be compared to tactical nuclear weapons and their use may be compared to 'The middle game' at chess. But there our objectives and those of chess players diverge. The players wish to play the middle game and to win it. We, if we are sane, wish above all to avoid having to play the middle game at all. Nevertheless we also wish to avoid getting into a position in which we shall be sure to lose if the game is played. This second consideration is very important, not only because of the consequences of losing, but also because, naturally, it will be a strong temptation to our opponent to begin to play the middle game if his experienced eye sees that we have got ourselves into a losing position. And once the middle game, involving the exchange of nuclear pieces, has begun, it will be hard to stop until one side has been totally destroyed.

In the third place there is 'the pawn game', and this we may compare to military operations with conventional weapons alone. In a sense the pawn game has been going on, in one part of the world or the other, ever since the East–West balance of power established itself, fifteen years ago. It would be highly desirable to stop it, to put the chessmen back in the box, and to play a different game, in which we were both on the same side and our only opponents were the ills of human life. In fact, that, it will be submitted, is in the long run the only hope for either of us. But to do that involves major changes in the outlooks of both players, changes of mind and of heart which cannot occur overnight. Meanwhile the pawn game—call it the cold war, punctuated by limited hot wars, or what you will—goes on. And at this level too we must see to it, for our lives' sake (and curiously enough for our opponents' lives' sake too) that we do not get into a losing position. For if we do we shall have only the alternative of surrender or of escalating up to the middle game of the exchange of the smaller nuclear pieces. And that will involve the extreme risk that the queens will be brought back on to the board again. For curiously enough the nuclear balance resembles chess in this respect also—that the banished queens may in certain circumstances return in wrath to the board. In fact it may not be too fanciful to write that in life as in the game the queens might be brought back by a pawn penetrating to the eighth square—by, that is to say, some secondary country acquiring and using nuclear weapons. And then not only the game but the players too will be all over.

One lesson of this grim game of nuclear chess, for which the whole world is the board, is surely that it is not much use being strong on any one of the three levels if you are weak on the others. You must be equipped to play the pawn game, the middle game and the end game. For the balance to prove stable, and war to be avoided, there must be symmetry at each level. Moreover, such all-round symmetry is necessary for there to be a possibility of gradually calling the game off by a process of mutual disarmament. This has been well shown in the disarmament negotiations. During most of the period Russia has been disproportionately strong except in the thermonuclear field. So of course she has been very ready to propose the abolition of thermonuclear weapons. For the West to have accepted this would have been equivalent to a player who was in a losing position, well down in the exchange of pawns and major pieces, to have accepted an exchange of queens. And even such a beginner at chess as myself knows better than to do that, since the disproportion in strength is of course increased.

There is one more analogy to chess, though a partial one. Just as White always has an advantage because he enjoys 'first strike' so it may never be possible to eliminate wholly, by securing greater and greater invulnerability, *some* advantage to the side that strikes first. But it should be possible to cut this initiator's advantage down to the small and indecisive advantage enjoyed by White. On the other hand, if both sides leave their thermonuclears vulnerable, it is as if White could take Black's queen at the first move. On the other hand, if the thermonuclears are invulnerable, we get the actual chess situation in which the queens are at the start well screened by their pawn defences and White has no more than the initiator's advantage of choosing his opening gambit.

7

A Reversal of N.A.T.O.'s Nuclear Strategy

What Should Be Done?

IT is much easier to criticize the present policy and military doctrines of N.A.T.O. than to suggest a viable alternative. Nevertheless, there is clearly an obligation upon the critic to do so: and the broad outlines, at least, of a new policy and of new military doctrines for N.A.T.O. are implicit in the above criticisms.

In the first place it is important to realize that the essence of the matter lies in what policies and doctrines as to the use, or non-use, of nuclear weapons are adopted by the N.A.T.O. high command. For the whole character of the N.A.T.O. forces, their numerical strength, the types of armaments which they will possess, their disposition, their training and for that matter their efficiency and morale, will inevitably depend upon this issue. To put the point bluntly: experience has shown that if the doctrine of an early and almost automatic first use of tactical, and then if necessary of strategic, nuclear weapons is adhered to, no conventional forces fit in quantity, equipment or quality, to meet a considerable emergency will ever be raised. Why indeed should the N.A.T.O. Governments put themselves to the expense and trouble of doing so, if their generals tell them that such conventional forces will never be used except at most for a few days' delaying action? If on the other hand the considerations set out[1] above, which take account of the fact

---

[1] It should be needless to say that there is nothing original about these

of nuclear parity, are made the foundation of Western military thinking, the need for adequate conventional forces becomes immediately, and imperatively, evident.

It is only in so far as it affects this basic issue that the question of N.A.T.O. as 'a third nuclear power' assumes importance. Whether or not some, no doubt small, part of the West's strategic nuclear deterrent force should be in some sense detached from the rest, as to its command and control, and, possibly, its geographical location, is a matter upon which a good deal can be said on both sides. Thus to detach a part of the force would be illogical and inconvenient. But if—though only if—the overriding condition of securing the very maximum possible degree of invulnerability were satisfied, and if some of the European nations felt greatly reassured, then there may be a case for arranging that, as under the present (1962) American proposal a few Polaris-carrying submarines are put under the command of N.A.T.O.

The 1960 American Proposals

The proposals laid before the other N.A.T.O. Governments by the Eisenhower Administration in the autumn of 1960 appear to have been of a very different character. Briefly what was proposed was that a large number of solid-fuelled, medium-range ballistic missiles of the Polaris, or similar, kind should be installed in continental Europe, no doubt in hardened or mobile sites, and that these should be placed under S.A.C.E.U.R.'s command—though their warheads would remain in American custody. It was explained that the object would be, not to make N.A.T.O. into a 'third nuclear power' but merely to 'modernize' the present *tactical* nuclear armoury of N.A.T.O., which essentially consists in nuclear-bomb carrying aircraft. It was, we were assured, to be a mere 'modernization' programme; and the Polaris-type missiles, although they

---

considerations. They are in the main common ground for most of the American defence experts, and for much informed, if as yet unofficial, opinion in Britain.

have a range of well over 1,000 miles and carry thermonuclear warheads of more than half a megaton in power, were described as 'tactical weapons'!

Who can doubt that if this policy were adopted all attempt to raise, train and equip serious conventional forces would be abandoned? The West would have proclaimed, with all the matchless eloquence of deeds, that it was pinning all its hopes upon deterring any Russian aggression—beyond a mere frontier incident—by a nuclear response. Moreover, this would be a nuclear response which however much we might label it 'tactical', would in fact be a strategic, thermonuclear response.

The real objection to such a policy is not that it would be provocative (though it would also be that) but that it would be fatally weak. For it would lack one indispensable prerequisite of effective deterrence, namely credibility. How could any American President in fact authorize S.A.C.E.U.R. to respond to say a medium-sized Russian conventional aggression by firing his Polarises? The President could not avoid the knowledge that he must reckon with a full Russian counter-response upon both Europe and America. He could not avoid the knowledge, that is to say, that in releasing S.A.C.E.U.R. to fire thermonuclear rockets, he was in fact initiating the full thermonuclear exchange. And how could he do that for any reason short of an unmistakable Russian move for full and immediate conquest of the world?

Therefore, the equipment of N.A.T.O. with a 'multi-gun battery' of medium range thermonuclear weapons, *instead of* (as it certainly would be) adequate conventional forces would, paradoxically enough, be in the nature of a 'green light' to our opponents for any aggressive action short of a decisive attempt to conquer Western Europe. Equally paradoxically, at the same time, and not unnaturally, it would be regarded by the Russians as an extremely provocative move. For it would in fact be a menacing addition to the West's first strike capacity. This policy would seem, therefore, to possess the fatal combination of being weak and provocative at the same time.

But if the proposal to equip N.A.T.O. with medium-range

land-based thermonuclear missiles points precisely in the wrong direction, what in fact would be a policy which would satisfy the considerations set out in the last chapter? We may at least make certain suggestions.

Two Suggestions

First, the provision of at any rate thirty first-rate, highly trained, really well-equipped divisions (or their equivalents) primarily designed and trained for the conventional role, on the European central front. The provision of adequate reserves could then be tackled.

Second, the provision of some short-range, genuinely tactical, nuclear weapons for the support of this force in case the enemy initiated the use of tactical nuclear weapons. This question of the provision and role of tactical nuclear weapons has always been, and remains, by far the most difficult issue of N.A.T.O. doctrine. On the one hand, it is clear that so long as the Russians possess weapons of this sort the West must possess them also. This is so both for the sake of the morale of our troops and also because it would be wrong to forgo the possibility, however slender it may be, that a war which had been taken to the tactical nuclear level might yet be halted there, before the world as a whole had gone up in flames. What then should be the character of N.A.T.O.'s tactical nuclear weapons? No doubt this question can be answered only tentatively and provisionally, for technical innovation, as we shall note in the next chapter, is continually changing the terms of the problem. But for the 'sixties at least, there seems much to be said for developing intensively the existing form of the delivery of tactical or nuclear weapons, namely manned aircraft. It is strongly and impressively denied that for this purpose the manned aircraft is even approaching the end of its effective life. Developed for 'contour flying' (i.e. ultra low level attack) where it is undetectable by radar, and for V.T.O.L. (Vertical Take-off and Landing) it is likely to remain a most formidable, and above all flexible, weapon. It has several advantages over alternative systems of delivery. First, manned aircraft are genuinely dual-

purpose weapons. They can carry a conventional or nuclear
bomb load at will. Thus, if we are to take seriously the provision of thirty divisions, designed essentially for the conventional
role, these aircraft must be provided in any case. Second,
manned aircraft can be used either on the battlefield or some
way behind it. Third, they can carry almost any size of nuclear
weapons, including the smaller subkiloton fission weapon.
Fourth, they can be positioned well behind the armies under
separate command and control from the ground forces.

We may compare these characteristics with medium-range
(1,000 miles plus) ballistic missiles, such as the land-based
Polaris rocket, throwing thermonuclear warheads of more than
half a megaton. To call such weapons tactical is a manifest
absurdity, whatever the targets to which they may be directed.
Once they had been employed—on say the cities upon which it
was believed that the opposing armies were based—what
possible hope could there be of preventing the full thermonuclear exchange? Indeed it would surely be rash in the
extreme for the Western authorities to *initiate* nuclear warfare
in this way. To do so would give the Russians the great advantage of striking first at S.A.C. No, if *thermo*-nuclear weapons are
to be employed at all it would surely be indispensable to loose
S.A.C. at the outset in an all-out attempt to destroy as much
as possible of Russia's retaliatory power. But if so it is difficult to
see any particular role for land-based, and so at least semi-
vulnerable, medium-range ballistic missiles. They would
merely prove a not very effective addition to S.A.C. The effort
needed to provide them would, surely, be much better directed
to providing additional invulnerability and striking power to
the main strategic deterrent force.

At the other end of the spectrum of delivery systems we may
compare manned aircraft to the various forms of 'nuclear
artillery' which are being developed. These consist in rockets
and artillery pieces capable of throwing small nuclear weapons
over, relatively, short distances. The main objection to reliance
upon these delivery systems is that by their nature, they must
be more or less closely integrated with the actual fighting units

of the ground forces. Indeed in the case of really small weapons
such as the 'Davy Crockett' this may mean integration right
down to the battalion or even platoon level. But when once
nuclear weapons have been intermingled with the ground
forces to this extent it is difficult to retain any genuine capacity
for conventional warfare. The command and control of
battalion and platoon weapons must tend to fall, whatever the
paper regulations, into the hands of junior officers. It is
difficult to suppose that such officers would, or could, always
forgo their use, if defeat, with the possible destruction of their
unit, were the alternative. Hence their widespread adoption
would appear to spell the end of any attempt to create a considerable conventional capacity for the N.A.T.O. forces.

For all these reasons the further development of powerful
tactical air forces, capable of delivering either conventional or
nuclear weapons, would seem the best policy for N.A.T.O. to
adopt, in this most difficult region of the tactical nuclear weapon.
It may be objected that the Russian ground forces may soon be
found to have had small tactical nuclear weapons of the
'artillery' type integrated with them. (Although this does not
seem to be the case today (1962).) Are we, it may be asked, to
deny them to our troops? Certainly it would be impossible to
do so unless our troops could be, visually and audibly, assured,
during their exercises, of powerful air support, which, it would
be pointed out, could be used at short notice in the nuclear
role. But given such support—especially from V.T.O.L., short
take-off, and contour flying aircraft—an effective and convincing answer to the Russian potential at the tactical nuclear
level could be provided. It would no doubt have to be made
clear, and that publicly, that if the Russians used their 'nuclear
artillery', the Western response would not be to reply with
exactly similar weapons, but to drench the Russian front and
immediate rear with nuclear weapons carried in manned
aircraft.

It is necessary to record, however, that other defence experts
strongly deny the efficacy of manned aircraft in the above role,
at any rate until V.T.O.L. and/or short take-off aircraft are

available, owing to the vulnerability of airfields to first strike attack by medium-range nuclear rockets, and to the vulnerability of aircraft in flight to the new 'anti-aircraft artillery' of the guided rocket type. I should have thought that this point could have been met by really drastic (and no doubt expensive) dispersal of even existing types of aircraft. As to the further allegation that the new anti-aircraft rocket artillery is making the delivery of either conventional or nuclear weapons from manned aircraft more and more difficult, is this true if the low-level method of attack is adopted?

In the last resort the layman, somewhat confounded by the differing views of the experts, can only fall back on insisting upon the principle that the tactical nuclear deterrent, however delivered, should be held well back, under a separate chain of command, and never integrated with the front-line ground forces. Moreover such a deterrent, again however delivered, should be genuinely tactical in the sense that it should have a range of a hundred or so miles: that in a word it should clearly be for battlefield support and 'counter-battery' work, not for the strategic bombardment of the enemy's homeland.

Should We Never Strike First?

If such a provision of (a) ground forces genuinely adequate in both quantity and quality to put up the most determined resistance to a Russian conventional attack and (b) powerful air forces in support (or comparatively short-range rocket-artillery) capable of either a conventional or a nuclear role, were provided, I can visualize few circumstances in which it could ever be to the advantage of the West to initiate nuclear war. It has, therefore, been suggested that the West would have much to gain and little to lose by making a declaration that we would never use nuclear weapons first. Without prejudice to the political advantages of such a course, it may be useful to remember that the actual advantage, by way of stabilizing the military situation, would be likely to follow, not from such a declaration, which might or might not be believed, but from the adoption of military doctrines, and of a military posture of the type just outlined. For such a military posture would also make it clear to any informed observer that abstention from the initiation of nuclear warfare was in fact the firm intention of the West. It would be the provision (i) of invulnerable, characteristically second strike, deterrent strategic nuclear forces; (ii) of adequate conventional forces and (iii) of tactical nuclear forces held well back under separate command and, if possible, capable of the conventional as well as the nuclear role, which would in fact reassure the world.

Objections to the Proposed Policy

In order to gain so great an advantage, both for ourselves and for the world, it would be sensible to pay a price. And, no doubt, such a N.A.T.O. policy would, like all other alternative policies, involve disadvantages. We must therefore state, and then answer, the objections which can be urged against its adoption. The principal disadvantage which is usually urged against such a policy is that it 'offers the Russians the option of conventional war.' It is argued that, by indicating that our response to even a medium-sized Russian conventional attack will fall short of nuclear retribution, it increases the risk of conventional war, while decreasing the risk of nuclear war.

Indeed it has been suggested that a sort of scale exists on which it is possible by moving in one direction to decrease the risk of war of any kind breaking out, but only at the cost of increasing the catastrophic character of the war if it does nevertheless break out. If, so the argument runs, it is considered desirable to do this one will weaken one's conventional forces and strengthen one's nuclear forces, so that the enemy will perceive that should he commit even a limited act of aggression, the response must be nuclear. Then the dread of such a response will, it is hoped, deter him from moving at all. The weakness of this argument is that the enemy may appreciate that, on the contrary, since we have debarred ourselves from responding to even a limited challenge except by nuclear means, we shall not in fact respond at all. We shall have lost more in credibility than we shall have gained by way of inspiring dread.

By moving along the scale in the opposite direction (i.e. by decreasing our nuclear and increasing our conventional forces) the objectors' argument continues, we shall admittedly make any war which does break out less catastrophic, but only at the cost of increasing the risk of the outbreak. For we shall have, allegedly, decreased the deterrence which we are exercising upon the enemy by indicating to him that if he makes a limited move he is incurring the risk of a conventional response alone, instead of a nuclear holocaust.

At first sight it may seem difficult to decide in which direction along the scale it is desirable to move. But in fact there is a cogent reason for believing that it is in the interests both of the West and of peace to move in the direction of strengthening the conventional forces. The decisive consideration is that it is, in present circumstances, probably fallacious to suppose that the deterrent effect upon the Russians will be decreased, on balance, by indicating by our posture that we should respond conventionally to a conventional challenge. It is true that this is a much lesser threat; but then, on the other hand, there is a far greater probability of our actually carrying it out! The net deterrent effect will, I repeat, gain more by way of credibility than it loses by way of terror.

Summary

It will be seen that the argument, that it is wrong for the West to shift the balance of our effort towards strengthening our conventional forces relative to our nuclear forces, rests upon the view that it is, still, the threat of nuclear response, whether upon the tactical or strategic level, which mainly deters the Russians from aggressions carried out by conventional means. And this, the reader of the preceding chapters will observe, is only another way of making the claim that the West still possesses a significant degree of deterrence of the second kind. The validity or otherwise of this view has already been discussed. We saw that while it was impossible to say dogmatically that the West now possessed no deterrence of the second kind, even for aggressions short of attempts at a military conquest of the world, yet we were discussing what was, at best, a waning asset.

But what about the case of an outright Russian invasion of the West, with all the conventional forces which the Russians could deploy westwards, in a manifest attempt at general conquest? We maintained that such an attempt was highly improbable, partly because in this one case the West does still possess a measure at least of credibility for nuclear deterrence of the second kind. For in this case, it genuinely is conceivable that an American President might launch S.A.C. on first strike: hence it would be rash indeed for the Russians to start a general war in this way. If then the West made a binding declaration never to use nuclear weapons first, and if that declaration were believed, we should have divested ourselves of one particular and possibly significant aspect of our deterrent power. It cannot, therefore, be denied that the argument of 'giving the Russians the option of conventional war' has some real force in respect of this one eventuality of a general war initiated by the Russians on the conventional level. This consideration reinforces the view that what is wanted is not so much a formal declaration that the West will in no circumstances use nuclear forces first, as a revision of N.A.T.O. doctrine and posture such as would make it clear that the West had acquired the option of responding to a conventional challenge by conventional means. What is needed is not to give an option to our opponents, but to acquire an option for ourselves.

The option to use conventional forces alone may be of great importance, for given the prerequisite of such forces in adequate strength it is by no means clear that it would be to the disadvantage of the West to keep even a general war at the conventional level. The ablest American defence thinkers are now accustomed to point out that the West's most important remaining asset over the Russians is not in the nuclear field— where there is bound to be an approximation to effective parity. Our main remaining advantage is precisely in industrial potential: in the capacity to produce vast quantities of conventional arms over a long period. In this respect North

America, Britain, Western Europe and Australia taken together still have a very great predominance over Russia, and even over Russia, the satellite states and China taken together. Therefore, just contrary to what is often supposed, it would probably be to the advantage of the West to fight even a general war at this level, and to place the odium of any escalation to the nuclear level squarely upon the other side.

If we wish for a watchword, or slogan, for this whole matter it might be found in this apparent paradox: in the nuclear age there is no substitute for adequate conventional forces.

8

The Arms Race

A Qualitative Arms Race

WE now have to face the fact that the balance of power which we have been discussing is a moving balance. At each of the three distinguishable levels of violence, namely thermonuclear intercontinental bombardment, smaller, tactical, or battlefield nuclears and conventional arms, both the Eastern and the Western alliances are continually augmenting their powers. For the balance to remain stable they must do so at roughly the same rates.

This is 'the arms race' which since before the First World War has been a subject of denunciation. The present arms race is, however, of a different character to those which preceded it. In former periods it was mainly a question of mobilizing, training and equipping great masses of men with the standard arms of the day, such as the bolt-action rifle, the machine-gun and the various calibres of artillery. Naval warfare was more mechanized, but even here the race consisted very largely in building the largest possible number of capital ships, with their appropriate auxiliary vessels. Technical changes took place comparatively slowly and were by no means the main concern of the military authorities and governments which were engaged in the race.

Today it is hardly too much to say that the race is qualitative rather than quantitative. The pace of technical change is of a

different order. Herman Kahn (op. cit.) suggests that a technical
'revolution' in weapons is now occurring about once every five
years. Every five years, that is to say, the two super-powers
introduce new 'weapons systems', as they are called, which,
when they have been distributed in large numbers and their
uses mastered, will render obsolete the existing systems. At first
sight this seems an exaggerated statement. But when we,
recollect that we are still only seventeen years from the detonation of the first nuclear weapons, we must concede that the
speed of change has not been far short of this. It is often forgotten that the thermonuclear weapon constituted as large an
increase of power over the fission weapon, as the latter did over
the ordinary or chemical explosive. The thermonuclear weapon
did not appear, it is true, until 1952. But since then 'progress'
(towards mutual annihilation) has been more rapid. It is not
however in explosive power, but in the means of its delivery,
that technical change is now intense. The B47 jet bomber,
a delivery vehicle which renders the super-forts which
carried the original A bombs to Japan of antiquarian interest
only, appeared in 1951. The B52, which readily delivers from
any point on the earth's surface to any other, and then returns,
with flight refuelling, appeared in 1953. But by 1959 the
I.C.B.M.s were introduced, and in 1961 the (at present) largely
invulnerable Polaris-carrying atomic-powered submarine
became operational. At the same time, and unexpectedly even
to many scientists, during the nineteen-fifties the tactical nuclear
weapons made their appearance. It is true that technical change
in conventional arms has been slower. But that is mainly because much less attention has been given to them.

'. . . Some Recent Work of E. Fermi and L. Szilard . . .'

Thus the arms race is becoming much more a competition in
who can first create, and introduce, and then render operational
new weapons systems, than a competition in the piling up of
great stocks of existing weapons or in the mobilization and
training of millions of men. As a measure of this change we may
contemplate the fact that at least half the immense military

budget of the American aircraft industry is said to be spent, not upon producing combat aircraft at all, but on research and development.

This change in the nature of the arms race has important consequences. A nation's power is coming to depend increasingly upon its scientists and technicians. But these do not appear out of nowhere. They must be expensively and lengthily trained. And this can only be done in universities and technical institutes. This has led some experts to the remarkable conclusion that over the long term, the number, size and quality of a nation's universities are becoming the best index of its military potential. If this is considered an extreme statement let us contemplate the famous letter written to President Roosevelt in 1939 by Albert Einstein.

Some recent work by E. Fermi and L. Szilard, Einstein wrote, seem to call for . . . quick action on the part of the Administration . . .[1]

Einstein continued

This new phenomenon would also lead to the construction of bombs, and it is conceivable—though much less certain—that extremely powerful bombs of a new type may thus be constructed. A single bomb of this type, carried by boat and exploded in a port, might very well destroy the whole port together with some of the surrounding territory. However, such bombs might very well prove to be too heavy for transportation by air.

'Quick action' was taken by the administration. Within six years from the receipt of this letter a nuclear weapon had become not merely 'conceivable', which was all that even Einstein had supposed it to be in 1939, but had destroyed Hiroshima. This is surely by far the most rapid development and application of a piece of fundamental research in the history of science. It proved that the almost always incomprehensible ideas of some mathematician or physicist tucked away in some university might, if backed by the resources of a super-power, really and truly produce an invincible weapon in six years.

[1] Quoted in *1970 Without Arms Control*, Report of the National Planning Association, Princeton University Press.

Henceforward, it has been impossible for traditional, non-scientific, and often anti-scientific military authorities to deny the supreme importance, not merely of technics, but of basic, theoretical scientific research. The 'E. Fermis and L. Szilards', with their equations, became, at one immense bound, the decisive element in national power. After this the apparently bizarre assertion that 'the state of universities' is, over the decades, the most important single factor in military potential, becomes comprehensible.

Professor Morgenstern (op. cit.) has a foreboding passage on the effect of this extraordinary transference of the arms race from the barracks to the study. He writes:

> In ancient times it was the adventures of the warrior, his wanderings through foreign lands, which pulled so many toward warfare. Now the same kind of fascination lies in the work the great experimental stations do all over the world—always connected with some potential or actual warlike application. So we get two things at once: we gradually discover more laws of the universe, and we have a spirit of another, though morbid, adventure thrown into the process.
>
> The scientists working in those new, fabulous fields, fervently hope that their new weapons and devices will never be used, knowing too well the consequences. But the risk is taken: the weapons are being invented and eventually pass out of their hands into those of the policy makers, who have not developed comparable new methods to neutralize them, in particular, methods for working together with the enemy, who is subjected to the same influences and the same dangers. Safety will not be achieved by the conventional ideas and methods of disarmament and diplomacy, which are trivial and totally inadequate compared with the new elements of the situation. Fundamentally new ideas are necessary for organizing human society.

Professor Blackett has vehemently challenged this suggestion that the greater part of contemporary scientific work has become entangled in the arms race. He writes:

> The existing advances in high-energy nuclear physics, in visual and radio astronomy, in organic and bio-chemistry, in molecular biology, in embryology and in munology and a dozen other fields are wholly independent of war preparations. (*Encounter*, April 1961.)

His disclaimer is reassuring. Nevertheless, Professor Blackett would probably not wish to deny that a painfully large amount of the world's available scientific effort is at present connected, either directly or indirectly, to the arms race. It was this which Professor Morgenstern was emphasizing, not, as I understand him, in order to suggest that the continuance of the arms race had become necessary to science, but in order to show that 'fundamentally new methods of organizing society' are now a necessity if we are to escape from the arms race and all that it involves. In other words, given the institutional framework of the nation-state, within which contemporary scientists work, their godlike impulse to know is bound to be compounded with their extremely human role of citizens of this or that nation-state, or of members of this or that social class.

Their scientific passion engenders painful conflicts of conscience over the question of what is their duty in the nuclear age. Baffled to know where their social loyalties should lie, whether to their nation-state, to their class, to all humanity, or to some abstract ideal, they often appear to decide that, come what may, they should get on with their job.

We may recall what is to my mind the most significant sentence of the whole voluminous report of the Oppenheimer hearings.[1] It will be recollected that a prolonged and severe controversy raged in 1950 as to whether America should devote her resources to the development of further types of fission weapons or should make the attempt (which might or might not succeed) to produce a fusion, or thermonuclear, weapon. All sorts of considerations, military, political, economic and psychological, played a part in the controversy. Dr Oppenheimer was not in favour of making the doubtful attempt to produce 'The Super' as the thermonuclear weapon was called. For all sorts of reasons—because it looked technically unpromising, because it was morally repulsive, because it would commit Russia and America to an intensification of the arms race, because it would concentrate all attention on unlimited,

[1] In the matter of Robert Oppenheimer (U.S. Government Printing Office, Washington 1954), p. 242 *et seq.*

nuclear, air war, to the exclusion of preparations for limited
war—not only Oppenheimer but also many of his scientific
colleagues were in favour of pressing ahead instead with the
development of a whole range of fission weapons. It was largely,
no doubt, because of the suspicion that this cool attitude was
really motivated by his former communist sympathies that
Oppenheimer was investigated. But as a matter of fact his
attitude seems to have been conditioned above all by scientific
considerations. So long as the prospect of making the fusion
process work remained dubious and scientifically unattractive,
he was against it. We find him writing thus to a colleague
(Conant of Harvard) 'I am not sure the miserable thing will
work, nor that it can be gotten to its target except by ox cart'.
A few months later in 1951, Dr Edward Teller showed that
there was a scientifically attractive and sound way by which
'The Super' could almost certainly be made. Immediately
Oppenheimer's attitude was transformed. 'It was technically
so sweet that we had to have it', he testified.[1] Thus Oppenheimer's repugnance for the H-bomb, his military views, and
his doubts as to the wisdom of Western policy, were all over-
borne by the 'sweetness' of a scientific solution. Or at any
rate so it seems. The truth is that it would have run counter to
their whole training and ethos for these scientists to have
forborne to explore the huge new possibilities for the control
of natural forces which the exigencies of governments engaged
upon the arms race had put into their hands.

All this is not to say that their scientific appetite is the only
thing which influences the scientists. In this case (as Professor
Blackett points out in *Atomic Weapons and East-West Relations*)
Oppenheimer was probably also influenced by the consideration that if the H-bomb was scientifically possible, and not even
overwhelmingly difficult, to make, the Russians would be
likely to make one if the Americans did not. Thus the scientists'
lust to know, while a genuinely important factor, is all entangled
with their simple national loyalties to their own nation-states.

[1] In the matter of Robert Oppenheimer (U.S. Government Printing
Office, Washington 1954), p. 242.

The Impetus of the Arms Race

Naturally there are many other, and more substantial, propulsions behind the arms race than the will to discovery of the scientists. I have only instanced this factor in order to show how deeply a technical and scientific arms race becomes interwoven with our whole social and intellectual life. Even institutions such as our universities, which seem farthest away from the military field, become vital to the (relative) security of both sides.

But of course the main drive behind the arms race is precisely the *competitive* attempt of a number of nations, or of two or more alliances, to achieve security for themselves. Equally obviously such an attempt must be self-defeating. Both sides cannot have a margin of superiority over each other. And yet at least some margin of superiority is the least that either side must strive for in order to feel secure. But this observation, which has been made a hundred times by anti-militarists, does nothing to free nations which are fast caught in an arms race. For it remains true that if either of them relaxes, the other will secure, first a margin of superiority and then incontestable predominance, so that the first nation or alliance will become powerless. Therefore, so long as the world is organized as it is today, so long as the world is articulated, that is to say, into a system of sovereign nations or alliances, and no mutual disarmament treaty is negotiated, no nation which is unwilling to surrender unconditionally to the will of another can relax its efforts. The best it can hope for is the maintenance of the stability of the balance. Both sides assume, or observe, that their opponent is augmenting his strength at such and such a rate. So they have to set themselves the task, as a minimum, of matching that rate. No more unattractive prospect can be imagined. For while the penalty of failure is destruction or subjugation, the prize of success is merely the continuance of the race. This simple but inexorable logic binds sovereign states and alliances to the treadmill of the arms race. It is this, far more than any more complex or covert explanations, which accounts for this terrible phenomenon.

It remains true that, as an arms race proceeds, all sorts of other forces and interests gather round it. The intense, if unwilling, scientific involvement which we have noted is new. But in addition, large contracts must be given out to armament makers. Particular firms, factories, and for that matter districts, as a whole, become geared to this remunerative activity. Again, the armed forces themselves become, in effect, major corporations, inevitably playing their part and exercising their influence on national policy. But on the whole such influences as these have been over-rated. 'The merchants of death' are not, today at any rate, very important, as compared with the undeniable necessity (within the context of a world of national states and alliances) of a nation or alliance preventing itself from being left behind in the race. The special interests of the armament makers (including the interests of the wage earners dependent upon them) and of the armed forces, considerable as they are, would be overruled by their governments if it were not for the genuine necessities of the race. Governments, both communist and non-communist, would so overrule them, for they have an incentive to do so. The arms race is expensive and no one likes paying for it. This brings us to the question of the economics of the arms race.

The Economics of the Arms Race

It would be wrong to exaggerate the economic consequences of the arms race. No subject has produced statements more widely divorced from reality than this. Writers at the liberal end of the political spectrum (and not they alone) often say that if their own nation, or others, continue the race, they will 'go bankrupt'. Bertrand Russell, in his *Common Sense and Nuclear War* writes, for example, that if the present arms race continues, 'before very long, the population of each group will be reduced to subsistence level' (p. 32). Unfortunately, perhaps, nothing could be further from the truth. The simple arithmetical facts are that the more important nations are at present spending on arms at rates varying between 5 and 15 per cent of their national incomes. (Russia 15 per cent (probably),

America some 10 per cent, Britain 7.2 per cent, France 5.6 per cent, West Germany 4.9 per cent.) If they spent this money on other objects, say, motor cars, or education, television sets or roads, houses or amusements, steel works or automation, they would become 5 to 15 per cent richer. That is all. If they spent it all on consumers' goods they would become, by this sort of margin, richer immediately. If they spent, or invested, it all on capital goods they would become no richer immediately, but would be able to make themselves richer by a much wider margin later on. In practice, no doubt, they could do a bit of both. If on the other hand they failed to spend the money at all, they would become much poorer than they are now. For an ever-growing percentage of their workers would become unemployed.

This latter consideration brings us to the other, and contradictory, assertion often made, especially by communist or near-communist writers. We are told that the present 'false prosperity' of the capitalist world is only sustained by 'vast expenditure on armaments', and would collapse into mass unemployment and slump, as in the nineteen-thirties, if the capitalist nations agreed to disarmament. Well, so it would if the governments concerned did not spend or otherwise distribute the money which they would save on armaments. If they neither stepped up their home investment rates, nor spent the money on health, education and housing, nor lent or gave it to the undeveloped world, nor correspondingly reduced the taxation of the mass of the population, then undoubtedly demand would fall off cumulatively and another great slump would be upon us. But most people of most political persuasions understand these simple facts today. So there is not much chance that anything of this sort would happen.

One very important person who has come to understand all this, somewhat unexpectedly, is Mr Khruschev. In a much-neglected passage in his major speech on disarmament to the Supreme Soviet in January 1960, from which we have already quoted, he said:

Some people in the West contend that disarmament is fraught

with grave consequences for the economy of capitalist countries. They allege that if they stop the production of arms, guns, submarines and other means of destruction, that would lead to ruin, to the loss of employment and means of subsistence for hundreds of thousands of people. However, only people who can see no other way of developing the economy save by subordinating it to the interests of war preparations can talk in this vein.

The least one can say about such contentions is that they are utterly unsubstantiated. I had a chance to talk with many representatives of the American business world, whose viewpoint on this question is far from being as gloomy as that and who are confident that United States industry could well cope with the task of switching the entire economy to the production of peaceful gods.

Indeed, isn't there reason to expect that the switching of production capacities to the manufacture of peaceful goods would make it possible sharply to reduce taxation of the population, increase the capacity of the domestic market, and at the same time spend more for education, health and social insurance? And wouldn't it increase tremendously the possibilities for international trade, freed from artificial restrictions prompted by considerations which have nothing to do with economic profit? How many countries in the world need peaceful goods, not weapons.

(So much for the theory of ever-increasing misery!)

As a matter of fact Mr Khruschev, with the enthusiasm of the convert, has somewhat oversimplified the problem. If for example a very conservatively inclined government, which had signed a disarmament treaty, used the billions or millions saved simply to cut the taxation of the rich, there *would* be a real danger that the money would neither be invested in new means of production nor spent on consumer goods. In such conditions the rich might well attempt to hoard a part of their, apparently, increased incomes. And then the slump would come. However, it is immensely encouraging that Mr Khruschev has come to realize that it is at any rate perfectly open to any government, however capitalist, to substitute useful social or individual expenditure for expenditure on arms.

Having, however briefly, cleared up these odder misconceptions we now come to the very real costs of the arms race. No one, in the West at any rate, likes to be even 5 or 10 per cent less rich than they otherwise might be. There is therefore a very real pressure on all democratically elected governments to cut down their expenditure on armaments. Moreover, now that taxation in most Western countries falls quite heavily upon the rich, this pressure comes from them quite as much as from the wage earners. Therefore, to return to the statement made at the end of the preceding section, if it were only the opposition of the vested interests of the armament manufacturers, the armed forces or the scientists, that had to be overcome, most governments would be ready enough to disarm. The fact is that governments do not disarm because they dare not. Until and unless they can achieve a watertight, inspectable and controllable treaty on a mutually agreed level of armaments, there is little that any government, which cannot accept the prospect of being at the mercy of other governments, can do to free itself from the arms race. That race will by no means automatically end itself in 'national bankruptcy' whatever that phrase may mean. It will not even prevent, as it has not prevented over the past fifteen years, a steady, indeed by any previous standards a rapid, rise in the standard of life. All this is true of both communist and capitalist states. Therefore, in default of action of a far-reaching character designed to change the whole frame of reference of the world situation, there seems but a doubtful prospect of an end to the race.

To Summarize this Part of the Argument

The arms race will not ruin us. But on the other hand it will never bring us security. The most it can do, and that only if the greatest possible pains are taken, is to preserve the stability of the balance between the two great alliances, as, whether by skill or luck (mainly in my opinion the latter) that balance has been preserved so far. And meanwhile the race absorbs, if not a particularly high proportion of our total resources, yet some of our highest talent, our finest skills and our best human material. It is a miserable business.

The 'Nth Country' Problem

We have so far considered the arms race in terms of a duel between the two great blocks of communist and non-communist states. But the world is so divided, or polarized, only to a certain degree and in a certain context. In other contexts all nation-states, whether they are members of one or other of the alliances or not, pursue their own defence policies and create, insofar as they can, their own independent armaments. To this extent the arms race becomes not a duel but a free-for-all.

The critical issue in this connexion is that of whether or not countries other than Russia or America will seek to provide themselves with nuclear arms. This is now known as 'the Nth Country' problem. Britain was the third country to acquire a nuclear potential, France is the fourth, and the experts appreciate that a good many others (China, Sweden, Italy, India, Japan, and—if not restrained by treaty—West Germany), will soon be able to do so if they wish. Hence they call the issue the 'Nth Country' problem, instead of the 3rd, 4th or 5th country problem, in order to denote the indefinite number of nations which may soon be able to manufacture their own nuclear weapons.

The consequences of this development, if it occurs, are not so easy to foresee as was at one time supposed. It used to be thought that such a spread of nuclear weapons would mean a rediffusion of power from the 'big two' towards the more familiar international situation of a fair number of nations, say six or eight, each of which was a formidable power on its own. And of course it remains true that any nation which acquires nuclear weapons becomes immensely powerful in relation to a nation which does not. Any nuclear nation, even if it possesses quite a limited stock of weapons, and rather unsophisticated ways of delivering them, can coerce a non-nuclear nation almost at will.

On the other hand it is now being realized that in relation to Russian and American power, the acquisition of some nuclear weapons by smaller countries may for some time mean little after all. For as we have seen the nuclear arms race has now

passed right out of the phase of a competitive building up of
stocks of the weapons (since both sides have ample supplies)
into a phase of the competitive development of more and more
sophisticated means of delivery. What matters in the power
equation between Russia and America is the number, and
much more the quality, of their bombers, their I.C.B.M.s,
their Polaris-carrying submarines, and the degree of invulnerability against first strike which each 'weapons system' can
achieve. And in *this* race it is difficult to see how other nations
can effectively compete. The cost and effort of attempting to
catch up with, and then to keep up with, the 'big two' in the
development of these proliferating new weapons systems really
does seem outside the capacity of any other nation—for the
present at any rate. Britain signalled her discovery of this fact of
contemporary life when in 1960 she abandoned the development of her liquid-fuelled rocket Blue Streak, in the foreknow-
ledge that it would be obsolete before it could become operational. Henceforward, Britain must become increasingly
dependent upon access to American research and development
for the means of delivery of her nuclear weapons, *against an
opponent of Russia's degree of development*. France is of course at a
far earlier stage of nuclear development. But in due course she
too will encounter the same situation.

Hence, either for good or ill, power does not after all seem
likely to be at once diffused by the spread of nuclear weapons. It
looks as if it would remain essentially polarized in Russian and
American hands for some time to come at any rate.

How long is that time likely to be? Perhaps something of the
order of magnitude of ten years may be suggested. For we shall
find that, as we pursue the subject in other contexts (Parts
Three and Four below) in the nineteen-seventies further
scientific advances may alter this situation again. Not only do
the scientists threaten us with relatively cheap and easy (as they
say 'Woolworth') nuclear warheads, but also with relatively
cheap and easy means of delivering them. Therefore, after
about ten years the spread of nuclear weapons might after all
lead to a marked diffusion of power.

A Secondary Arms Race

In any case the spread of nuclear weapons must immediately have other and grave consequences. In the first place it may start a secondary arms race between all countries other than the big two. It is true that nearly all technically advanced countries are now grouped in one or other of the alliances headed by Russia and America. But recent events have shown that this is by no means the same thing as the sinking of their national identity or sovereignty in these alliances. Britain, so far at any rate, lays store by the retention of her own nuclear capacity. More strikingly, France has shown fanatical determination to acquire her own nuclear capacity. Unless she totally misunderstands the conditions of the main arms race (which is not impossible), this cannot be because she hopes in the proximate future to make herself an independent power of the same order of magnitude as Russia or America. She must be thinking of power in relation to nations other than Russia and America. And in *this* context she is quite right in supposing that the possession of nuclear capacity will greatly increase her power.

Again, within the communist alliance it is becoming perfectly clear that China has by no manner of means sunk her national independence or sovereignty in the alliance. She contradicts Russia freely and accordingly, it may be assumed, is most anxious to achieve independent power and above all independent nuclear power. In her case it can be argued no doubt that in the very long run she might catch up with the big two in what might be called 'net nuclear capacity'. At any rate she might suppose that she might catch up, though even for a vast country like her, at an early stage of development, the task of overtaking the immense lead established by Russia and America would be formidable indeed. Far short of that, however, independent nuclear capacity would obviously be most important for China. Quite simple means of delivery would give her very great power over against both India and Japan, and in general in her own part of the world.

In fact the mere prospect of China's acquisition of nuclear capacity is beginning to raise the issue within major nations which are not members of either alliance such as India and Japan. China has been, it would seem, incautious in physically threatening the integrity of Indian territory at this early stage. The vigour of Indian reaction would seem to indicate that if and when Chinese nuclear capacity is announced, India, in spite of all her pacifist, anti-nuclear attitudes, will be likely to set about acquiring nuclear capacity herself. What else could she do? (As a matter of fact she is already well advanced in the preliminary task of building the reactors etc. which form the necessary industrial base for such a capacity.)

Japan is a more complex case. She evidently still feels herself to be under American domination, and bitterly resents it. Nevertheless, as that domination relaxes, as it is doing, her traditional rivalry with China may be expected to reassert itself, especially if China remains for many decades fanatically and dogmatically communist, and Japan remains a highly successful capitalist society. Again, the year of China's acquisition of nuclear capacity will be a critical moment for Japan. It is difficult to see the forces of Japanese nationalism, which are surely still strong beneath the surface, in both her right and also in her left wing parties, forbearing to set themselves the goal of acquiring nuclear capacity. Finally, firmly neutralist nations, of which the leading examples are Switzerland and Sweden, are at present considering not only whether they should acquire nuclear weapons but also which kind will best suit their needs. Thus, unless something is done about it, the world seems set for a secondary nuclear arms race between the medium-sized nation-states. This is a complication which nations such as Britain, who might look with favour upon the conception of discontinuing her nuclear programme, relying upon America in this respect, and making her whole contribution to the alliance in conventional weapons, must take into account.

Finally, I repeat that most defence experts foresee with apprehension a time in, say, the nineteen-seventies, when even quite minor and undeveloped nations may well be able to possess themselves, in one way or another, of nuclear weapons, and of simple but by no means necessarily ineffective ways of delivering them. (It has been said that in certain circumstances a suitcase may be a very good vehicle of delivery.) What such experts fear is that one or other of the super-powers, or of the nuclearly-armed medium powers, may start supplying, for one pressing reason or another, some smaller and less developed nation which it particularly wishes to strengthen. But nothing is more obvious in the history of the last seventeen years than that arms supplied to smaller, and supposedly client, states by their patrons, for one purpose, may be acquired and used for quite another purpose. For example the West has been supplying the Arab states with arms on a substantial scale for years and years with the object of strengthening them against Russia. But the Arab states *acquired* these arms almost solely in the context of their contest with Israel. This became undeniable as soon as they began taking Russian arms as well. For Russia did not supply these arms to strengthen the Arab states against herself. And in fact of course the arms have been used almost exclusively in the two wars with Israel. Moreover, the same argument can be used, *mutatis mutandis*, for the arms which the West has supplied to Israel. Whatever purpose the West had in mind, the Israelis thought exclusively of the arms in terms of their struggle with the Arabs; and have so used them. It is only too easy to foresee what the world will be like if similar policies are pursued with nuclear weapons. What will be the chances of the prevention of recurrent nuclear war in a world in which Egypt and Israel, Iraq and Egypt, India, China and Japan, half a dozen South and Central American states, one or two states in Africa, and all the medium-sized highly developed nations, possess nuclear weapons and at any rate some means of delivering them?

Thus the spread of nuclear weapons through the nations of the world is a daunting prospect, in spite of the fact that such nations are unlikely at any rate for a decade to present any direct menace to the two super-powers, because of their probable inability to keep up with the development of the means of delivery. A secondary nuclear arms race amongst the medium powers, and then what might be called a tertiary arms race amongst the minor powers, would be bound to increase the general insecurity to a most serious extent. Do we not here catch sight of the conclusion that a world of sovereign nation-states is simply incompatible with human survival in the nuclear age? Moreover, the fact that the super-powers will still be all-powerful, as against anyone but each other, may give us the clue to the one road of escape, although to follow that road will be for many people highly distasteful. But if the rivalry of the two super-powers is still unabated, when the possession of nuclear weapons has become widespread, so that they are incapable of combined action (using the United Nations as their joint instrument) even for the elementary, temporary and *ad hoc*, purpose of preventing the smaller nations from pursuing their feuds with nuclear weapons, it will be difficult to refrain from despair.

Summary

The present arms race, both in its scientific and technical intensity as between the super-powers, and in its tendency to diffuse nuclear weapons widely amongst the nations of the world, is a uniquely alarming phenomenon. Most, though not all, historical experiences confirm the view that even non-nuclear arms races have led towards war: an uncontrolled nuclear arms race will lead to extinction. What is to be done about it? The answer is of course to stop it. But how? In respect of the duel between the great alliances, the duellists are, as we have seen, caught fast in mutual, and it must be admitted, well-founded, distrust and apprehension. In respect of the tendency to equip other nations with these weapons, how are we of the alliances, locked in our mutual antagonism, to combine to deny them to the rest of the world?

It is true that sustained efforts have been, and are still being, made directly to stop the nuclear arms race by means of disarmament. Disarmament conference after conference is held, now between the principals only, now with the medium powers present, now on a wider basis. No success has as yet been registered. Our next task must be to examine the question of disarmament. For certainly disarmament is a prerequisite of the prevention of war. We may discover, however, that certain other pre-conditions have to be satisfied if the efforts which our distracted world is making to stop the arms race are to have an opportunity to succeed.

PART TWO

Disarmament

9

'Neither for the Kingdom of Christ . . .'

THERE is one way in which the West can end the arms race
tomorrow. And that is to disarm immediately irrespective
of what other nation-states may do. This is what a particular
school of thought, which used to be called pacifist and is now
often called 'unilateralist', advocates.

There is in principle only one thing to say about this
proposal: it is the obvious thing to do, so long as we are willing
to face the consequence; which is surrender to the will of any
nation that does not also disarm itself.

The most serious advocates of pacifism have always unhesitatingly accepted this consequence. It is set out with in-
comparable force in the manifesto of the original members of
the Society of Friends to King Charles the Second of England
in 1660. They wrote:

We utterly deny all outward wars and strife, and fightings with
outward weapons, for any end, or under any pretence whatever;
this is our testimony to the whole world. The spirit of Christ by
which we are guided is not changeable, so as once to command us
from a thing as evil, and again to move unto it; and we certainly
know, and testify to the world, that the Spirit of Christ, which leads
us into all truth, will never move us to fight and war against any
man with outward weapons, neither for the kingdom of Christ, nor
for the kingdoms of this world.

Is it possible to overestimate the unflinching honesty which caused these intensely religious Quakers to write that they would fight *neither* for the Kingdom of Christ *nor* for the Kingdoms of this World? They squarely faced the fact that he who renounces the use of physical force must be unwilling to defend in that way what he values highest of all, his 'Kingdom of Christ', as well as what he may value far less, his 'Kingdoms of this World'. If this fact is faced then there must be deep respect for the traditional pacifist view. And if some of us have spoken and written with less than this respect about some of those who hold the present day 'unilateralist' standpoint, it is because they have not always seemed to rise to the same heights of impregnable frankness as did the Quakers of the seventeenth century.

If then, we disarm unilaterally we must be prepared to surrender both 'the Kingdom of Christ', which in our present day secular idiom we might call the non-material values which we cherish most, as well as 'the Kingdoms of this World', which we might call 'The Affluent Society'. Nevertheless, since what is at issue may be nothing less than the ending of the arms race, and with it the risk of nuclear war, we should carefully consider whether the true pacifist is not right in deciding that it would be better to be ready to surrender both of these 'Kingdoms' rather than to be ready to fight for them.

Let us take first the 'Kingdoms of this World'—the affluent society in which we live. It has never seemed to me wise for those of us who have long been materially comfortable to belittle the value of that new level of material comfort, and above all of material security, which the wage-earning majority in the Western World has just achieved. The affluent society may be all that is said of it—vulgar, crass, thoughtless, philistine. But it may be hazarded that only those who have themselves long been affluent will see it so. The wage earners, who for the first time in history have got their heads above the grim waters of primary poverty, will see it differently. They at any rate will hesitate many times before taking any action which might put in jeopardy the maintenance of their new-found and after all very modest affluence. Those of us whose purses have always been well filled may say that he who steals them steals dross: it is above all the wage-earning masses of our Western societies who will dissent.

But what of 'the Kingdom of Christ' which, wrote those unrelenting Quaker logicians, we must also be prepared to leave physically undefended? It would be almost as blasphemous for an unbeliever as for a believer to say that any of us, in West or East, today possessed the 'Kingdom of Christ', in the sense that we had established a reign of justice, liberty and fraternity upon earth. All we can claim (and all that the communists can claim either) is that we have aspired. It is our type of aspiration which is at issue. If we surrender undefended our own aspirations to a better society, seen with our eyes, reached for by our hands, conceived by our brains, is not some ultimate betrayal involved? We may be right or wrong in setting so high a value upon the liberty to dissent, upon our political mechanisms for achieving a measure of self-government, upon the variety of our ways of life. But we do. For us these things are the tiny glimpse of the Kingdom of Christ which is all we have. If we give them up, do we even remain ourselves?

Nevertheless, the pacifist in the nuclear age can and does put us an ultimate question. All this he may grant, and yet he may still say that all this must not be defended at the risk of nuclear war. Better, he may say, to give our fates into the hands of the communists to settle as they think best, than to be dead. No doubt it is only a rough answer to this contention to say that to induce the peoples of the west to surrender is too remote a possibility to be worth talking about. Conceptually, at any rate, unilateralist propaganda might convert the peoples of the whole western (or alternately of the Soviet) alliance, including the American people, to its view. It may be said, therefore, that it is our duty to persevere in such propaganda however distant its goal may seem. But I cannot find much interest in the proposal. Some goals are not only of such doubtful desirability but also of such improbability of attainment that their discussion seems barren. The goal of inducing a voluntary surrender of the entire Western (or Eastern) alliance by means of pacifist propaganda is of this kind. It is of doubtful desirability, not because it can be argued that it would be better to be dead than to submit to communism: it would not; but because what we are being asked to do is to exchange the *certainty* of surrender to communist authority (or to any other authority which retained nuclear weapons) against the (probable) elimination of the *risk* of nuclear war. If nuclear war were certain if we did not surrender then the balance of the argument would be different. But as every one of these pages is devoted to showing there are ways, difficult indeed, but any rate *less* unlikely of fulfilment than the goal of surrender, which, if we pursue them successfully, will avoid both surrender and war.

The improbability of inducing the voluntary surrender of the Western (or Eastern) alliance as a whole (and nothing less can eliminate the risk of nuclear war) needs little argument. Remarkably, the most eminent figure, by far, in the British Campaign for Nuclear Disarmament has himself vigorously proclaimed the fact that to secure the surrender of either the East or the West by means of pacifist persuasion is an end too remote to be worth striving for, even if it were in principle desirable. Bertrand Russell writes in his recent book *Has Man a Future?* (p. 90, Penguin Books):

> There is a slogan invented by West German friends of peace: 'Better red than dead'. One may guess that in some sections of Russian public opinion, there is an opposite slogan: 'Better capitalists than corpses.' I do not think it necessary to inquire into the theoretical validity of either slogan since I think it out of the question that the one should be adopted by western governments or the other by the governments of the east. Neither slogan presents justly the problem which east and west, alike, have to face. Given that military victory by either side is impossible, it follows logically that a negotiated *détente* cannot be based on the complete subjection of either side to the other, but must preserve the existing balance while transforming it from a balance of terror to a balance of hope.

It also follows logically, however, from these words of the unilateralist leader that the ultimate pacifist question as to whether it were not better to convert the West to surrender rather than to risk nuclear war is not one which, in practice, we need even attempt to answer; for we have no such choice. It is in fact just as impossible that the Western world will surrender to the communists as that the communists will surrender to the Western world. All that is possible is what is discussed in this book, namely that the two worlds shall at first live together in a balance of power and then, before it is too late, learn just sufficiently to co-operate to enable them to organize an authority capable of keeping the peace. Almost all practical men of affairs, on both sides, will regard even this second objective as straining to the utmost the bounds of the possible.

And so the real choice before us is not at all the rhetorical choice of surrender or death. It is this: either we must pursue the dusty, arduous and complex task of finding some sort of a way in which men may live in peace in the nuclear age, since they can no longer live at war, or we must wash our hands of the rough, ugly business of the real world and how it may be preserved. But this is, surely, the role played not by Jesus but by his judge?[1]

---

[1] I have discussed in some detail the specifically political aspects of unilateralism, more especially as it affects the British Labour Party, in a pamphlet entitled *The Pursuit of Peace* (Fabian Society, 3s 6d, 1960). I there discuss the alternative 'unilateralist' proposal that Britain alone, rather than the western alliance as a whole, should abandon nuclear weapons and drop out of her alliances. This view is often called 'neutralism'. It will be noticed in chapter 13 in the context of British defence and disarmament policy. For in fact it has little to do with the issue of unilateralism proper.

IO

The Old School of Thought

The 'If only . . .' Theme

IF we cannot stop the arms race on our own, can we not stop
it by agreement with our potential enemies? Such an agreement is the objective of that world-wide movement for disarmament which has been pursued ever since the end of the
First World War. Eminent men, like the late Lord Cecil and
Mr Philip Noel-Baker in Britain, for example, have given their
lives to this movement. Disarmament conference after disarmament conference has been held. Soviet Russia, ever since
1927, has declared that general and complete disarmament by
mutual agreement is one of the major objectives of her Government. No government which was not fascist has ever admitted
that it was opposed to disarmament. Little progress towards
disarmament has been made. Why?

To give a full chronological history of the attempts which
have been made since 1918 at multilateral disarmament, would
require a long book devoted to the subject. Moreover, it would
be a book which would be as painful to write as it would be
arduous to read. For upon the surface the history of disarmament has been a history of missed opportunities: of opportunities, moreover, narrowly missed, and missed as often as not
because of more or less accidental circumstances, such as the
mistakes, the prejudices, or simply the mistimings, of individual
statesmen: it has been, apparently, a history of heart-breaking

'might-have-beens' in the course of which agreements which might have saved the world failed by a hair's breadth. That, at any rate, is in essence how the course of these international negotiations has often appeared to the most ardent advocates of disarmament. Mr Philip Noel-Baker, for example, gives that impression in his major work *The Arms Race, A Programme for World Disarmament* (Stevens, 1958). Instead, therefore, of attempting to write another history of the disarmament negotiations, we may be content to describe one or two turning points, in order to illustrate this remarkable characteristic of, it would seem, almost fortuitously missed opportunities.

The first instance is of purely historical interest. This is how the World Disarmament Conference of 1932 appeared to Mr Noel-Baker writing in 1958.

The Geneva Disarmament Conference ultimately met in February 1932; it was not till March 1933 that the British Government laid before it a comprehensive Draft Convention which Sir Anthony Eden had prepared. There was a general consensus of opinion at the time that, if this had come at the beginning instead of at the end, the Conference could hardly have failed; 'had only this laudable desire for action and contribution found earlier expression,' says Mr Wheeler-Bennett, 'the history of the Disarmament Conference might have been very different.' But the British Government, like the French, took too long to make up its mind that disarming itself was better than allowing Germany to rearm; by the time it had done so, Hitler was in power, and the Conference was dead. (Op. cit., p. 43.)

Thus Mr Noel-Baker attributes the failure of disarmament between the wars to a delay of eleven months in presenting proposals which were in themselves sound and adequate. This seems difficult to believe. It should not be supposed, however, that the closest scrutiny of the record would show that Mr Noel-Baker was wrong in his facts. On the contrary, in this as in the other instances to be cited, the surface of the record would indicate that the world continually missed its salvation by a hair's breadth and a mischance. 'If only . . .!', we are almost forced to exclaim. Indeed, unless we have the unpopular habit

of looking beneath the surface, the refrain of 'If only . . .'
will haunt us whenever we look at the record of the world's
attempts at disarmament.

The I.A.D.A. Plan of 1946

The second example is also, unfortunately, now of mainly
historical interest: but it is more recent history: it is within the
history of the nuclear age and it may therefore have more
direct lessons for us today. It is startling, in 1962, to recall that
at the very start of the nuclear age, in 1946 the United States
Government made what was, apparently, an offer of total, and
perforce unilateral (for she alone possessed the bomb), nuclear
disarmament. The offer was conditional upon the creation of
an international agency to be called the International Atomic
Development Authority, to be set up under the United Nations,
and having drastic powers. These powers were first for the
suppression of any attempt on the part of other nations to
acquire, or, on the part of the United States to re-acquire,
nuclear weapons, and second, for the possession of a world-wide
monopoly in the ownership, control and operation of all
nuclear processes for peaceful purposes. On these two conditions the United States offered to destroy its entire stock of
A-bombs and bomb-making, fissionable material—nor was it at
that time impossible to verify that such total nuclear disarmament had, substantially, taken place. For the United States'
stock of nuclear material was in 1946 very small, and was the
only stock in existence in the world. The United States then
enjoyed a complete monopoly in the production and possession of nuclear weapons, a monopoly which she was not to lose
for three more years.

This was the famous 'Lilienthal' or 'Baruch' plan, as it was
alternatively called. In fact the plan was largely inspired by
Dr Robert Oppenheimer, the scientist who had played what
was, perhaps, the leading part in the production of the atomic
weapons. (And this is an ironic fact, for it meant that this plan,
which became anathema to the Russians, had been inspired by
an American scientist, who, as investigation was to show, had

had, only a few years previously, pro-communist sympathies, though only tenuous and innocent connexions with communist organizations.)

What specifically did the American Government propose? Mr Noel-Baker (op. cit., p. 192) sums up the Oppenheimer-Lilienthal-Baruch proposals as follows:

It would be hard to guess from Communist speeches that what the United States had actually proposed was that the source of power in a new, world-wide industrial revolution should be handed over to a publicly owned International Authority, in which all nations should have fair and equal rights and shares; to which the United States would give, for nothing, the most valuable industrial secret ever known; to which it would hand over capital assets worth at least $4,000 m. It would be just as hard to guess that the United States had proposed to give up the A-bomb, which it alone possessed; to distribute the vitally important strategic industry of atomic energy on an agreed and equitable basis around the world; and to dedicate all the knowledge and experience at its command to ensuring that no more nuclear weapons should ever again be made. The greatest capitalist nation had proposed the international socialist control of the source of world prosperity for centuries to come; the greatest military power had proposed a total nuclear disarmament, in order that the rule of law through the United Nations should prevail.

This is to put the proposal in the most favourable light, to say the least. Nevertheless, it cannot be denied that this is, substantially, what was proposed. It is remarkable, therefore, that the Russians unhesitatingly and vehemently opposed the plan and have never wearied, from that day to this, in vilifying it. How are we to account for the Russian attitude?

In the first place we must emphasize the conditions which the Americans attached to their offer. The proposed 'International Atomic Development Authority' really was to be a world-monopoly which was alone to conduct (with the exceptions noted below) all the processes of nuclear power production, in order that no state should be able to divert fissionable material to war-like purposes. This was because the authors of the plan considered that this was the only way in which it could be ensured that no more atom bombs would ever be made. Mere inspection and control would never do this, they supposed: it was necessary that the entire process, from the mining of the uranium ore to the production of electric power should be owned and operated by the International Atomic Development Authority (I.A.D.A.).[1] For the United States Government would only destroy its stock of bombs if it could be sure that no one, including itself, could ever be in a position to make any more.

It was the creation of this world monopoly for the production of nuclear power to which, essentially, the Russians objected. They did so for a number of reasons. First, both Mr Baker and Professor Blackett (in his immediately post-war book *Military and Political Consequence of Atomic Energy* (Turnstile Press, 1948) emphasize that the Russians feared that I.A.D.A., on which they would be represented, but in which they, and the other communist countries, would be in a minority, might distort, hamper and even stop altogether, the development of nuclear power in Russia. Professor Blackett in particular wrote that this was a major Russian apprehension. For he considered that the development of nuclear power would be indispensable to Russia, while it would be a mere luxury, or possibly even an inconvenience, for America.

If this was indeed an important Russian reason for rejection the sequel has been ironic. For in fact up till now (1962) the Russians have made little use of the nuclear generation of electricity. They have preferred extensively to exploit their coal and oil resources. And in this they may well have been well advised. For, now that we are familiar with it, what is a nuclear power station but an elaborate, roundabout and so far rather uneconomic, method of boiling water? The older method of lighting a fire under the water seems well able to hold its own so far. (This is not to deny that ultimately improved processes of nuclear fission or fusion will become a main source of the

[1] National Governments were to be permitted to build and operate nuclear power stations on their own, but under licence from I.A.D.A. and using nuclear fuel produced by I.A.D.A.

world's power: but clearly that time is not yet.) So the Russians need hardly have feared that their economic development would be 'strangled' by a hostile I.A.D.A. which was in a position to limit the number of nuclear power stations which they should be allowed to build. But this was all difficult to foresee in 1946; fear of seeing a possibly important Russian industry owned and controlled by a non-Russian body was no doubt one of the factors which determined their violently hostile reaction to the I.A.D.A. proposal.

Nevertheless, it may be surmised that it was fear of putting great power into the hands of a probably hostile international body in respect of the *military*, rather than the peaceful, uses of nuclear energy which really weighed with the Russians. And here it is important to appreciate the very real grounds for Russian fears. The plan, as originally put forward by the Americans, contemplated the prior setting up of the whole elaborate and far-reaching machinery of I.A.D.A., by which world-wide uranium mining and processing, the production of fissile material, and about half of the actual production of power by nuclear means, would pass into I.A.D.A. ownership, *before* the American Government began to surrender or destroy its stock of bombs. Professor Blackett (op. cit., p. 140) cites a U.S. War Department document submitted to a conference in the spring of 1947 which estimated that five years would elapse *after* this international control had been set up, before the last American bomb had been destroyed. Such a time scale was clearly unacceptable to the Russians, if only because it gave them no assurance that when all the conditions had been fulfilled, and I.A.D.A. was duly in possession of the world's (including Russia's) uranium mines, processing plants and nuclear power plants, the American nuclear stockpile would in fact be destroyed. For it was left to the unfettered discretion of the I.A.D.A., *voting by simple majority*, to declare whether or not the conditions necessary to the destruction of the American stockpile had or had not been fulfilled. Moreover, the decision of the I.A.D.A. as to whether this or that state was violating the provisions of the plan, in this or in any other respect, and so might, in the extreme case, be subjected to sanctions, including armed attack, was expressly exempted from the veto which prevailed in the Security Council. Thus for all questions connected with nuclear energy, and these were the life and death questions of world power, the I.A.D.A., voting by simple majority, was to be the supreme authority of the world, able not only to decide whether or not any state was in default of its obligations under the proposed treaty, but able to call, as a last resort, upon all other states to make war upon such a state. Naturally it was not contemplated that the I.A.D.A. should call upon the rest of the world to make war on Russia, or any other state, which, for instance, it declared to have failed to hand over all its uranium mining and processing plants. In that case, it was thought, the authority would merely free America from the obligation to destroy her stockpile. But it *was* very definitely contemplated that the I.A.D.A. would and should call upon all states to make war upon any state which it declared was embarking upon the production of its own atomic bombs and would not 'cease and desist' from so doing. This last provision, for what was called 'condign punishment' for any state which was attempting clandestinely to become a nuclear power was of the essence of the plan. And necessarily so, for clearly it was impossible for all other sovereign states to abstain from making the new and supreme weapons for themselves, and for America to destroy her existing weapons, unless they were assured that *every* state was doing likewise. Finally one must never forget that the Russians believed, probably correctly so far as the ensuing five or ten years were concerned, that the Americans would command a majority in the authority which would wield these vast powers.

Thus the plan as it stood required a degree of trust in American good faith which it was naïve to suppose that the Russians would or could exhibit. Was, then, the vehement Russian rejection of the plan justified after all? This does not follow. For it is important to recall the immense relative advantage to Russia which would have been secured if some version of the plan could in fact have been put into effect. Here, it is repeated, were the Americans, in 1946, when they were the only country in the world which possessed them, offering to abolish nuclear weapons, and proposing to set up the most far-reaching arrangements to ensure that neither they nor anyone else should ever be able to produce them again. Let us envisage what would have happened to the military balance if, sometime towards the end of the nineteen-forties, this had been done. The very military situation which the American Government showed itself, during the first half of the nineteen-fifties, determined at all costs to prevent, would have arisen. In say 1947 the Russians enjoyed, far more than they do now, an immense superiority in conventional armaments. If nuclear weapons had been abolished, there would have been nothing to balance this Russian conventional predominance. It is hardly too much to say that Russian supremacy would, at that date, have been difficult indeed to challenge. It was, then, surely paradoxical in the extreme for the Russians to refuse out of hand to consider a plan which promised, at any rate, to produce this highly favourable situation for themselves. After all they could have met the admittedly unacceptable features of the plan in a number of ways. For instance they could have proposed that the first American A-bomb should be publicly destroyed on the 'vesting-day', when I.A.D.A. entered into ownership of its world-wide interests: that one more American weapon was to be destroyed at stated intervals, and that the whole I.A.D.A. arrangements should automatically become null and void if the destruction of their stockpile was not punctually carried out by the Americans. After all, I repeat, in early 1946 the American stockpile must have been very small indeed. For we know that it consisted in only two weapons in August 1945. If I.A.D.A. had been reasonably rapidly established, it may be conjectured that there would have been fewer than a score of American weapons to destroy.

It is interesting, incidentally, to note that at this period no one raised the objection to this type of nuclear disarmament which is proving insurmountable today. No one suggested that the Americans would secretly withhold a part of their stock and use it to terrorize a nuclearly disarmed world. And this for several good reasons. First, it would not have been difficult to calculate fairly accurately what the American stock must be. So they could not have hoped to withhold more than, say, one or two weapons without detection. Secondly, even if they had done so, one or two Hiroshima-size A-bombs would not have been nearly enough to prove a decisive factor in a world war. Thirdly, the rest of the world, including Russia, was nuclearly disarmed already, so that they could not have held back stocks. Total nuclear disarmament, as an isolated measure, including the destruction of stocks, was, perhaps for the first and last time, a possibility at that moment. It is true that even if some such Russian amendments as these had been accepted and the plan put into effect, the Russians, and the rest of the world also, including America, would have been faced with the fact that I.A.D.A., a world authority which they did not directly control, was in full possession and control of their nuclear industries. And I repeat, it was thought (erroneously as it turned out in respect of civil uses) that this would matter far more to the Russians than to the Americans. But to weigh against this undeniable disadvantage, the Russians would have made the enormous gain of having abolished for ever the American nuclear stockpile. It is startling that they made no attempt whatever to exploit this potentially huge advantage by proposing to amend the plan. The simplest explanation of their conduct is perhaps the soundest. Their extreme, if by no means always ill-founded, suspicion of American, and generally Western intentions, made it impossible for them to act intelligently.

Having said this we must ask a question with far-reaching implications. If the Russians *had* accepted the plan, subject to some such amendments as the above, would it have been likely to have been implemented? No one can tell. But it is difficult to resist the impression that even if the Russians had given the most constructive reply which could be reasonably demanded of them, the I.A.D.A. would not in fact have been established. The very fact that the I.A.D.A. plan really would have meant that America gave away the whole unique (if temporary) advantage of her nuclear monopoly—that same fact which made it fool-ish of the Russians to turn down the scheme at sight—must have meant, I fear, that the American Government would have found it very difficult to accept the indispensable Russian amendments. There were plenty of people in influential positions in America who were extremely suspicious of and hostile to the plan, even as it was, since they believed that it gave far too much away. They would have put heavy pressure on the American Government to refuse anything which the Russians proposed.

This raises the whole question of whether the American Government was sincere in putting the plan forward, in the sense that they genuinely hoped that it would be adopted. The answer must be that the authors of the plan—above all the atomic scientists—were passionately sincere in this sense. On the other hand a great many important people in the American 'establishment' were profoundly thankful when the Russians rejected the plan. Similarly it can be asserted that the Russians would merely have been indulging in an exercise in 'political warfare' (which may perhaps be defined as the gentle art of putting the other fellow in the wrong) if they had sought to make the necessary amendments to the plan instead of rejecting and denouncing it. But we shall find that this can always be said of the offers and counter-offers of disarmament negotia-tions. Such negotiations can always be regarded either as genuine efforts to come to an agreement or as mere exercises in political warfare. Usually they have both aspects. (Neverthe-less, as we shall note, some of the particular turning points in the negotiations have been much more of the one character and some much more of the other.)

Is Disarmament Possible?

All this raises one of the main issues to be discussed in this chapter. Is disarmament by agreement possible between sovereign states, and if so to what extent? Undoubtedly *some* measures of agreed and mutual disarmament are *sometimes* possible between *some* sovereign states. For they have occurred. The Rush-Bagot treaty of 1817 between the British Empire and

America, limiting the warships to be kept on the Great Lakes to a low minimum, and the Washington Treaty of Naval Disarmament of 1922 between America, Britain, Japan, France, and Italy again limiting the number, size and type of warships, are the two instances of successful disarmament by agreement which are usually (and somewhat monotonously) given. But the total prohibition of by far the most powerful weapon in the world, such as would have been effected by the I.A.D.A. plan, would have been an instance of disarmament by agreement of a different order of magnitude. Are such decisive measures of disarmament as this really possible between sovereign states?

It is too soon even to sketch an answer to such a question. But we should note the crux of the issue upon which the I.A.D.A. plan broke down. If it had been carried out in full it would, I repeat, have been of immense military advantage to the Russians. But that advantage could only have been obtained at the price of setting up an authority which would have exercised the very considerable world-power involved in owning and controlling the entire nuclear industry. The Russians saw that they could not hope to control such an authority themselves and suspected that the Americans, because of their world-wide influence, could and would control it. Therefore they preferred that no such authority should be set up and that the world should enter the nuclear age articulated into many sovereign states coexisting, sometimes peacefully, sometimes belligerently, in 'a state of nature'.

In a word while the I.A.D.A. scheme fell far short of the establishment of a world authority, or any sort of world government, it undeniably pointed in that direction. Indeed Professor Blackett (op. cit., p. 193) who strongly sympathized with the Russian objections to the plan, ends his book with these words. 'Though it is, of course, impossible to predict the form that any system of world government might take in the future, or how it will come into being, it is easy to predict that it will not begin with world government in the weapons and one commodity, which was the essence of the majority report of the Atomic Energy Commission of the United Nations.'

It will be found that I, on the contrary, am inclined to believe that if there is a possibility of our moving, before nuclear war overtakes us, towards some kind of minimally effective world authority, it will be by picking out, precisely, the nuclear field, and by restricting such a world-wide authority's powers, as closely as possible, to this field. Be that as it may, Professor Blackett performed a great service by exhibiting his deep insight, as early as 1948, into the nature of the nuclear disarmament problem. For he realized from the outset that the plan proposed for nuclear disarmament raised the question of world authority. How could it do otherwise? How could America possibly abandon, unilaterally, her nuclear monopoly unless some authority were set up which really was in a position to ensure that no other country could illicitly acquire nuclear weapons? Maybe America, if it had come to the point, would not have abandoned her nuclear monopoly even then: but clearly this was a minimum stipulation, which it was quite unrealistic to ask her to waive. And how could an authority securely exercise the power to prevent any nation acquiring nuclear weapons unless it were given the immense position, recourses and privileges proposed for I.A.D.A.? Unless in particular it was freed from the veto provisions of the Charter and could, by simple majority vote, impose sanctions, including, in the last resort, the coercion by armed force of any state which it considered to be producing nuclear weapons? (The Russian arguments on the veto merely amounted to saying that America or Russia, or indeed any other state, should in the last resort be judges in their own case as to whether or not they were violating the plan by producing nuclear weapons.) But if the I.A.D.A. were given such powers as this would it not be on the way to becoming a world authority in embryo? Of course it would be: that was precisely what the Russians objected to, because they considered, perhaps correctly at that date, that it would not be a world authority which they took an effective part in exercising, but would be a world authority exercised *over* them. That was what set the Russians talking about the sacredness of national sovereignty like so many diplomatists of the old school. The whole story is instructive, or would be if we showed any capacity for learning its lessons.

'*The Moment of Hope*'

The next phase of the disarmament negotiations which it may prove instructive to recall began in 1952, when the assembly of the U.N. appointed a Disarmament Commission to deal with conventional as well as nuclear weapons. This, and the immediately following, episode were in my opinion less of the character of sincere and genuine efforts to reach and implement disarmament agreements, and more of the character of exercises in political warfare, than had been the I.A.D.A. plan, or than the 'Test Ban' negotiations were to be. Indeed it is difficult to write of them without irony and bitterness. Perhaps it is inevitable that mighty governments should attempt to score off each other by putting each other in the wrong on disarmament. But when we remember what is at issue 'the deception of the people' involved is hard to bear.

The first few years after the breakdown of the I.A.D.A. plan had been spent in an interchange which it is hardly too much to say consisted in the Russian Government saying to the American Government 'Let us abolish nuclear weapons', thinking, but not saying, 'for there you predominate' and the American Government saying to the Russian Government 'No, let us abolish conventional weapons', thinking, but not saying, 'for there *you* are supreme'. This completely barren exercise was interrupted on June 11th, 1954, when the British and French delegates to the sub-Committee of the Disarmament Commission submitted a document which has come to be known as 'The Anglo-French Memorandum'. This document proposed both the total abolition of nuclear weapons and major reductions in conventional forces, under 'a control organ with rights and powers and functions adequate to guarantee the effective observance of the agreed prohibitions and regulations'. The American Government at once accepted the proposals. The Russian Government at first refused, but then said that it was willing that they should form the basis of discussion.

Obviously everything depended on the extent of the reduction in the conventional weapons, on which Russian strength
still largely depended, the timing of these reductions in relation
to the abolition of nuclear weapons, and the establishment of the
'control organ', to see if both kinds of weapons really were
abolished and that they stayed abolished. There was not
much trouble about the extent of the reductions. Agreement
was reached on manpower ceilings of 1 million to 1.5 million
each for Russia, China and America and 700,000 to 800,000
each for France and Britain. What mattered was the timing.
After almost a year's argument the French and British delegates put forward, on April 19th, 1955, a timetable under
which a 'cut off' of new production of nuclear weapons should
take place when one half of the reduction in conventional
strengths had been made. When 75 per cent of the reduction in
conventional strengths had been made, the 'elimination' of
nuclear stocks was to begin. Both processes (i.e. the remaining
reductions in conventional strengths and the elimination of
nuclear stocks), the document continued, 'shall be completed
within the limit laid down in the Disarmament Treaty'. (In
other words by a date to be agreed.) All this was dependent
upon 'the institution of an effective system of control'.

These proposals were pressed by the French, British, and
American Governments with some vehemence upon the
Russians. The American delegate said for instance, 'Will it
(Russia) accept the drastic reductions which the United States
is prepared to accept, such as a ceiling of from 1 million to
1.5 million men . . . fifteen days have elapsed since the
Franco-British proposals on 75–25 per cent?' If, he continued,
there was no answer from the Russians, they would have to
'arrive at no other conclusion than that there is no desire to
negotiate'.[1]

And then on May 10th, 1955, the Russians played their ace.
They accepted the Western proposals almost in their entirety.
They accepted the manpower ceilings of between 1 and 1½
millions: they accepted the '75–25 per cent' timetable for the

[1] Cmd. 9650, p. 438. Quoted by Noel-Baker (op. cit.).

synchronization of nuclear and conventional disarmament: they accepted most of the Western proposals on control. They accepted very nearly the lot. (Naturally there were things in the Russian document on which the West would have had to make counter-proposals—there always are: but in general it was acceptance.) Embarrassment and then consternation spread through the Western camp. The Western governments insisted upon a recess of the sub-committee. After all, something unprecedented, something untoward, had happened. Somebody had accepted somebody else's disarmament proposals. What was to be done?

The sub-committee did not meet again until August 29th. Thus the West obtained nearly four months' respite. When the Commission did meet the West simply changed the subject. Let us talk, said the American delegate, about President Eisenhower's remarkable proposals for the prevention of surprise attack, made at the Geneva Conference, which had taken place in the interval. Let us talk about 'open skies': let us talk about 'open societies': let us talk about cabbages and kings: let us talk about anything except the impossibly embarrassing fact that the West has made extensive disarmament proposals, that the Russians have accepted them and that we ought now to be drafting a comprehensive disarmament agreement.

Naturally enough the Russians were not going to let the West get away with that one. In the end they dragged out of the American delegate the fact that the West had withdrawn its offer. On September 6th the American delegate said: 'The United States does now place a reservation upon all its pre-Geneva substantive positions taken in the sub-committee or in the Disarmament Commission or in the U.N. on those questions in relationship to the levels of armaments.' This is officialese for 'the deal's off'.[1]

---

[1] Mr Selwyn Lloyd who was then Foreign Secretary denied to the House of Commons that this withdrawal of support for the Anglo-French proposals by the United States Government amounted to 'a volte-face'. To say that it did was, Mr Lloyd said, 'becoming one of the great myths of history'. The reader can judge for himself. Mr Lloyd went on to criticize

Mr. Noel-Baker entitles the chapter in which he recounts these events 'The Moment of Hope'. I cannot help feeling that 'the moment of despair' would be a more appropriate title. For here we have proof that even when a bold and comprehensive offer of disarmament is made by one side, and then accepted by the other, the only result is to make the sponsors of the offer withdraw in confusion. Here is the proof, that in this round of the disarmament negotiations at any rate, what was being attempted was political warfare, or the putting of the other man in the wrong, and not the conclusion of a disarmament agreement.

The reasons given by the West for the volte-face are also interesting. The Russians had themselves pointed out, in their acceptance paper of May 10th, that there was a danger of one side or the other clandestinely retaining some of its stock of nuclear weapons. So there was, and is. In fact that danger was by 1955 so great that this particular form of nuclear disarmament by means of the destruction of stocks was already almost certainly impracticable. But what could be more preposterous than for the West suddenly to pick up from the Russians this fatal objection to their own proposals, which they had been, till that moment, pushing for all they were worth? Does this not show conclusively that the Anglo-French proposals were not put forward with any idea that they would ever be accepted, still less implemented, but as a weapon of political warfare by which the Russians were to be put in the wrong? Moreover, the Anglo-French proposals proved an effective weapon for this purpose, until the Russians produced their devastating counter-stroke of accepting them. What, however, were the Russian motives in accepting the Western proposals? Did they think

---

the terms of the Russian acceptance of May 10th, 1955, on the grounds that the controls proposed were inadequate and that the timing as between conventional disarmament and the coming into force of a ban on the use of nuclear weapons was unsatisfactory. Some of the criticisms may well have been justified. But of course if the western governments had really meant their proposals they would have tried to improve Russian counter-proposals in further negotiation instead of withdrawing the whole offer.

that there was any chance of their being implemented? Almost certainly not. It was probably a daring and, as it proved, extremely successful move in political warfare. No doubt the Russians considered the question of what would happen if the West called *their* bluff, in turn, and accepted the Russian acceptance. They supposed, perhaps, that there would be plenty of opportunities of causing the process of drafting the actual Disarmament Treaty to break down, long before they would actually be faced with the prospect of reducing their armed forces to $1-1\frac{1}{2}$ million men in return for an unenforceable promise on the part of the Americans to scrap their nuclear weapons.

All in all 'the moment of hope' appears to have been one of the most discreditable episodes in the whole story of the disarmament negotiations. The West put forward proposals which, as the sequel showed, they never dreamt of having to implement: proposals the insincerity of which was mitigated, if at all, by an only too genuine omission to have thought out the problems of nuclear disarmament in any serious way. The Russians merely seized their opportunity to bring off a brilliant stroke of political warfare.

The Moment of Farce

It must not be supposed, however, that the Russians had it all their own way in the political warfare battle which, it is tragic but necessary to admit, the general disarmament negotiations had largely become. In 1960 the West had its revenge. Disarmament negotiations were resumed as a result of the meeting of Foreign Ministers in the summer of 1959. These negotiations were, at the insistence of the West, held 'outside the framework of the U.N.' in a committee of ten nations. No arrangement could have proved worse. There was no agenda, no rules of procedure, no order of debate and the Chairman was changed every day. It is true that M. Jules Moch, the French delegate, made a constructive speech on the opening day, March 15th, 1960, and an agreed 'Western' paper was duly produced. It was essentially an 'Arms Control' rather than a disarmament paper. (We shall discuss the difference between the concept of arms control and disarmament in Chapter 12.)

In the 1960 discussions the argument turned on whether the disarmament treaty should go the whole way to total disarmament, if necessary in phased stages, or begin with a few small modest steps by way of limiting and controlling the arms race. In fact there is much to say on both sides of this issue. But in political warfare an arms control advocate is at a hopeless disadvantage. The Russians therefore had by far the best of the argument and Mr Eaton, the American delegate, was reduced to alleging that the Russians were not willing to accept a system of inspection and control. The difficulty of this allegation was that it was untrue. The Russians had themselves proposed detailed inspection and control arrangements. The Committee adjourned on April 27th. Everybody knew that the British and French delegates had been vainly trying to get the Americans to produce presentable proposals. The Committee of Ten, it was arranged, was to meet again on June 7th.

In the meanwhile the U2 episode and the abortive Summit Conference took place. On June 3rd, Mr Khruschev revealed that he had intended to put a disarmament paper before the Summit Conference but would now put it before the Committee of Ten. This he duly did. This was a far-reaching document and, as general disarmament documents go, a good one. There were to be three stages of disarmament. In the first stage there was to be the abolition of the means of delivery of nuclear weapons. This was M. Moch's suggestion: possibly impractical in its original form but well worth pursuing (see below). In the second stage the reduction of conventional forces to 1.7 million each for Russia and America, and the abolition of nuclear stocks, was proposed. In the third stage virtually total disarmament was to be reached. Moreover, the earlier, and obviously propagandist, Russian proposal that all this was to be done in four years was dropped. There were detailed, and so far as possible (which in some cases is not saying much) practicable, proposals for inspection and control.

What relation to the realities of 1960 these extremely ambitious proposals had is another matter. But they were not something which could be shrugged off if world opinion was not to be fatally alienated. Nevertheless, this is what the unfortunate Mr Eaton tried at first to do. He argued that the Russians were trying to get nuclear disarmament without conventional disarmament, and were avoiding inspection and control. Again the trouble with these arguments was that they were demonstrably untrue. It is an open secret that the British and French delegates became more and more embarrassed with these tactics and in the middle of June prevailed upon Mr Eaton to go home for new instructions. He returned to Geneva on June 26th. The United States Government had decided to play, in part at least, the gambit used by the Russians in 1955. Mr Eaton came back with a paper in his pocket which went a good way at any rate to accept the Russian proposals. 'General and complete disarmament under effective international control' was categorically accepted as 'the ultimate goal'. Moreover, general and complete disarmament, it was now agreed, should 'proceed through three stages containing balanced, phased or safe-guarded measures, with each measure being carried out in an agreed and strictly defined period of time'.

It is not too much to say that the Americans (rightly or wrongly) thus accepted the Russian 'disarmament' approach as opposed to their own 'arms control' approach. It is true that the American three stages were differently phased. The First Stage, for instance, had the 'cut off' of new nuclear production instead of M. Moch's abolition of the means of delivery. The Second Stage had the same manpower ceilings as the Russians had proposed, namely 1.7 million for Russia and America, with some mutual destruction of nuclear means of delivery. The Third Stage was, as in the Russian paper, to be virtually complete disarmament. There were still differences between the Russian and American drafts but these were now negotiable— if there had been any serious intention on either side that a 'comprehensive and complete' disarmament treaty on these lines should or could be negotiated. Once again, as in 1955, the crucial moment had arrived when someone had to a considerable degree accepted someone else's disarmament proposals. And the result was the same. The Committee of Ten was to meet on June 27th. Without even waiting to hear exactly what the West's new proposals were, but, it may be surmised with some confidence, having got wind of the fact that they came embarrassingly near to being an acceptance, the Russians simply took to their heels! They broke up the Committee of Ten and went home, uttering loud cries that the West was once again proving itself an incorrigible warmonger.

Here then was a second demonstration, with the roles of the protagonists reversed, that the one infallible way of breaking up a general disarmament conference is to accept the other man's proposals. For then you put him in an impossible position. His only choices are to try and change the subject or, when that fails, to withdraw his own proposals, as the West did in 1955, or to break up the Conference and go home as Russia did in 1960. But what does this mean? Can there be any doubt that it means that these elaborate and at first sight immensely attractive schemes for comprehensive and complete disarmament, with their resounding general principles and their 'three stages' and all the rest of it, are essentially exercises in political warfare rather than *operational* schemes which might actually be put into effect? A close study of their actual provisions would confirm—if further confirmation were needed—this bitter conclusion. For although they nowadays include fairly strong words about the necessity of inspection and control, no real attempt is made in them to say how this control is to be exercised at the crucial points. For example they all include, at one 'stage' or another, the destruction of nuclear stocks. But they do not include any proposal as to how an inspectorate is to enforce this provision; and this for the very good reason that no one has ever been able to suggest an even plausible way of doing it. Similarly the international control organization which they usually propose to set up would instantly run into the same dilemma as did the I.A.D.A. scheme. It would either be ineffective or become a world authority in embryo. In the case of a general and comprehensive disarmament scheme this would be true *a fortiori* for the I.A.D.A. only had the nuclear industry to supervise: in this case it would be the whole range of national armaments. If the Russians, for very substantial reasons, would not contemplate ceeding one part of their national armaments to a world authority which they did not control, what hope is there of their, or for that matter the Americans', ceding the whole of their national defences to such an authority?

How can we avoid the lamentable conclusion that these offers and counter-offers for treaties of general and complete disarmament are never meant to be taken seriously as schemes which might actually be implemented? It is not the mistakes, prejudices or 'mistimings' of this or that negotiator or statesman which are at the root of the repeated failures. It is that the negotiators and statesmen have no belief in what they are perhaps inevitably doing. They are playing the game of political warfare, busily putting each other in the wrong before the bar of world opinion. We are not witnessing, as Mr Noel-Baker seems to imply, a high drama in which each act has, it is true, so far ended in failure, but which might at any moment open a new era for humanity. We are not witnessing a Greek tragedy but an international farce.

Nevertheless it would be wrong to conclude that the politicians and officials of both sides who conduct these negotiations are tricksters, playing a heartless game. For the most part they are men like ourselves of all degrees of clarity or confusion of mind: in many cases believing at times in the possibility of achieving disarmament by these methods, at other times disillusioned and angry, usually at what they regard as the bad faith of the other side. In succeeding chapters we shall have to take up two major issues in this connexion. First, is it inevitable that all disarmament negotiations should be of this profoundly disillusioning kind? We can say at once that this need not be so. On one condition there is no need for even general disarmament negotiations (such as were resumed in 1962) to be like this. But that condition is that the negotiations should be prepared and conducted with the full, professional, seriousness which nations at present devote to their defence preparations alone. It has been well said that until and unless nations devote even a few per cent as much of their resources, in highly skilled manpower, in research, in money—generally in national effort—to disarmament as they devote to their defence policies, nothing will be accomplished. There are fortunately some signs, which we shall notice in Chapter 13 that the major nations concerned are beginning to think at least of approaching the problems of disarmament in this way.

Finally, even if the history of the negotiations for general and complete disarmament is profoundly discouraging, have there not been negotiations for particular, limited steps in disarmament which have been at least relatively encouraging? There have: in particular during those same years in which the above barren proceedings were dragging on, one international negotiation which, though it failed, was evidently serious, in the sense that the possibility of success was genuinely contemplated at some stages, and even by both sides, was taking place. This was the 'test ban' negotiation. It may have lessons to teach us.

I I

The Test Ban

Far More Difficult and Far More Important

DURING the late 'fifties and early 'sixties another kind of disarmament negotiations was going on: and these negotiations were not mere exercises in political warfare. They were the negotiations, begun at a conference of scientific experts in Geneva on October 31st, 1958, for the cessation of nuclear tests. No student of their record will doubt that they were of a different character from the proceedings at the various general disarmament conferences which we have just described. The serious and detailed character of the proposals made, the closeness of the bargaining, and the very protraction of the negotiations, combined with the fact that, so far as we know, no tests were conducted during the almost three years of negotiation by the governments concerned (America, Russia, and Britain), so that the objective of the negotiations was actually reached, though only *ad interim*, reveal the fact that the possibility of the actual signing and implementation of an agreement to ban nuclear tests was at various times seriously considered by both sides.

The conclusion of an agreement to ban the further test of nuclear weapons has emerged from these negotiations as something which is at once far more difficult of achievement, but also far more important, than is usually supposed. It is hardly too much to say that, if the draft treaty or something similar, which was discussed by the three governments, were *really* to be signed and implemented, a new world situation would begin to come into existence. This may seem an extravagant claim. But as we shall attempt to describe below, the implementation of such a treaty would inevitably lead towards the establishment of an effective concentration of nuclear power (and so of power *tout court*) in the hands of America and Russia. I believe that the first step in the history of the modern world towards the replacement of 'the state of nature' in which sovereign states have hitherto lived would thus have been taken and I ask the reader to suspend his incredulity as to this sweeping claim until he has considered the evidence to be presented in the rest of this book.

The above assertions are based on a particular conception of the consequences of a test ban treaty. It is often said that, even if America, Russia, and Britain had signed such a treaty in, say, 1958 or 1959, nothing very much would have been accomplished. For, it is noted, France in those very years was conducting her first nuclear test explosions, while China, and possibly some other nation-states, were actively preparing a nuclear capability. Therefore, it is asserted, any treaty to refrain from testing on the part of the original three nuclear powers must have quickly broken down when other states were seen to be proceeding with their programmes. It is, however, just this consideration which would have given such importance to the conclusion of a treaty. Clearly such a treaty would have broken down after a few years unless its three original signatories had been able to secure the adherence to it of all or nearly all the potentially nuclear powers. Indeed it is probable that for such a treaty to endure they would have had not only to stop China from beginning to test and to induce France to stop testing, but also to induce Britain to abandon her existing nuclear capability (and in my view Britain in such circumstances would have lost nothing and gained much by doing so). For of course the two existing nuclear super-powers could hardly have indefinitely refrained from improving their own capabilities in producing nuclear warheads (though this may not be a crucially important matter, see below p. 174), while watching the rest of the world busily creating and then improving its capabilities by means of tests.

It is just this necessity to extend a test ban treaty till it is universal, and so represents an insuperable obstacle to the diffusion of nuclear capability through the world, which lends the possibility of such a treaty its far-reaching importance. For once such a treaty had been signed America, Russia, and Britain would have had to look round for ways and means of securing adhesions to it, or of enforcing its provisions upon everyone who was unwilling to adhere. There would probably have been intense resistance on the part of France in the West and China in the East. The question is, could such resistance have been overcome, given the will on the part of America and Russia to overcome it? Perhaps the existing super-powers would not have developed sufficient joint determination for such a task. But in that case, it would have been pointless for them to have signed the treaty at all. On the other hand, there is little doubt of the *ability* of the two super-powers, backed as they would be in this case by Britain and by many of the uncommitted states, to have had their way if they had exerted themselves.

We have little experience of the degree of coercive power which the two super-powers, acting together, can exercise in the contemporary world. But there is just one such instance, that of Suez. In that case, America and Russia being, uniquely and momentarily, of one mind, had no difficulty in stopping the actual military operations of two of the next most powerful states in mid-career (see p. 286 below). Their means for inducing the abandonment of the attempt to acquire nuclear capability, or in the case of Britain and France to abandon a small existing capability, would probably prove ample if they could employ them unitedly and determinedly. Thus we may regard the conclusion of a Test Ban Treaty as a long step at least towards the prevention of the diffusion of nuclear weapons; for unless it were that, it would be nugatory. It is this which gives it its far-reaching importance.[1]

The Course of the Negotiations

The early months of the test ban negotiations provide one more of those apparently heart-breaking 'might have beens' of disarmament. During August 1958, the Russian and American scientific experts very rapidly came to the conclusion that it was possible to establish a control system which could detect violations of a test ban treaty. The difficulties of agreeing upon this particular, and at first sight very modest, step of disarmament appeared much less formidable than those involved in the measures (the destruction of nuclear stocks for instance) discussed in the last chapter. For it was thought that any nuclear explosion anywhere would be readily detectable by a scientific monitoring system which, though fairly far-reaching, was not held at that time to be incompatible with security. Moreover, the sanction for the enforcement of the ban could be a simple one. It was quite unnecessary to threaten drastic measures such as making war on a state which was found to have resumed testing. All that would happen if anybody resumed testing would be that the other signatories of the treaty would resume also. It was therefore thought that there was little need to set

---

[1] What, it may be asked, would an American and a Russian Government actually *do* to enforce their will in this, or any similar, respect, upon a recalcitrant nation-state? I should not have thought that once the all-important, and so far unfulfilled, condition of their having a *joint* will, had been achieved, they would have much difficulty. Naturally they would not begin the process of coercion by crude threats. They would, for example, first of all lead the overwhelming majority in the Assembly of the United Nations, which they could together mobilize, to demand compliance. When that failed, as it likely would, they would begin to talk sanctions. These might begin by the way of the withdrawal of their protective alliances—from China in the case of Russia, from Britain or France, in the case of America. This would really be alarming to the recalcitrants. But if this failed they could pass on, acting no doubt through the United Nations, to economic sanctions including actual economic non-intercourse. It is most unlikely that they would actually have even to rattle the terrible sword of ultimate nuclear power in it scabbard. No, the difficulty lies in the achievement of a joint will, not in its implementation once achieved. The whole question of effective world power is discussed in Chapter 19 below.

O.P.W.—M

up an international authority with formidable powers of inspection, control and enforcement, such as one side would be likely to jib at (as in the case of the proposed I.A.D.A.) for fear that the other side would in practice control it.

In this situation it did not seem by any means beyond the wit of man to arrive at an agreement—provided there was a genuine desire on both sides to do so. But was there? The best answer to this question is probably that there were serious and important people, on both sides, who did so desire, and who thought an agreement possible; but that equally there were serious and important people on both sides who did not. At least this was the position in the West, and there is some evidence, though much of it hearsay, that this was the position in Russia also.

The West Chooses 'No Bread'

It will be impossible to give anything in the nature of a 'round by round' commentary on these negotiations, if only because the full Geneva Conference, to which the above experts' report was referred, held, in the nearly three years of its existence, over 350 meetings. But it may be possible to record without distortion the essentials of what happened. It looked, I repeat, during the early months of the negotiations, as if a treaty might be quickly agreed upon. And then came the only too familiar recoil. A particular school of American scientists, of whom Dr Edward Teller was the most extreme and articulate spokesman, was strongly opposed to the conclusion of a treaty. They set to work, and in a few months they came up with the conclusion that test explosions could be conducted underground without detection. (Also in outer space. But the real difficulty lies in the underground explosions.) Naturally, such explosions would remain undetected at a given distance only if they were small enough and if the hole in which they took place was big enough. But given a big enough hole and a small enough explosion, it was shown that the thing could be done. I say that this conclusion was 'shown' or proved, not because of any technical competence to hold an opinion on the matter, but because the best scientific opinion in the West appears to take that view, and also because in the course of the negotiations the Russian scientists appear to have accepted it. Thus the American scientists of the Teller school undeniably found what they were looking for. But were they right to look for it? This may seem a strange question to ask. If, it may be objected, it turned out in fact that certain tests were undetectable by the methods proposed, then surely it would have been far too risky to sign and implement a test ban treaty which ignored the fact? Surely the American scientists concerned are highly to be commended for preserving the West from a most dangerous error? The issue is not so plain.

In the first place we must recall what the actual consequences of their intervention have been. It is true that there has been no test ban treaty: but, then, there were no tests either—so far as we know—for over three years. The net result of our refusal to accept the admittedly only partially effective measures of control which were originally proposed has been, in effect, that the West for three years unilaterally stopped testing, relying entirely on Russia's word that she had done the same! It is certain that if anyone had proposed in 1958 that America and Britain should stop testing for three whole years with no more than the barest Russian say-so that she would do likewise, they would have been laughed out of court. They would have been ridiculed not only by Dr Teller and those who, to a lesser or greater degree, thought like him, but also by most informed opinion in the West. Yet that is what happened. The intervention of this school of American scientists may have been inevitable and they may have been actuated by the highest motives: but the results of their intervention were paradoxical to say the least.

For let us recall that there remains no difficulty in detecting the kinds of tests which, until 1961, had actually taken place. It remains just as true as ever it was that no one can set off, say, a megaton weapon in the atmosphere without the whole world knowing about it, as they have always done in the case of previous tests. Moreover, even the partially effective inspection and control system which the original concept of the treaty was to have set up would have given us, of course, a far greater assurance still of detecting the resumption of these tests in the atmosphere. We have rejected all that because we could not have an assurance of detecting certain types of underground tests. The West chose, for three whole years, the 'no bread' of a wholly uninspected test ban, rather than accept the 'half loaf' of a partially effective inspection system.

The Proposed Inspection and Control System

It would not be fair to suggest, however, that no further efforts to conclude a treaty were made. On the contrary, after the American scientists presented their new conclusions as to what range of tests were detectable by what means, the Conference, after a good deal of delay on the part of the Russians, made an effort to arrive at a system of inspection and control which would meet, as nearly as possible, these new criteria of effectiveness. It is unnecessary to go into the highly technical details of these negotiations. Suffice it to say that it was in the end agreed that it was impossible, with present techniques, to detect tests *below* a certain size in holes *above* a certain size.[1] In effect this meant that it was hopeless to try to detect test explosions which gave an earth tremor, or shock wave, of less than 4.7 units on the scale used in the detection of earthquakes. It was ultimately agreed that both sides should simply promise not to conduct tests below this magnitude for a specified number of years (the number was never agreed) while the scientists tried to discover ways of detecting them.

But the difficulties of detecting even those underground tests which caused more than a 4.7 shock wave turned out to be great. They involved setting up a most elaborate system of control posts, some manned and some unmanned, over all the territories of the signatory states. Moreover, all these posts could do was to report that there had been, in or about such and such a place, a shock wave of such and such an intensity. In

[1] More especially if they were what is called 'decoupled': but we need not go into that.

many cases it would be impossible to say whether what had occurred was a nuclear test explosion or an earthquake. Therefore it was necessary for some 'authority' to have the right to inspect this suspicious occurrence 'on site', as it was called: that is by sending actual inspectors to the area. And protracted arguments took place on the number of times a year such an authority could exercise this right. The West suggested twenty, subsequently reduced to twelve; the Russians suggested three. Finally the question came up, as usual, as to just how this authority should be controlled and composed, and as to who, specifically, was to do the inspecting.

The Committee struggled seriously and gallantly with these issues; it struggled for months and years. But in retrospect it can be seen that ultimate failure was almost inevitable once it had been concluded that this degree of inspection and control was indispensable. In particular, if the 1961 American estimates of the relatively modest scale of Russian strategic capacity are correct (see p. 46 above), we have a ready explanation of the Russian's unwillingness to allow their territory to be inspected to this degree. For it is undeniably likely that teams of inspectors visiting, several times a year, any part of Russia in which a shock wave had been recorded, might locate one or more of the Russian I.C.B.M. sites. And if there are indeed less than fifty of these missiles in existence—grouped probably in sites containing several missiles—the discovery of even a few of these sites would begin to destroy the invulnerability of the main Russian strategic deterrent. Such are the awkward consequences of the Russians' having adopted a policy of the 'minimum deterrent', dependent for its invulnerability upon secrecy. It is difficult to suppose that Russia was ever going to accept this degree of inspection and supervision over the whole of her territory at the hands of an authority which she did not securely control, and undertaken by particular administrators of that authority whom she suspected might be deeply hostile. (It is also interesting to speculate as to whether the United States Congress, when it came to the point, would have been willing to accept such an agreement.)

In the event, however, the negotiations, in effect, broke down in the first half of 1961. They did not necessarily break down on such issues as the length of the 'moratorium', as it was called, nor on the admittedly undetectable small underground explosions nor on the number of 'on site' inspections: these issues *might* still have been negotiable. What proved unnegotiable was a new Russian demand as to the recruitment of the executive officers who were to carry out the inspection and control. (The composition of the 'authority' itself had been agreed all right.) In 1961 the Russians made the new stipulation that the Principal Executive Officer of the authority should be replaced by three equal officers and be appointed in accordance with their new principle of the 'troika'. That is to say, one was to be a Russian appointee, one a Western appointee and one an appointee from the neutral or uncommitted countries. It was assumed by the West that the Russians meant that each of these executives was to have a right of veto over the decisions of the other two. If this interpretation were correct the Russian-appointed executive could veto a decision to hold any on site inspections at all: or to report that the results of such an inspection showed that a nuclear explosion had taken place. It must be agreed that in this case it would have meant that Russia, or the other signatories of the treaty, need only be inspected when they wanted to be.

The Russians, however, denied that this would be the effect of applying their 'troika' proposal to the administrators of a test ban treaty. They maintained that *each* of the three administrators would still have an absolute right to demand on site inspections—up to the agreed number—even if his colleagues did not agree. On paper this seemed to make the troika arrangement acceptable: but in this case what was the point of proposing it? An apparently ineradicable, and not unnatural, suspicion became rooted in the minds of the Western negotiators that the real purpose of the new Russian stipulations was to put Russia in a position to block, if necessary by means of administrative obstruction, any on site inspections which they did not want. And mainly on this issue the negotiations, in effect, broke down. For the Russian proposal to transfer them to the sphere of the general disarmament negotiations meant, it is to be feared, to transfer them out of the sphere of real negotiations and into the sphere of political warfare. It was taken by the West to mean that the Russians had lost interest in the actual conclusion of a test ban treaty. This was the Russian recoil.

But Does Inspection Matter?

Is it true, however, that the Russian 'troika' stipulation of March 1961 makes an agreement impossible? This is almost certainly true in the sense that once it had been made there was little possibility of the American Congress accepting such a treaty. How could any American administration even ask Congress to accept elaborate control machinery which, it seemed likely, was only to operate when the Russians wished that it should? Curiously enough, however, serious arguments can be advanced to show that even such a treaty as this, and much more the sort of treaty with the relatively simple, but enforceable, provisions which might have been obtainable in 1958-9, would have promoted rather than detracted from American and Western security, and would have constituted the first real step towards disarmament and peace and for that matter towards a world authority established by the Russian and American nuclear powers.

It is clear that any such view must rest upon the at first sight paradoxical opinion that an effective system of inspection and control for a test ban treaty does not matter very much. This, however, is precisely the opinion of some careful students of the matter. For example Mr Brennan and Mr Halperin in their contribution to *Arms Control Disarmament and National Security* (George Braziller, New York, 1961) take, in effect, this view. (And these men, it must be recalled, are the reverse of sentimentalists or pacifists: they are extremely hard-headed American defence experts.) They write '. . . are the potential net gains—political, psychological and military—of a test ban sufficient to compensate for the potential military costs of unrestricted clandestine Soviet testing? If this question can be answered in the affirmative, the inspection problem becomes nearly vacuous. And we believe that it can . . . a test ban would appear to be quite safe for national security even with no inspection whatever. . . .'

This remarkable view is sustained by careful arguments. They amount, in effect, to saying that the inducements, and therefore temptations, upon Russia (and *mutatis mutandis* upon America) to test clandestinely are far smaller than is usually supposed. In the field of large strategic nuclear weapons this view is supported by some fairly technical, but still intelligible, calculations which tend to show that improvements in the actual nuclear warhead are not now a very significant factor in the arms race. It may be theoretically possible to increase the explosive power of a thermonuclear device of given weight by a factor of 5. But this improvement, potentially obtainable by unlimited testing, compares with an improvement in this 'power weight ratio' as it is called by a factor of 1,000 over the Hiroshima type bomb which has already taken place. Besides, once again, even the most primitive inspection system, or even none at all, would probably detect megaton explosions, if they took place in the atmosphere. Theoretically they might take place undetectably in outer space. But the cost of such a test explosion programme there would be literally astronomical. The fact is that it is in terms of improvements in the means of delivery rather than in terms of improvements in the warheads themselves that the arms race in the strategic field is above all taking place.

Clandestine Testing for Tacticals?

Brennan and Halperin agree, however, that the field in which clandestine test explosions might produce what at first sight would seem to be significant improvements, is in the development of tactical nuclear weapons. No doubt unrestricted testing might produce families of lighter, smaller, more convenient tactical nuclears. Moreover, it is in this field that it would be undeniably possible for the Russians, or anyone else, to test underground without too much risk of detection.

But then how much would even the one-sided development of tactical nuclear weapons matter? Brennan and Halperin are of the school of thought which strongly opposes the view, adumbrated by Dr Teller and Dr Kissinger (who no longer holds it) and adopted, as we have seen, by N.A.T.O., that the West could make up for its, allegedly, inevitable inferiority of numbers by the adoption and development of tactical nuclear weapons. In Chapters 6 and 7 of Part One we have set out the reasons for supposing that the adoption of this military doctrine by the West was a disastrous error. Brennan and Halperin go further and put forward the view that it would have little effect upon the military balance if the Russians, by clandestine testing, unilaterally produced a new family of improved tactical nuclears. They do not, of course, suggest that now that tactical nuclears have become standard equipment in the forces facing each other across Europe we can abandon them. But they do suggest that our existing types and stock of tactical nuclears, and means of delivery, are amply sufficient to obliterate 'a field army of 25 Divisions' *however dispersed*. (Probably the same can be said of the Russian tactical nuclears.) What particular advantage would such armies gain then by the development, even unilaterally, by means of clandestine tests, of handier, smaller, lighter nuclear weapons?

An Equalization of Nuclear Power against America's Interests?

Finally they advance a consideration of major importance. The real gainers from unhindered testing, and the consequent development of a new family of light and handy tactical nuclear weapons would not be Russia or America but the smaller, poorer states which at present have no or few nuclear weapons of any sort. It is only too possible that the scientists, given unhindered testing, research and development, will produce new nuclear weapons which are not only handy, small and light, but also *cheap*. Brennan and Halperin write of the possibility of 'Woolworth' bombs and warheads. Nor, in the long run, need these relatively cheap and easily produced nuclears be confined to the tactical field. If the scientists in the end master the problem of setting off the fusion process without using a trigger or detonator of fissionable material, we might have 'Woolworth' H-bombs in the megaton range.

Undoubtedly almost any test ban treaty would tend to make such developments impossible. And this greatly disturbs the anti-test ban treaty school of thought in America. For example, Representative Holifield, the Chairman of the Joint Congressional Atomic Energy Commission, in advocating the resumption of testing by the United States said, on June 14th, 1961, that the continued moratorium was stifling developments undreamed of at the present time. 'Concepts are now being considered by our scientists which could be as revolutionary as the hydrogen bomb in 1949' (*The Times*, June 15th, 1961).

It is only too possible that the scientists will prove him right. But what has not, it seems, come anywhere near Mr Holifield's consciousness is the suspicion that nothing could be more contrary to American interests than such a development. (We could hardly expect him to realize that it would also and equally be contrary to Russian interests: for that would involve a realization that there might be instances of a joint American–Russian interest.) Yet who can deny that even if it were to be America, as it probably would be, which first developed the new types of 'cheap and easy' nuclear weapons, it would be quite impossible to prevent the spread of the new technique, first to Russia (if indeed she lagged behind at all which is far from certain) and then to every industrially advanced nation? Thus the American advantage would be quickly and sharply reversed. The balance with Russia might, it is true, be unaffected one way or the other, though the arms race would be carried to a higher level. But the American (and Russian) predominance as against all other nations would be most markedly reduced. Indeed, Brennan and Halperin go so far as to argue that if, for instance, 'cheap and easy' thermonuclear weapons, without fission triggers, were to be devised, a sort of equalization in powers of destruction between small and relatively poor nations and the super-powers would occur. For Sweden and Switzerland, or *a fortiori* Britain, France, Italy, or Germany could produce or procure enough of such weapons to destroy, or 'overdestroy', America or Russia: moreover, most of the more advanced smaller powers could probably provide invulnerable means of delivery, such as nuclear-powered submarines. Where then would be the advantage of the super-powers? We should be in a sort of equalitarian world in which the smaller could destroy the larger power as easily and surely as the larger the smaller.

This may well be an exaggerated view. As Mr Albert Wohlstetter pointed out in an important article in the April 1961 issue of *Foreign Affairs*, such smaller powers would probably have great difficulty in acquiring means of delivery for their 'Woolworth' weapons, which would make them effective, especially as second strike deterrents, against a superpower. This may be true: nevertheless we are here considering a future in which the scientists had succeeded in making the production of the nuclear warheads themselves much cheaper and easier. Is it not possible, indeed probable, that they might have done the same thing for means of delivery? Might they not have made it possible to produce means of delivery which were sufficiently invulnerable and sufficiently 'unstoppable' to present an acute menace even to the super-powers?

Be that as it may, it cannot be denied that Brennan and Halperin must be correct in asserting that the diffusion of 'cheap and easy' nuclear weapons must tend at least towards an equalization of nuclear power—and so of power between all industrially advanced nation-states. The governments of the smaller powers might be attracted by such a prospect, though they would be profoundly irresponsible, in my opinion, if they worked for it. For such an equalitarian nuclear world would be appallingly unstable. At any rate, though the resumption of testing may well be in the narrowly conceived national interests of poor and medium powers, it is certainly directly contrary to the interests of the existing super-powers and above all of America which still, probably, has some lead in nuclear techniques. Brennan and Halperin somewhat ruefully point out that that lead has already been enormously reduced, if not eliminated, by Russia, a relatively poor state, during the past fifteen years, precisely by means of technical progress making it easier and cheaper to produce nuclear weapons. The conclusion is inescapable that it would be in the direct interests of the state or states which are today in the lead to freeze nuclear weapon technique at the existing state. And this even an ineffectively inspected test ban treaty would go far to accomplish. For the difficulties of the two super-powers acting together in preventing illicit testing by beginners should not be formidable and would require a much less elaborate network of inspection posts and rights of on site inspection than would the effective mutual inspection of the super-powers. True the existing nuclear powers might, as we have seen, continue to make some probably not very significant advances by means of clandestine underground testing; but even a treaty without watertight inspection and control provisions would almost certainly make it impossible for new states to enter the nuclear arms race. (Especially if it was backed by the 'cut off' of the production of fissionable material (see p. 200 below.))

Nevertheless, the whole concept that the *prevention* of further technical progress in a particular field might be in American interests runs clean contrary to the whole bias of American opinion. Implicit in Representative Holifield's statement of June 1961 for example is the pre-supposition that the dazzling prospects of technical progress in the development of nuclear weapons is 'a good in itself', which America must in no circumstances forgo. Moreover, this whole view, that it would have been—and may still be—worthwhile to accept and implement a test ban treaty even if it contains inspection and control provisions of a manifest inadequacy, depends on too sophisticated a process of reasoning to make it possible to present it to the United States Congress, or, for that matter, to any other legislative assembly. It would be impossible, I fear, for a United States Administration to ask for the ratification of a treaty that even seemed to give Russia a veto on inspection, on the grounds that that inspection did not matter after all! It just would not be practical politics.

A Real 'Might-have-been'

Therefore we must probably accept the fact that when the opportunity, or apparent opportunity, to conclude a test ban treaty in 1958 or 1959, with relatively simple but genuinely enforceable control and inspection provisions, was missed, largely, perhaps, because one school of American scientists was given time to demonstrate that these control provisions were not watertight in respect of underground explosions, the immediate prospect of a treaty was lost. For the real answer to these scientists, namely that it did not much matter *whether in this particular instance* the controls were watertight or not, was not one which could win the approval of the American Government or the American people.

But how much may have been lost when this opportunity was missed! For here was the one case in which a joint American-Russian interest in survival might have come to the surface and been embodied in a treaty. As we have noted above, the very fact that the treaty would have been nugatory unless it had been accepted by, or enforced upon, the rest of the world, while it meant that even the actual implementation of the treaty would be only a beginning, also represented an immense opportunity. Here was a possible way out from international anarchy, which in the nuclear age may prove incompatible with human survival: a way out, moreover, not into the never-never-land of a power vacuum of perfectly sovereign states living for ever in perfect peace with each other, but into a genuinely conceivable world of the concentration of power into fewer and fewer hands. The conclusion of a test ban treaty in 1958 or 1959 might have constituted a break through into a period of real progress towards a mutually agreed lowering of the level of armaments, together with, part as cause and part as effect, a corresponding lowering of the temperature of the cold war.

It was not to be. One more failure in the story of disarmament negotiations has to be recorded. But on this occasion the failure was not absolute. Certain gains from the test ban negotiations can be recorded. In the first place the world got a breathing space of three years from test explosions, with the, on the whole, insignificant exception of the French tests in the Sahara. And that has been something. For a continuation and intensification of the testing of thermonuclear weapons in the megaton range in the atmosphere, by not only America, Russia and Britain, but soon by other states also, might have begun—and may yet begin—in the end to produce those dreadful medical consequences which we were told, prematurely I think, were being produced up to 1958.

It Ended With a Bang

As all the world knows only too well the Geneva test ban negotiations were disrupted in the autumn of 1961, and they ended with a bang rather than a whimper—in fact with far the greatest bang in human history.

Mr Khruschev, uninhibited as ever by his previous protestations that Russia never, never would be the first to resume testing started a new, long and varied series of tests including the detonation of a 50-megaton weapon. What was his motive? No doubt the Russian military authorities were strongly pressing to be allowed to test: they no doubt claimed that they would obtain valuable military advantages from a new series: it is of the nature of military authorities so to do. But it is doubtful if this pressure alone would have been decisive. As noted in Part One (p. 48 above) the most plausible explanation of Mr Khruschev's remarkable decision was that the Russians rather suddenly felt themselves to be relatively weak in the nuclear field: that they saw the objections to the doctrine of minimum deterrence which they had in effect adopted, and got nerves. It is said that responsible and reasonable Russians when asked to explain the resumption often begin their reply with some such words as '. . . when my country is in danger . . .'. Unless some realization of nuclear inferiority, and its disadvantages, had dawned on the Russians, what is the explanation of this sudden feeling of danger? It is true that the Berlin crisis had markedly increased tension and had led to a moderate augmentation of the American defence programme. But after all this was a crisis which the Russians had themselves produced out of the whole cloth by demanding an end to the *status quo* in Berlin. It does look as if the Russians, having committed themselves to a forward policy on Berlin, suddenly felt qualms as to the adequacy of the ultimate nuclear strength with which they could back their diplomatic thrust.

On that hypothesis the resumption of testing makes sense. True the objective military gains will be, if the Brennan-Halperin school of thought is correct, as I believe it is, not very important. And anyhow they will be long-term. But the diplomatic gains by way of covering up Russian nuclear deficiencies and giving, on the contrary, an impression of immense Russian nuclear strength were no doubt both large and immediate. And this, perhaps, was what Mr Khruschev needed. He may have needed it as a reinforcement of his position on several different fronts. He may have needed this resounding answer to critics at home: to his Chinese critics abroad: to doubters of his toughness in the neutral world: to satellites in distress in Eastern Europe, such as the wretchedly unsuccessful government of Herr Ulbricht in East Germany for instance. It may well be that such diplomatic prestige gains have made the resumption seem well worth while in Russian eyes. For it seems clear that they attach a minimal importance to the effect of this 50-megaton shock on the peace movements of the world to which they give such lavish verbal support.

If this is even an approximately true appreciation of the situation there is nothing here which the West needs to become unduly alarmed about. Of course the Russians' resumption put an end to the 1958–61 round of negotiations. But the main obstacles to taking up test ban negotiations again are those described above rather than the resumption of Russian testing itself. Of course the resumption proves the wearisome absurdity of the communists' claims that theirs are 'the peace-loving states' as opposed to 'the wicked, warmongering capitalist states'. But no one who does not wish to be has been deceived by such claims for a long time now: and those who do wish to be will continue to be so deceived. Nothing much has been altered.

Prospects for 1962

Unfortunately, however, the Russians, not so much by their tests themselves as by what they have claimed to have achieved by them, have injected a new and acute issue into the negotiations. For they stated that they had produced an effective anti-missile missile. No claim could be more calculated to alarm their opponents and to drive them to resume testing themselves. For as we noted in Part One (p, 83 above) the discovery of a 100 per cent effective anti-missile missile would go far to render the discoverer omnipotent and his opponent impotent. Therefore, any suspicion that the Russians were even on their way to such a discovery was bound to set the Americans testing also lest they be fatally left behind. No American Government could have allowed the indefinite continuance of unilateral Russian testing once this Russian claim had been made.

And yet it is still probable that the gains, either towards the production of a sufficiently effective anti-missile missile, or for other warlike purposes, of further testing, either underground or even in the atmosphere, are far smaller than is usually supposed. It seems probable that the main problems of the production of an anti-missile missile lie in the delivery vehicle and in the field of the radar detection and identification of the missile, rather than in the further perfection of the warhead itself. No doubt this argument cannot be pushed too far: no doubt there are some advantages to be got from the further limited improvement in the power-weight ratio of the warheads which, we are informed, is possible: no doubt it is useful to test the radius of destruction of warheads of different sizes. But these are probably not the critical problems in the production of an anti-missile missile. Moreover, they all necessitate testing in the atmosphere. And in that field a water-tight test ban treaty is attainable without elaborate inspection and control provisions.

For it is well worth noting that when one of the super-powers determined to resume testing she turned, not to any clandestine underground tests, but to full-scale tests in the atmosphere. And the whole world in fact knew immediately, without any control or inspection system whatever, that she had done so. This suggests that the detection of the kind of tests which really matter (in so far as any further tests by the two super-powers may be held to matter) could be readily detected by a relatively simple and modest control and inspection system.

Why then should not a test ban treaty, with simple inspection and control provisions but limited to atmosphere testing, be signed at the coming (1962) round of disarmament negotiations? That indeed is what I personally believe should be done. The present (mid-1962) position in regard to the further perfection of large warheads, and the knowledge of their effects, would be stabilized and both sides could go on testing small warheads, for the not very important (see p. 93 above) purposes of tactical nuclear weapons, underground.

Writing in the first half of 1962 little optimism, however, can be felt about the prospects of the signing of such a test ban treaty. After all it would be asking a very great deal of the Americans to accept such an arrangement after all that has happened. They would have to accept that the Russians by, unilaterally, without warning and in defiance of their own declarations, breaking the test cease-fire, had, if we believe their claims, made the most sensational advance possible in the arms race, or, if we believe the American assessment of those claims, had made *some* advance; and yet America was to deny herself any right of reply. Moreover, the argument is now inevitably used by American opponents of a treaty that whenever it suits them the Russians will suddenly begin to conduct another major series of long-prepared tests. No doubt all the world will at once know that they have done so, but nevertheless Russia will have stolen one more march towards parity and the predominance of nuclear power, while America will require several months of preparation in order to reply with her own series of tests. Probably this argument is not so strong as it sounds. I repeat that the further perfection of the actual nuclear warheads is by no means so critical a matter that the nuclear balance would be disturbed by one side stealing even two marches of a few months over the other by unilateral testing. But this again is a sophisticated argument which it would be difficult indeed for the American Government to make either Congress or public opinion appreciate.

Finally it is not certain that the Russian Government is itself any longer interested in a test ban treaty. True a simple treaty banning atmospheric tests is on offer from the Russian Government—but their statements increasingly sound as if they hardly even expected such an offer, in the current circumstances, to be entertained.

For all these reasons it is difficult indeed to be optimistic over the chances of any sort of test ban treaty emerging from the round of disarmament negotiations which began on March 14th, 1962. I fervently hope that the reader of these pages, in the autumn of 1962, will be able to convict me of undue pessimism: but I fear that he will not. Probably we shall by then have to regard this whole effort—stretching from 1958–62—to secure a test ban treaty as exhausted. But in my opinion it is imperative that the subject be raised again at the first favourable opportunity.

Thus the profound tragedy of what has happened lies not so much in the resumption of testing by the Russians—outrageous, by all civilized standards as that decision was—but in the failure on the part of the two existing super-powers to come to an understanding that their interests pointed directly to the achievement and maintenance, by whatever means, of the standstill in nuclear testing. For only so could they maintain their joint nuclear hegemony and stop the spread of nuclear capacity through the world.

A Multi-nuclear World?

It would be, surely, to delude ourselves to think that, now that the armistice on testing has been so rudely broken, testing can be long confined to the four existing nuclear states, unless a new test ban treaty is negotiated and signed. This is because each new state, as it reaches nuclear capability, will, like France, find it indispensable to test its weapons. China, for example, we may be sure, will be no less determined than was France to test as soon as she can. And when China tests how can India refrain? Therefore, over the years, the absence of a test ban treaty will mean that we shall face the prospect of what might be called a multi-nuclear world. No prospect could be more intimidating. It is not merely that one by one the one hundred or more nation states will reach the position of, for example, Britain today, which can manufacture most, though not all, of the current range of nuclear warheads and bombs. It is rather that uninhibited scientific development will in the end supply any and every even half-way capable state with a whole range of cheap, handy and perhaps incomparably destructive nuclear weapons! That in the end, say, Egypt and Israel, Brazil and Cuba, Pakistan and India, may enjoy something approaching parity of destructive power with Russia and America. For it is argued that the net destructive power which they may acquire, while still far less than that of the super-powers, may be absolute in the sense that any increase in it would be a work of mere supererogation.

This last implication, namely that the world in the absence of a test ban treaty, or some similar agreement, between Russia and America, will become not only multi-nuclear (this is agreed) but that there will be an approximation to a parity of effective nuclear capability, and a consequent blurring of the distinction between the existing two super-powers and the rest, is disputed. Some defence experts believe that America and Russia will, on the contrary, draw further and further away from the rest, above all in means of delivery: that consequently there may never be any new super-powers: that American and Russian predominance will be permanent.

The layman is not entitled to dogmatize on this issue. But on the whole this dissenting opinion seems to neglect the consideration that, though the means of delivery of emergent nuclear powers may remain far less sophisticated than those which

Russia and America will be continually developing, yet in due course—in say ten or twenty years—they will become, at least in the hands of such powerful states as China, India or a united Western Europe, sufficiently effective, and sufficiently invulnerable, to have produced a measure of parity of effective nuclear power amongst a group of nation-states. In any case the more sceptical experts do not in any way deny the extreme instability of a multi-nuclear world, even if the new nuclear powers remain comparatively 'Balkan' in scale as compared to the original two. They point out that even the diffusion of nuclear weapons by gifts from the super-powers would produce the gravest instabilities. Therefore, the experts are at one in dreading the prospect of a multi-nuclear world. This whole issue of the power of the super-powers, its probable duration, and the consequences of nuclear diffusion, will be discussed in Chapter 19.

This is the prospect which the failure to conclude a test ban treaty in the late nineteen-fifties or early nineteen-sixties has opened before us. It is a prospect which threatens the continued existence of the human race: but it threatens also the predominance of the two existing super-powers. And yet America and Russia have shown themselves impotent to avert it, which they could almost certainly have done by the conclusion of a test ban treaty. They were hamstrung by their mutual and, it must be admitted, by no means ill-founded suspicions and antagonisms. They have been, up till now, almost completely preoccupied by their intense rivalry and competition. Hardly a suspicion that they might have joint interests as against the rest of the world, and that those joint interests might coincide with the overriding interest of the human race in its own survival, has dawned on them. And yet how can mankind hope to survive unless there dawns upon the super-powers a consciousness of the overriding necessity of some kind of mutual understanding, if only for this one purpose of preserving their own predominance by preventing the development of a multi-nuclear world? That is why we cannot, surely, allow ourselves to regard the failure of the test ban treaty negotiations of 1958 to 1962 as final. In some way or other these negotiations must be taken up again. The Russian and American Governments may in time learn, and in time teach their respective peoples, that even an incomplete and defective treaty, which is probably all that is attainable, is indispensable. Such a treaty may not do much to diminish the intensity of the conflicts and suspicions between Russia and America. They will probably have mutually to assume that the treaty is being evaded by the other party, whenever evasion is practicable without detection, and will have to come to the realization that these evasions are unlikely to have a marked, still less a decisive, effect on the balance of power between them. But such a treaty would go far to prevent the spread of nuclear weapons around the world.

In other words a test ban treaty would merely check to some degree the arms race between Russia and America themselves. But it might well succeed in averting the nightmare development of a multi-nuclear world, in which every power, great or small, would have an almost equal power of destruction over every other. And then Russia and America, having united for this single purpose of preventing the proliferation of nuclear weapons both in type and in their distribution throughout the world, might be able to begin to build some degree of mutual understanding upon this narrow, but real, basis of mutual self-interest.

Thus we must never let the test ban issue rest: for it has shown itself to be the one disarmament issue on which success really did come into sight. On the other hand, just as we shall see that it is barren to consider even disarmament as a whole in isolation from the whole complex of international relations, so it is also barren to regard a test ban treaty in isolation from the wider issues of disarmament. We must therefore consider the views of a new school of thinkers on disarmament which has arisen in the West.

12

Another School of Thought

Arms Control Instead of Disarmament?

I T is hardly to be wondered at that after all the disappointments
and frustrations described in the last two chapters a new
view on the subject of disarmament has appeared. It developed
first amongst the American defence thinkers, whose work has
been referred to in Part One of this book. Many of these men,
in spite of, or indeed because of, their close preoccupation with
technical defence questions felt strongly that something *must*
be done about the arms race. Many of them had either been
actually opposed to, or at any rate sceptical of, most of the
proposals for disarmament which had been made at the various
disarmament conferences. Yet they saw the fatal drive of the
race. These men have gradually evolved the concept of what is
called 'Arms Control', rather than Disarmament.

As a move in political warfare the change of title could hardly
be more disastrous. It has caused not only the Russians but
many lifelong supporters of disarmament in the West to assert
that these men have abandoned 'real' disarmament in favour
of some bogus, or at least extremely half-hearted, attempt to
stabilize armaments at their present level. And it is true that
most if not all of the ideas and proposals of arms control are
more modest and limited than those of the older school of
disarmers. That in itself would be no reason for dismissing
them. It would be foolish indeed to reject anything which made
a genuine start at disarmament—even if the first step were no

more than an agreed arrest, or even slowing down, of the up-
ward spiral of the arms race. To suggest otherwise would,
surely, be like denying that it was a good thing to apply the
brakes, slow down and then stop a motor-car which was going
headlong towards a cliff, before turning the car round and
driving it in the opposite direction. But it is nevertheless necessary, in my view, always to envisage measures of arms control
as no more than preliminary to putting the arms race into
reverse by means of positive measures of disarmament. Thus the
'arms controllers' have, partly, themselves to blame for the
disrepute into which their views have come in some circles.
For they have tended to promote arms control as a substitute
for, rather than as the beginning of, disarmament. And they
have done so partly at least because the word disarmament
carries a pacifistic, anti-national unrespectable connotation
with it in these circles in America: a connotation which they
wished to avoid. Yet the only real difference between the concept of arms control and that of disarmament appears to be
that the former lays more emphasis upon the necessity for
specific measures promoting rather than disturbing 'the
stability of the balance'. For the rest the proposals—test ban,
'cut off', limitation of numbers of conventional forces, etc.
etc.—which are discussed are bound to be much the same,
whether they are called measures of disarmament or measures
of arms control. The only clear-cut difference is between the
arms controllers and a minority of disarmers who suppose that
total disarmament amongst sovereign states is possible at one
fell swoop. Thus the arms control versus disarmament controversy seems to be sterile or semantic. What matters is to
find particular measures by means of which Russia and America,
with their allies, can first control the arms race, halt, and then
reverse it. But now that we can see the obstacles in the light of
bitter experience it is clear that it will not be easy to do so.
Before making the attempt it will be well to compare and contrast the point of view of a non-American writer who, while he
cannot be classed as an arms controller, has a very different
point of view from, for example, that of Mr Noel-Baker.

A Less Sanguine Approach

It may be convenient to cite the recent work of Mr Hedley Bull, *The Control of the Arms Race: Disarmament and Arms Control in the Missile Age* (published for the Institute for Strategic Studies by Weidenfeld and Nicolson, 1961).[1] (Mr Bull is an Australian working at the University of London.) This difference in approach to the whole subject is vividly illustrated in Mr Bull's opening pages. He is by no means willing—as we have hitherto done—to assume as self-evident that disarmament is desirable. On the contrary he lists the various reasons which are usually advanced in its favour, and comes to the conclusion that they are of varying degrees of validity. For instance he notes that disarmers usually contend that armaments constitute an intolerable economic burden upon the nation which sustains them—there is not much in this, he concludes: that war is morally wrong—some wars are and some are not he writes: that large military establishments tend to corrupt liberal and democratic institutions—there is some force in the contention: and finally that armaments are themselves the, or at least a, cause of war—this, he holds, is only true in a very conditonal sense and to a very limited degree.

It is at once obvious that we have encountered a very different attitude from that of Mr Noel-Baker for example. Still, Mr Bull has reached the conclusion that for a variety of reasons some measures of disarmament, so long as they do not tend to disturb the stability of the balance, are desirable. Nevertheless, few impartial readers of his book will doubt that increasing in every possible way the stability of the balance of power is what Mr Bull really believes in. The particular *level* of armaments at which the balance is maintained is for him a secondary matter. Nor, he considers, will the lowest level be likely to be the most stable: rather the contrary.

Moreover, to be acceptable, Mr Bull continues, measures of disarmament, in addition to leaving the stability of the balance

---

[1] I was a member of the Study Group of the Institute for Strategic Studies out of the discussions of which Mr Bull's book grew. I appended a dissenting comment to the book's approach and conclusions.

undisturbed, must be inspectable and controllable. And here, like everyone else, he comes up against the major difficulties of achieving methods of inspection and control which are at once effective and compatible with national sovereignty. Finally he classes 'constitutions for world governments' among 'gestures, research, therapies and cures' which represent 'a corruption of thinking about international relations and a distraction from its proper concerns'.[1] No wonder, then, that Mr Bull is pessimistic about the advancement of particular measures of disarmament. For such measures are thought to involve in varying degrees the institution of a degree of inspection and control which would, undeniably, involve the sovereign states of the world, including the super-powers, submitting, to a lesser or greater degree, to agencies which they do not control.[2]

Symptom and Cause?

What must we say as to this douche of cold water which Mr Bull, and those who think like him, have poured upon the warm enthusiasms of the older school of disarmers?

Let us consider first his proposition that arms and the arms race are not a very important cause of war and (as he also considers) that even their complete abolition would not ensure peace? No serious student of the subject supposes that nations fight each other *because* they possess arms. Clearly arms are the instruments *with which* they fight, and the competitive race to arm themselves better and better is a symptom rather than a cause of their rivalries, conflicts and mutual apprehensions. But does it follow from this that disarmament is a largely futile

[1] Mr Bull may mean merely that the drafting of paper constitutions for world governments, without any consideration of how any sort of world authority might come into existence is futile. I agree as to the futility of that sort of thing. But taking his book as a whole I think it is fair to say that he means much more than this. (See the further quotation from his book, p. 194 below.)

[2] As we have seen in the last chapter, a test ban treaty for very special reasons need involve, in my opinion and unless Brennan and Halperin (loc. cit.) can be shown to be mistaken, a much lower level of inspection and control then all other measures. But how can one convince governments of this?

attempt to deal with the symptoms of the disease while leaving its cause untouched? This appears to be a *non sequitur*. A medical analogy is both familiar and helpful here. There are illnesses, I understand, in which it is urgently necessary to attack the symptoms—say a raging fever—before there can be any hope of eradicating the disease. For the symptoms will themselves react back, exacerbating the disease, perhaps fatally, unless they are successfully tackled. In just the same way there can, surely, be little doubt that the existence of the massive armed forces which contemporary states find themselves forced to maintain, as a result of the competitive pressure of the arms race, react back and predispose them to war. Beyond a certain point they almost inevitably distort not only and not chiefly the economic, but also the whole of the political, social and cultural life of the community. How could it be otherwise? In so far as the central and decisive activity of a community tends to become the assertion of its armed power over against other communities, there will be a predisposition to trials of strength, as against peaceful or even co-operative co-existence.

Therefore, whether the *level* of the balance of armed strength is high or low is a far more important factor than Mr Bull and his school allow. He is right of course in his contention that the achievement of a low level should not be aimed at without regard to the stability of the balance. But how much importance need we give to this consideration? It is true that it can be shown that, in the abstract, a balance between a few nuclear weapons would be, other things being equal, less stable than a balance between a higher number of such weapons. But I believe that the point is in practice academic and indeed misleading.[1] For the other factors never are equal: they are on the contrary so important and so variable that they will usually overshadow the theoretically greater stability of more weapons rather than fewer. Therefore, I adhere to the older, common-sense, view that the lower the level of armaments on both sides the less will be the predisposition to use them. Who can really

---

[1] In the narrower context of the number of I.C.B.M.s to be held by each side Mr Bull accepts this view (loc. cit., p. 169).

doubt that if it were possible to, say, halve the level of both the nuclear and the conventional armaments in each of the alliances, even while leaving all the other factors unchanged, there would be a considerable reduction in the danger of war? It may be, of course, that our instinctive conviction that this is so springs partly from a realization that in that event the other factors would not in practice be left unaffected: that such a reduction in levels would necessarily be associated with a considerable improvement in the relations of states: that it must react both as cause and effect, not only upon the warmaking capacities but also upon the *intentions* of the states concerned. But this is simply to introduce a theme with which we shall be increasingly concerned (and which Mr Bull and his school of thought accept and indeed emphasize) namely that it is deeply misleading to consider the question of disarmament in isolation from all the other factors making either for peace or war.

The Russian View of the Matter

This consideration applies, on the other hand, to the Russian contention that if only all states would agree to and implement a treaty of total disarmament, peace would be secure because henceforward they simply could not make war even if they wished to. At one level it can be replied that such totally disarmed states *could* make war on each other, and that the state which most quickly learnt to manufacture weapons and train its manpower would win. But the real answer is rather that the whole conception of a world of totally disarmed, totally sovereign, states is so illusory and misleading as to be almost a contradiction in terms. The state of nature, or international anarchy, in which completely sovereign states by definition must live, necessarily means that each must look after itself. It is inconceivable that such states could ever wholly deprive themselves of the means of doing so. The truth is that to demand total all-round disarmament is to demand some sort of world authority.

Naturally the Russians know all this as well as we do: or rather they know it a good deal better, for Marxism is a particularly explicit political philosophy on such issues. Why then do they tirelessly ask for the impossible? They do so, in a sense, as an act of conscious political warfare. But also it is a demand which they, no doubt, feel that they—and they alone—are fully entitled to make. For it is an aspect of Marxist theory that only a world of communist states can possibly form a co-operative world federation, but that they both can and will, almost automatically, do so. Therefore, the logic of their demand for total disarmament leads, they believe, straight to the necessity of a world of communist societies.[1] The fact that forty years of experience of communist societies indicates that they habitually use just about as much force, and threat of force, amongst themselves as do other societies, and are as jealous of their national sovereignties,[2] is not the sort of fact that can be expected to impinge on the mind of a trained communist.

What the Realists Ignore

The Russians reject, as we have seen, any approach to an authority, capable of giving the world the possibility of the rule of law, until and unless all major states have become communist. Mr Bull, and some of those who think like him (and they include most practical men of affairs) do not explicitly reject the creation of such an authority (though some do): but they regard its attainment as too remote and improbable to have much to do with the problem which faces the world here and now. Indeed Mr Bull writes that 'we cannot expect that the establishment of a universal government by contract among the nations rather than by conquest will be brought about by governments incapable of the most modest forms of co-operation'. (He sees the possibility, but not the desirability, of world

[1] Marx said that the demand that men should shed their illusions involved the demand that they should change the conditions which made those illusions necessary. In the same way the demand for total disarmament involves the abandonment of the conditions which make armaments necessary, namely a world of sovereign states living in a state of nature.

[2] Note for example Mr Khruschev's remark to Mr Walter Lippmann in April 1961: 'I will never entrust the security of the Soviet Union to any foreigner.'

government by conquest.) No doubt both the Russians and these Western thinkers are being realistic, in the sense that (a) there can be nothing like complete disarmament while the world is articulated into sovereign states living in a state of nature: (b) that a sharp discontinuity exists between the world as we know it and a world in which an indispensable minimum of sovereignty had passed into the hands of some single authority; and (c) that the transition from the former to the latter sort of world would be indispensable to any decisive modification of the international state of nature. The Russians suppose that it is unrealistic to raise the issue until after the world has become at least predominantly communist. Mr Bull and his school of thought at heart, I believe, think that it is unrealistic to raise it at all. No one can prove that they are wrong. But if they are right, the prognosis for the future of our species in the nuclear age is dark.

For, as we have seen, the most promising specific proposals for disarmament such as the I.A.D.A. plan of 1946, or the test ban negotiations of the last three years (1958–61) always in the end came up against the questions of inspection, control and enforcement. It always turned out that unless some agency, authority, commission—call it what you will, in the impartiality and integrity of which both sides could have at least a degree of confidence, could be set up, it was impossible to make progress. It would however be a disastrous error to suppose that there is nothing between leaving things as they are and the creation of a fully-developed world authority. It will be suggested below that what may yet be possible is the gradual emergence of an elementary sense of common purpose, in a strictly limited field, between the Russian and American Governments. And that on the basis of this limited sense of common purpose some rudimentary organs of world authority may yet be built.

Mr Bull wrote of the proposal, implicit in the test ban, to limit the number of nuclear powers to two: 'It is difficult to see how a limitation of the nuclear club that was to last even a short time could be brought about except by the discovery by

Russia and America of a common purpose in imposing such a limitation.' Precisely. But we have seen that such a common purpose, firmly founded upon their own national interests, lies behind the test ban negotiations, waiting to be discovered by the Governments of the two super-powers. This common purpose, which is simply to stop the spread of nuclear weapons through the world, since that spread will fast erode the predominance, and then menace the very existence, of the super-powers (and the existence of all the rest of us also, can be made effective only by some sort of treaty. Such a treaty would arrest, by the device of the test ban, the acquisition of nuclear capability by new powers (and probably the relinquishment of their nuclear capability by the third and fourth nuclear powers, Britain and France). The conclusion of such a treaty has proved, for the time being, outside the reach of the Russian and American Governments, because of the intensity of their well-founded mutual suspicions. For it would involve some, though in practice a small, element of mutual trust. Nevertheless, as the perilous consequences of failure, namely what we have called 'a multi-nuclear world', impinge on the consciousness of the two Governments, we may expect them to return, perhaps again and again, to an attempt to reach at any rate this limited degree of understanding.

Unfortunately their time is by no means unlimited. Already their duopoly of nuclear capability has been breached by Britain and France. And in 1962, rumours persist that a fifth potential member of the nuclear club—the potential super-state of China—may soon [1] present the unrefusable application form of a successful test explosion. It is true that, as we noticed in Part One, this is not to say that Russian and American predominance in nuclear power is immediately threatened, for their lead in means of delivery will be hard to overtake. Nevertheless, as Brennan and Halperin convincingly argued, unrestricted research, development and testing must be expected in the long run to tend to equalize nuclear destructive power

[1] Though perhaps not *so* soon as is often supposed: but, surely, within ten years as a maximum.

between at least all advanced states. Therefore, the period in which the rudiments of world order can be built on the self-regarding interest of Russia and America to preserve their predominance—which interest coincides, in my view, with the interest of the human race in its survival—is limited.

If nothing much has been done until several new powers achieve approximate parity of nuclear destructive power, the more complex task of evolving the rudiments of a world authority on the basis of the common interest of a group of powers will have to be undertaken.

13

Defence and Disarmament Policies

Disarmament May Be Defence

THE main concept put forward in the last three chapters, namely that there is a foundation of common interest between America and Russia, which, if we dig deep enough, can be discovered beneath their searing antagonisms, can be applied to other measures of disarmament as well as to a test ban treaty. It is simply that a test ban treaty appeared, and still appears, to be the best 'growth point' from which a rudimentary world authority might be developed.

The purpose of this chapter will not be to discuss other possible measures of agreed disarmament, except by way of examples. For such specific measures must arise out of the opportunities of the international situation. It is probable that the very tensions and crises which are only too certain to arise will provide the best opportunities to arrive at this or that measure of possible disarmament. But such opportunities will only be taken if the leading nation-states approach the question of disarmament in a different and more realistic spirit than they have done hitherto.

First of all it will be indispensable to think of the defence and disarmament policies of our respective nation-states, and of our alliance, as two sides of the same coin. These policies have after all one purpose, namely the security and survival of the peoples of our nation-state and of our alliance. Sometimes we may come to the conclusion that this purpose can be promoted by means of defence policies alone: by means, that is to say, of competing in the arms race lest we find our state or our alliance at the mercy of its opponents. But, we have seen, the arms race must be in the long run a self-defeating method of achieving security. Therefore we must pay at least equal attention to what we may think of as a negative arms race, i.e. disarmament. We must realize that we may sometimes achieve the same objective, namely security and survival, by means of some measure of mutual disarmament, as at other times we may be forced to seek by adding some new weapon to our nuclear or our conventional armouries.

Such an attitude would involve much more far-reaching changes, not only in our attitudes of mind, but also in the actual machinery of our Governments, than is always realized. It would be too much to say that in present-day governments disarmament is nobody's business. But only just too much. There are small sections of most Foreign Offices charged with thinking out and presenting their nation's disarmament policies and, under President Kennedy's administration, there is something more in America. But the objective of attaining national security and survival by means (partly) of agreed disarmament has never been integrated into the machinery of government in a way even remotely comparable to the way in which defence policy has always been so integrated. It would need a revolution in our thinking to do it. What is really needed is that our defence planning staffs should see disarmament not as the opposite of defence policy, but as an alternative and indispensable way of attaining the same ends as those sought by the maintenance of armaments. What is needed is some new machinery of government by which a degree of sustained attention can be given to disarmament, in the widest sense of the term, and including especially such measures as a test ban treaty, 'disengagement' and the 'cut off' (see below), comparable to that habitually devoted to defence policy.

Second, if the frustrations of the past decades are to be avoided the problem of disarmament must be approached far

O.P.W.–O

less abstractly, and with far more appreciation that this is but one facet of the question of how the relationship of nation-states must be adapted in order to make survival possible in the nuclear age. And this will mean, specifically, basing disarmament proposals upon a discovered mutual interest in survival between the leading nation-states. It is only, in my opinion, by means of this 'harder', more concrete approach, by means of harnessing the self-interest, become mutual interest, of two or more of the super-powers, that disarmament can become something more than one of the causes of 'the stage army of the good'. It may be possible to illustrate this proposed approach by means of discussing the prospects of the present, 1962, round of disarmament negotiations. We can only do so here by giving examples of the sort of disarmament proposals which seem hopeful.

'Pugwash' Hopes for the 'Cut Off'

It would be an error to suppose that the prognosis for the 1962, round of disarmament negotiations is entirely negative. In particular some of those Western defence experts who attended the 'Eighth Conference on Science and World Affairs' at Stowe, Vermont, in September 1961, have come back encouraged by their discussions with the Russian scientists and defence experts whom they then encountered. (These used to be called 'the Pugwash Conferences' for the earlier meetings were held at Pugwash, Canada.) Perhaps the most useful part of these discussions will prove to be the fairly specific proposals for a 'cut off', as it is called, in the further production of fissile material of a quality suitable for military purposes. This, the experts believe, is a genuinely inspectable and controllable proposition, in the sense that it would not involve a violation of security which, for the reasons given above, the Russians could not, today (1962), be expected to accept. The conference concluded that a production cut-off without the reduction and ultimate elimination of stockpiles would not, in itself, decrease the nuclear weapon potential of the present nuclear powers. But it would make it impossible for a new nation to build up its weapons stockpile, and, if strictly adhered to, would make it impossible for additional powers to build nuclear weapons by their own efforts. A very important benefit would be that experience would be gained with a control system which would be largely applicable in the later stages of stockpile reduction.

This seems an eminently constructive view. It is evident that such a 'cut off' of nuclear production would in fact be a strong reinforcement of a test ban treaty. Together they would prevent the growth of a multi-nuclear world. Moreover, they might pave the way for the much more difficult task of the reduction, and even eventual elimination, of existing nuclear stock-piles.

Such measures, like the test ban, would no doubt encounter the hitherto insuperable difficulty of securing an agreement on measures of inspection and control. Various ingenious suggestions have been made to overcome this difficulty. The most promising of these is perhaps the so-called 'Sohn Zones' plan for what is, in effect, a sampling technique, by means of which particular areas, instead of the whole, of a nation's territory should in turn be open to inspection. This scheme is at the time of writing being seriously discussed in the 1962 round of disarmament negotiations. We can only hope for the best.

Out of Crisis, Disengagement?

In a very different context, ought we not to strive to produce out of the very tensions of the Berlin crisis a measure of local nuclear disarmament or disengagement as it is usually called, in Europe? It is true that at first sight the mere pulling back and away from each other of even the smaller tactical nuclear weapons by a hundred miles or so does not seem significant. For some of these weapons have a range of many times that number of miles. But this is to look at the matter from too narrowly technical a point of view. This is really a part of the implementation of that general reversal of policy on the part of N.A.T.O. which was discussed in Chapters 6 and 7. If limited nuclear weapons are in the hands of front-line units the tendency will always be to use them at once in the event of any considerable attack. If they are held well back under separate command, the defending side will retain the option to use conventional means against a conventional attack. Again the placing of the weapons is bound up with the question of who is to decide whether to use them or not—the question of 'whose finger is to be on the trigger'. At present the position is that the warheads of N.A.T.O. tactical nuclear weapons are under American control. This is as it should be. There is really no alternative arrangement except to equip each and all of the N.A.T.O. allies including France, West Germany, Britain, Belgium and Holland, not only with means of delivery, but with the actual nuclear warheads and with their custody, so that the forces (very likely at battalion level) of each and all of these nations could start the nuclear exchange.

This, I fear, is what the West German Government is, in effect and unofficially, pressing for. This is because, as Herr Strauss, the German Defence Minister, is accustomed to explain, he has no confidence in N.A.T.O. building up conventional forces capable of meeting a Russian conventional attack. But, he implies, give him tactical nuclear weapons and the right to use them and the Russians could be held.

Once again Western defence thinking in general and German defence thinking in particular seem incapable of grasping the fact that the Russians also possess tactical nuclears.[1] If they did not, there would be great force in the argument that, however great the danger of 'escalation' might be, the N.A.T.O. ground forces, using tactical nuclears, would be at a decisive advantage against Russians using conventional weapons. But what reason is there to suppose that N.A.T.O., using tactical nuclears, would be at an advantage over the Russians using

[1] In one case, however, German defence thinking has proved to be ahead of Western defence thinking as a whole. In *Defence or Retaliation* by Helmut Schmidt (Oliver and Boyd, 1962), an English translation of which has just become available, what has been well called (by Mr Michael Howard) 'every sensible man's defence policy' has been set out with splendid clarity. And this is indeed the defence policy of German Social Democratic Party under the wise leadership of Mr Fritz Erler.

tactical nuclears, as of course they instantly would if we replied to their conventional attack in this way? And yet this conception that the West would gain some advantage by moving the war from the level at which both sides used conventional weapons to one at which both sides used tactical nuclear weapons, persists undiminished amongst the European (including the British) military planners. It is particularly strange that it should be above all the Germans who show themselves intent upon turning any considerable conventional clash in Europe into a nuclear exchange. For whatever country might possibly escape devastation, and its people extermination, in a war fought on the central front in Europe with tactical nuclear weapons Germany and the German people must certainly be destroyed. If ever there was evidence of a 'death wish' it is here.

British Defence Policy

There is one aspect of the present German defence policy with which it is possible to sympathize, however. And that is their protest against discrimination between the N.A.T.O. allies, by which they and they alone should be denied the custody of nuclear weapons. It is impossible to discriminate in this way between allies. It is not done at present, for custody is in American hands. But as the British and French nuclear programmes progress, there might well be a tendency to equip British and French ground forces with British- and French-made tactical nuclear warheads. This is why there is no really workable alternative to the present position in which the custody of the nuclear warheads is centralized in American hands. (If at some future date Western Europe, including Britain, unifies itself into a new super-power, that no doubt will be a different matter. Such a super-power would probably insist on equipping itself with a range of nuclear weapons. But if its defence planners had any sense they would go for an invulnerable sea-borne strategic deterrent such as Polaris—and a centrally commanded tactical deterrent held well back—see page 109 above. But this is in the future.)

It is unpleasant for a British writer to have to record the

fact, but it is British and French confusion of thought and intransigence which is, largely, responsible for the failure to adopt such a sane defence policy on the part of the West. At the end of 1961 Mr McNamara, the American Secretary of Defence, made another appeal to Britain and France not to proceed with their own nuclear deterrents, but instead to integrate in the American system. The appeal was rejected (*Observer*, December 17th, 1961). There is now no doubt that on a balance of considerations Britain and France ought to accept this policy in principle.[1] Just what should be done with the existing British nuclear stocks, with the inevitable future production of plutonium from British nuclear power stations (until and unless a universal 'cut off' can be agreed), and with Bomber Command, are questions which should be very carefully considered by the defence authorities of the alliance as a whole. What matters is that Britain and France should cooperate in, instead of obstruct, the present American Administration's defence policy for the central front in Europe which is far better thought out, far more rational and therefore likely to be far more effective, than their own. This for the reasons given in some detail in Chapters 6 and 7. A rationalization of N.A.T.O. strategy by giving due weight to adequate strength at each of the three levels of conventional, tactical nuclear and strategic nuclear weapons, would permit a measure of nuclear disengagement in Europe, and would do so without discrimination against our West German allies, in the sense that America alone would hold the key to the nuclear cupboard. For the rest we should all tirelessly explain to the Germans (when we have understood the thing ourselves) that the present American strategy of giving adequate importance to conventional

[1] The only circumstance in which a case might be made out for the retention by Britain (or France) of her own nuclear deterrent is in the dire eventuality of the general spread of nuclear weapons through the world. In that case Britain and France might no doubt be forced to retain theirs, not because they contributed anything much to the Western Alliance, but because the world had become so desperately insecure a place that no considerable nation could exist without a nuclear capacity. But that eventuality would create a world in which the human race would have a poor chance of survival whatever anyone did.

strength, far from leading to their abandonment, is in fact the sole way in which they can be protected without involving their certain extermination in the event of war. In a word just as there is no substitute for conventional strength for the purpose of preventing an act of Russian aggression of a size below that to which it is credible that we should respond with nuclear weapons, so also there is no substitute for conventional strength in order to make possible nuclear disengagement in Central Europe.

The Preservation of Outer Space

We should note one more suggestion relating to the positioning of nuclear weapons before coming back to further measures of possible disarmament in the more usual sense of the mutual reduction of weapons.

A suggestion which should certainly be pressed is the demilitarization of outer space. As no nuclear weapons have yet been hoisted up above the atmosphere it might be possible to establish an inspection and control system which made such a development impossible. There would then arise the question of the existing American—and perhaps Russian—reconaissance satellites. Such reconaissance satellites are clearly of much more use to the West. What *quid pro quo* would Russia be willing to give for their abandonment?

Scrapping Vulnerability

There is one more measure of disarmament which might be a possible starting point. And that is the mutual scrapping of stated numbers of those means of delivery of the strategic nuclear weapons which are inherently vulnerable. For example liquid-fuelled rockets (such as Thor) on soft fixed sites; after that perhaps some types of bombers; after that perhaps liquid-fuelled rockets in hardened fixed sites. One can conceive realistically of, say, one hundred liquid-fuelled rockets and one hundred bombers being delivered by each side to the other and publicly destroyed. There would thus be no difficulty as to inspection and control.

It is usually objected that this proposal simply means an

offer mutually to scrap obsolescent means of delivery; and that this would be a deception of the public which would suppose that a measure of effective disarmament was being undertaken when it was not. But this objection is based upon a continuing failure adequately to distinguish between means of delivery which are effective weapons on first and second strike respectively. It is quite true that liquid-fuelled rockets on soft fixed sites and, in many respects, some types of bombers on some bases, are becoming useless for second strike retaliatory purposes; for they would be destroyed by the opponent's first strike: they have little or no deterrent effect therefore. Nevertheless, they are still appalling weapons on first strike. The American, and British, weapons of this kind could probably devastate nearly every major city in Russia and the corresponding Russian weapons could probably do the same to the West. They have become, through their vulnerability, weapons of almost pure aggression, useless for any other purpose, but terrible in the extreme for this purpose. How can it then be said that the destruction of stated and equal numbers of them would not be a measure of genuine disarmament? It is true that they could not be eliminated altogether because it would probably be impossible to verify that elimination without a degree of inspection and control much beyond what is at present obtainable. But the mutual scrapping of even 100 or 200 of such weapons on either side would unquestionably contribute to both mutual security and also, which is very important, to the *sense* of security of both sides. The very existence of these characteristically first strike weapons is a grave mutual provocation. The world would gain very greatly in security if they were progressively scrapped, even though the arms race went on at full intensity in the provision of invulnerable, characteristically second strike weapons.

Naturally these are merely suggestions and instances of possible measures of disarmament which should be tirelessly promoted as opportunity serves. (Most of them are advocated by Mr Bull (op. cit.) though not by some of the American 'arms controllers', or, for that matter, by believers in immediate 'general and complete' disarmament.) They flow, to a lesser or greater degree, from the concept that those measures of disarmament have a real possibility of implementation which can be seen to be in the interests not only of the world at large but in the mutual interests of the super-powers. For the super-powers even when locked in their world-wide struggle, *have* a mutual interest, even if it is no more than the interest of mutual survival: and that mutual interest cannot avoid coinciding, at least in its essential respect, with the interest of the human race as a whole.

Perhaps, however, the real development of events will present opportunities, not for the measures of disarmament instanced above, but for other and different measures. What is important is that we should be continually and restlessly searching for measures which can start the process of disarmament. The real criticism of the arms control school of thought is that, in spite of its members' valuable work, their general approach reveals unmistakably that the balance of power is the only concept of international relations which they take seriously. In the nuclear age it is not enough.

Disarmament or Political Warfare?

The West might, no doubt, put forward these suggestions for concrete first steps in disarmament, as Phase I in a comprehensive plan at the resumed disarmament negotiations which are due to take place during 1962. This coming round of negotiations may, unfortunately, prove as barren as the preceding rounds—though we can but hope and pray that it will not. But even if this round breaks down the pressure of world opinion will again and again force both sides to resume. Therefore it is of immediate practical importance that the West should know what it is about in these matters.

Let us then face the fact that unfortunately, but undeniably, these future negotiations will, like past negotiations, have two aspects. On the one hand they will from time to time throw up some specific issue, like the test ban negotiations, or like the other suggestions made above, which both sides take seriously in the sense that they genuinely consider the possibility of the conclusion and implementation of an agreement. It should be the business of the West continually to put forward such issues, as opportunity offers, and press them to the limit. Who knows if one day success may not be achieved on one of them?

Moreover, paradoxically enough, unless it presses for proposals which it really would accept, the West will prove, in my opinion, very ineffective in the other aspect of future disarmament negotiations which—let us face it—will inevitably recur. And that is the political warfare aspect. It is not, alas, to be expected that either side will be able to abstain from putting forward large comprehensive plans, the main purpose of which is to 'expose' its opponents as reluctant disarmers. So far the Russians have undoubtedly shown themselves the more adroit and bold players in this political warfare contest. There is little reason to suppose that they will stop playing, or that the West, when thus challenged, can avoid a response in kind. The gambits are becoming well established. The thing to do when your opponent proposes one of these comprehensive plans is either to accept it, or to put forward a counter-plan which goes even further than his. Then he is forced, as was the West in 1955, either to change the subject, or to break off the negotiations, as the Russians did in 1960. No doubt in one form or another this game will go on. It has precious little to do with disarmament. But whether we like it or not we shall be forced to play the political warfare game. To fail to do so would give an unacceptable propaganda advantage to the Russians. They would exploit it to the full and very likely succeed in pillorying the West as the opponents of disarmament. Therefore we shall be bound in self-defence to put forward ambitious and comprehensive disarmament proposals. To fail to do so would be to disregard Bernard Shaw's well-known maxim: 'Never to be fair to your opponent: it gives him an unfair advantage'.

The 'Interests' Approach

It will have been noted, perhaps with disapproval, that the

approach to disarmament made in these pages is different from that made by most 'disarmers'. Where they have, for the most part simply assumed that disarmament, in the largest attainable measure, is in the general interests of humanity, and that only the follies, prejudices or ill-will of the world's leaders hold us back from it, we have sought some more specific and narrow 'interest'—such as the self-regarding interest of the superpowers in their own predominance and survival—on which to build. Or again, whereas some vision of a more or less totally disarmed world of still 'free', in the sense of fully independent, states, co-operating quite voluntarily through a United Nations type of world organization, has been implied in most 'disarmers' attitudes, we have repeatedly raised the concept of some sort of world authority, exercising a degree at least of coercive power, as indispensable if disarmament is to get very far.

In a word, ours has been a much less attractive and pleasant approach, which is likely to be far less popular. Why therefore make it? Simply because the older, traditional approach to disarmament has been tried intensively for forty years now and has ended in a series of heartbreaking failures and disillusionments. To seek for 'real', in the sense of relatively narrow and self-regarding, interests upon which actual measures of disarmament might be based, may well lay the present writer open to accusation of cynicism. But is it cynical to attempt to draw some lessons from forty years of almost unrelieved failure in the work of achieving any actual disarmament by means of treaties or agreements signed and ratified? Is it cynical to enquire why all the splendid, self-sacrificing idealism of outstanding men and women who, moreover, have been backed by an overwhelmingly favourable world sentiment, has gone for almost nothing? Must we pursue, without reflection, the same road which has proved time after time to be a dead end, in case we incur the accusation of cynicism? Is it not rather the duty of every idealist to study searchingly the melancholy record of disarmament in order to discover why no progress has been made?

At all events it is my belief that measures of disarmament, which I yield to none in claiming to be one essential part of any policy for the prevention of war, must be founded on some discovered mutuality of interest between the super-powers existing in the world at the relevant time. I believe that this mutuality of interest as between Russia and America can be discovered today: that it is beginning to be visible, amidst all their rasping disputes, in such things as their undeniable joint interest in stopping the spread of nuclear weapons, of the existing types, and still more in stopping the development of new 'cheap and easy' types of such weapons.

British Interests

This 'interests' approach to disarmament may shock another and opposite body of opinion, at any rate in Britain. Some readers may well feel that it is strange and reprehensible in a British writer to found his approach to the problem of disarmament upon the discovery of a common interest between the super-powers, partly at least in order to maintain their own nuclear supremacy. For the British national interest, in the traditional sense, is clearly contrary to this. If we think, exclusively, about maintaining and maximizing British power in the world (a limited but not in itself unworthy motive), we shall conclude that what is desirable is, precisely, the development of new types and kinds of nuclear weapons by the secondary but advanced nations, so that the above-described equalization of nuclear destructive power between technically advanced nations, irrespective of their size and populations, may tend to come about. No doubt this is a means by which Britain in particular might hope to regain a parity of world position with the super-powers. For Britain is particularly well placed to take a lead in such a development. She has much more nuclear know-how and experience than any other nation except the super-powers. Britain might be able to equip herself with an adequate number of nuclear weapons—perhaps of new and cheaper types—and with invulnerable means of delivery (for example in the next period, Polaris-carrying submarines). Such a nuclear capacity might give her, for some years at least, a destructive power, if not of the same order of magnitude as that of the existing super-powers, yet so great that she might in practice be able to destroy them almost as readily as they could destroy her.

Why then should a British writer desire to see such a development blocked by such arrangements as a test ban treaty and the 'cut off' of nuclear production? There are a number of reasons. First, if Britain developed a nuclear capacity of this kind, China, France, West Germany, Italy, India and probably several other states would almost certainly be bound to follow hard upon her heels. We should sooner rather than later have produced 'the multi-nuclear world' which, we submitted above, gave so little prospect of survival. Britain's particular advantage over the other secondary powers would be likely to be short-lived. Second, in the nuclear age a rigid adherence to special national British interests of the old sort is not really wise, even if we are thinking exclusively of the security and well-being of the British people. In the nuclear age the long-term interest of Britain in a stable peace, even if it is a kind of peace which is by no means perfect from a British point of view, is so overwhelming that she should be prepared to relinquish (at any rate if all other secondary nation-states do, or are compelled to do, the same) the possibility of regaining parity of ultimate power. She should do so, however, with her eyes open, realizing that she is advocating policies which involve sacrifices.

In general then the 'interests' approach to the disarmament problem should not mean that we assume that every nation must inevitably think and act exclusively with a view to maximizing its own power. It will be both possible and wise for nations to take longer-term and broader considerations into account also. But the 'interests' approach does mean that nations, so long as the world consists of sovereign states, never can and never will lose sight altogether of their own power. To suppose anything else leads to nothing but futility and frustration. For this is the basic 'interest' of sovereign states. And in matters of life and death, nations, like social groups, or indeed individuals, have no alternative but to consider, first, though not exclusively, this self-regarding interest.

'Interests never lie'

This is the *rationale* behind the watchword of the 'whips', or Parliamentary managers, of the Whig party in nineteenth-century Britain. The old Whig whips used to mutter 'interests never lie'. These hard-bitten and experienced men had found that the social groups, social classes—land owners, industrialists, court interests—what you will—with which they had to deal, followed predictable courses once the self-regarding mechanism that actuated them had been understood. It was only by taking into account these, the real factors in the situation, that the Whig whips could sustain the British Governments of that day. (Applied to internal affairs the maxim 'interests never lie' is therefore the British way of stating the theory of the class struggle.)

In the same way we may rest assured that any attempt to approach the interlocked problems of disarmament, of the development of some sort of world authority, and so of peace, will be as barren as have been the disarmament conferences of the last forty years unless we take into account and seek to build upon the real self-interests of the nations. That is why we have striven so hard to unearth, beneath deep layers of conflict and suspicion, some foundation of common interest between the super-powers. We could find only their interest to survive by abstaining from mutual destruction—and, more obviously, their interest to prevent other nuclear super-powers from arising. These are simple interests, but important ones. Can anything be built upon them? Before trying to answer that question, we must ask what it is that causes that conflict between the two super-powers and their allies which fills the world today. Is that conflict irreconcilable? What are the intentions, as distinct from the capabilities, of the super-powers?

PART THREE

Intentions

14

Communist Intentions

Capabilities or Intentions?

IT is a military maxim that, in framing a country's defence
policy, the capabilities alone, never the intentions, of other
nations must be taken into account. But this is one of those
maxims which, however dutifully they are preached in the
staff colleges, can never be adhered to in the cabinet rooms.

In order to understand why this must be so, we have only to
envisage what the consequences would be for British defence
policy in the nineteen-sixties if our statesmen attempted to
ignore the intentions of other nations. In that case we should
have to prepare ourselves to meet an American threat at least as
seriously as we actually do prepare ourselves to meet a Russian
threat. After all American *capabilities* for the coercion of Britain
under threat of nuclear bombardment are even greater than
Russia's. S.A.C. could render the British Isles uninhabitable
any afternoon. The American Government would have to
reckon with, at worst, the risk of the loss of a few American
cities in retaliation. Yet in fact nobody in Britain gives a
moment's thought to our defencelessness in respect of America.
Why? Simply because we know that the Americans will not
attack us. In fact, we take account exclusively of American
intentions and not at all of American *capabilities*. If we followed
the military maxim and did the opposite, we should be living
in quaking fear of S.A.C.

O.P.W.—P

It follows therefore that somewhere behind all the considerations which have been discussed in previous chapters there lurks some inexplicit estimate of Russian intentions. Both we in Britain and the Western Alliance as a whole evidently worry about Russian intentions. If we did not, we should be unconcerned with Russian capabilities. We must now, therefore, attempt to bring into the open this underlying fear of Russian intentions, in order to see if, and to what extent, it is ill or well founded.

There exists a school of thought in British public life which frequently expresses the belief that all these fears of Russian intentions are quite ill-founded. Adherents of this school of thought might even be willing to accept much of the logic of the preceding chapters. But they would say that that logic was founded upon a fundamentally false premise. They would say that if there was any danger of Russia's attempting to attack us then indeed the whole chain of consequences which we have considered might follow. But, they would add, there is no such danger. Russia, they conclude, is a completely pacific state, armed only in self-defence and as a precaution against the armament of her potential opponents: we could scrap our own armaments without fear or hesitation, secure in the knowledge that Russia would take no advantage of our impotence.

This view of Russian intentions is at the one pole of political opinion. At the other pole there are those who suppose that Russia is a state dedicated to the military conquest of the world for communism: a crusading state, much more aggressive even than most of the nation-states of history, because driven by 'a sacred mission' to impose her way of life upon the world wherever and however she can; a state restrained by fear of the military strength of the Western alliance alone. In the face of such disagreement, it is evidently important to arrive at some appreciation, or estimate, of Russian intentions; for no policy for the prevention of nuclear war can leave them out of account. Moreover, Russia is now only one (though still much the stronger) of the communist super-powers. We must consider also Chinese intentions. We need not pay so much attention to the secondary members of the communist alliance. Finally we must attempt a similar estimate of American intentions, of the intentions of America's allies, and, broadening out from that, of the intentions of the other considerable nation-states of the world.

A Nation-State-With-A-Mission?

It will be noted that neither of the above schools of political thought regard Russia as a normal nation-state. One regards her as a much misunderstood angel of peace, the other as the devil incarnate. In one sense our enquiry may then be stated in terms of the question: to what extent, if at all, can present-day Russia be treated as a nation-state of the familiar type? Let us first recall that the Soviet Government, whatever it may now have become, was not established as the government of a nation-state of any kind. On the contrary the establishment of 'The Union of Soviet Socialist Republics' was intended to put an end to the existence of Russia as a nation-state. What was to be put in her place was a union of self-governing socialist republics, to which any and every future socialist society might be expected to adhere, irrespective of whether or not the capitalist, or feudal, nation-states, to the territories of which they had succeeded, had or had not formed a part of the Russian Empire.

Lenin, Trotsky, and the other founding-fathers of Soviet Russia were deeply in earnest in this conception. For good and ill they really were internationalists. It is true that Lenin himself, in distinction from many of his senior colleagues, such as Trotsky and Stalin, was a deeply-rooted Great Russian. (See his article on 'The National Pride of the Great Russians'.) But even Lenin was unquestionably a communist long before he was a Russian. This was not because he denied or ignored the existence of nationalism, but because, as a Marxist, he believed that, for the working class, national conflicts were overshadowed by class conflicts. Trotsky wrote of him (*Pravda*, April 23rd, 1920)—'Lenin's internationalism is by no means a form of reconciliation of nationalism and internationalism in

words, but a form of international revolutionary action. The
territory of the earth inhabited by so-called civilized man is
looked upon as a coherent field of combat on which the separate
peoples and classes wage gigantic warfare against each other.
No single question of importance can be forced into a national
frame.'

Unquestionably this was the original vision of Marx. It is
inscribed in the Communist Manifesto itself.

. . . modern industrial labour, modern subjection to capital, the
same in England as in France, in America as in Germany, has
stripped him ('the worker') of every trace of national character. . . .
The working men have no country. We cannot take from them what
they have not got. . . . National differences and antagonisms
between peoples are daily more and more vanishing. . . . The
supremacy of the proletariat will cause them to vanish still
further. . . .

Time has dealt more cruelly, perhaps, with this theme of
militant internationalism, which runs through the whole
original body of communist theory, than with any other. One
hundred and fifteen years have passed and 'the worker' has on
the whole more 'national character' than ever. Far from having
no fatherland, it would be truer to say that he has come to feel
that to have a nationally independent fatherland is a prerequisite for having everything else. Nevertheless, communists
have never abandoned their original vision of a world unity
founded upon the demand that the workers of the world should
unite. Thus Lenin, and still more Trotsky, were deeply imbued
with international faith, founded the Soviet Union in its light,
and would have been profoundly shocked at the idea that their
foundation could develop into a nation-state. To what extent
has the Soviet Union, nevertheless, done just this? And, if so,
how and why has such a transformation taken place?

'The Soviet Design for a World State'

From time to time hard-working American professors redis-
cover the above-described internationalist basis of communist
theory, and are profoundly shocked by their discovery. They

are then apt to proclaim that they have unearthed a dastardly conspiracy to conquer the world. This, for example, is the attitude of mind exhibited by Professor Elliot R. Goodman in his recent book *The Soviet Design for a World State* (Oxford University Press, 1960). The Professor's erudition seems only matched by his lack of insight into the nature of the contemporary world situation. He produces a hundred quotations to demonstrate what anyone who has ever read Marx or Lenin knows already, namely that communism is an international creed, which regards the nation-state as something to be transcended. So far as that is concerned we shall be inclined to reply 'so what?' Must not any thoughtful student of the post-nuclear world do the same?

The tone of hectic conspiracy-hunting which pervades not only Professor Goodman's work, but also his whole school of thought, is a great pity. For it may cause many people to refuse to reflect upon several by no means new but still important considerations which his school of thought advances. In the first place Professor Goodman, in particular, emphasizes and documents the undeniable fact that original communist doctrine looked forward not only to the dissolution of all existing nations but to the re-integration of all peoples into a World Federation of Socialist Republics of which the Soviet Union was regarded as the nucleus.

Second, Professor Goodman by no means disregards the extent to which the Soviet Union over the past forty years has appeared to depart from its internationalist principles. He deals at length with the Stalinist concept of building socialism in one country; with the apparently ruthless sacrifice of the interests of the extra-Russian communist parties to Russian national interest; and with the subjection of the other nations of the Tsarist Empire to the dominance of the Great Russians. But all these undeniable events are, he considers, evidence of the extent to which the internationalist ideal has been distorted, rather than of its abandonment. He is convinced that the communists of the 1960s are as firmly determined as were the communists of 1917 to build a world state upon the basis of the workers' class solidarity. Only now, he writes, theirs has become a determination to build a 'Russified' world state.

There is force in this contention. To the extent to which the old universalist ideal is preserved at all, it has undoubtedly been heavily Russified. But Professor Goodman does not seem to allow sufficiently for the extent to which this very development has made the original communist internationalism unacceptable and inapplicable outside Russia. This is shown by his inability adequately to account for the fact that the nations which became communist after 1945 have not become members of the Soviet Union, but have either remained 'satellites' or become genuinely independent. He is convinced that this is a mere temporary status on the way to their full incorporation. But this conviction does not enable him to account for the fact that, on the whole, the countries of Eastern Europe have in most cases achieved a little more, rather than less, national independence of recent years. Above all how does it account for the two cardinal facts that Yugoslavia has become undeniably independent, and that no one even suggests the incorporation of China in the Soviet Union?

Professor Goodman and his school fail to differentiate between the internationalism and universalism of communist *intentions* and the way in which the world is in fact developing. Blinded by the intensity of their hatred and fear of communism they miss the evergrowing divergence between what is actually happening in the world and what the communist leaders would still, no doubt, like to happen. And this is again a pity for it is the key to an explanation of the paradox that the communists, though complete internationalists in theory, in practice oppose any and every move towards the establishment of even the most embryonic form of world authority, and appear upon the world stage as unyielding champions of national sovereignty. The explanation is that communists believe exclusively in a post-revolutionary internationalism. Only socialist societies, which have finally overcome all capitalist resistance within themselves, can, they are convinced, come together in a world federation (and ultimately in a unitary world society). They lay it down

that it is as impossible as it would be undesirable for the capitalists to do any such thing.

We shall discuss the consequences of communist internationalism, strictly conditional as it is on a prior world revolution, in subsequent chapters. Here it will be best to form our own
view of actual, present-day Russian and Chinese intentions in
regard to war and peace without the distraction of the passions
which, as it seems to me, distort so much of the thinking of
Professor Goodman and his school of thought on this subject.
We may return, then, to the question of whether *in fact*—and
however much it has been contrary to the intentions of its
founders—the Soviet Union has become a nation-state. For to
the extent that she has she must be dealt with like other nation-
states.

Refuge, Bastion and a Base

There is little doubt that the transition of the Soviet Union into
the Russian nation-state, in so far as it has occurred, has taken
place indirectly and unconsciously. What happened was that,
as the years went by after the revolution, the Russian leaders
began to think of the Soviet Union as the unavoidably national
incarnation of their essentially international communist ideal.
The two events, both entirely unexpected to the original
Bolshevik leaders, which caused this paradoxical development,
were (i) the postponement of the revolution in the rest of the
world and (ii) the consolidation, nevertheless, of communist
rule in, roughly, the territory of the former Russian Empire.

The result has been that the Soviet Union has come to be
envisaged by communists, both within and without her
borders, as, indeed, a nation-state, but as a nation-state of a
special and exceptional character. The Soviet Union had had
to become, it was felt, a nation-state in spite of herself. But if
she had been forced into this role she must never forget that she
was a nation-state-with-a-mission. Her mission was to act as
the national refuge, bastion and base for the quintessentially
internationalist communist movement.

As a matter of fact, this kind of 'nation-state-with-a-mission' is not a new phenomenon in history. On several occasions particular nation-states have come to incarnate essentially international ideas and causes. We may think of two examples, in one of which the ideal so incarnated was conservative, in the other revolutionary. The Spain of Philip II incarnated, as refuge, bastion, and base, Roman Catholicism both as faith and cause. His Spain was the base of the Counter-Reformation in its desperate international struggle with Protestantism. And Philip probably felt himself a Catholic even before he was a Spaniard. For he sometimes appeared to sacrifice Spanish national interests to the interests of the international Catholic Church, if and when these interests conflicted. A second example is afforded by Republican, and to a decreasing extent even Imperial, France between 1789 and 1814. The republican leaders, and even Napoleon for some time, felt themselves to be the leaders of the anti-feudal forces of the world, engaged in a struggle with the old order, as well as, and in some cases even more than, the leaders of France.

Hence there is nothing particularly exceptional in the mixture of passionate nationalism and (at least initially) passionate internationalism, which has characterized the Soviet Government. Experience suggests that 'nation-states-with-a-mssion' are apt to have two characteristics. They are even more self-assertive and aggressive than other nation-states. And they are apt to commit serious mistakes, owing to the mixture of motives by which they are actuated. National interest, like many other compelling interests, is most effectively pursued single-mindedly. To this extent it is more difficult for nation-states-with-a-mission to hold their own, in the long run, with the more ordinary variety of the species. On the other hand they have obvious short-run advantages, such as increased fanaticism and, often, groups of adherents, either secret or open, within their rivals.

Be that as it may, a nation-state-with-a-mission is unquestionably what Soviet Russia has in fact been, during most of the forty-odd years of her existence. She has been neither, that is to say, what her founders intended her to be, namely the mere nucleus of a new, world-wide, international, indeed anti-national, communist society, nor on the other hand has she been a mere nation-state like another without any particular ideological and international ties, duties, or responsibilities. For I believe that even when she has most ruthlessly sacrificed the apparent and immediate interests of communist parties in the rest of the world, as she so often has, she has done so in the fairly sincere belief that, by preserving herself at all costs, she was in the long run furthering the interests of communism all over the world.

The Sense of Mission Cools

The next question is, to what extent is the Russia of the nine-teen-sixties still a nation-state of this special character?

The proceedings of the meeting of the eighty-one communist parties in the autumn of 1960 and of the Twenty-second Party Congress of the Communist Party of the Soviet Union in the autumn of 1961 should throw light on this question. And to a certain extent they do. They make it perfectly clear that there is now a sharp difference of opinion between the Russian and the Chinese communist leaders upon precisely this issue of the extent to which communist nations should be nation-states-with-a-mission. No one can any longer doubt that the Chinese believe that the mission to spread communism through the world should be pursued much more militantly than do the Russians. But of course the Russian communist leaders still believe in that mission to a certain extent. The question is, to what extent? And here the interpretations which can be put, and which have been put, on Mr Khruschev's pronouncements at these conferences, of those of other Russian spokesmen, of the statement of the eighty-one parties in 1960 and of the new Twenty-Second Congress of the C.P.S.U. in 1961, differ widely. How widely may be judged by the following contrast. Professor Merle Fainsod (the eminent American Sovietologist), writing in a special supplement of *Problems of Communism* (published by the Information Agency of the U.S. Government), speaks of 'the ambiguous formula of peaceful co-existence which Khruschev has chosen as his springboard to world power. . . .' On the other hand the Albanian leaders, speaking it may be surmised on behalf of their Chinese patrons, characterize the same pronouncements as 'bourgeois pacifism' (quoted in the *Guardian*, January 11th, 1962). Moreover, according to Satyukov, speaking at the Twenty-second Congress, Molotov in his letter to the Central Committee protesting against the new draft programme also asserted that it contained 'pacifism and even revisionism'.

Evidently you can pay your money and take your choice: you can regard the present Russian doctrine of the possibility of co-existence as 'a springboard to world power' or as a betrayal of the whole programme of international communism. Both views seem extravagant. For my part I do not believe that the new evidence which we now have has done more than confirm the commonplace conclusion that Russia is still a nation-state-with-a-mission, but that on the other hand she now has a considerably lessened sense of that mission. Only those with very special causes to plead will deny that Russia still feels a mission to assist the spread of communism through the world, or, on the other hand, that she feels this mission less compulsively, and even less ardently, than once she did.

All this may be incontrovertible, but it may also be not very helpful for the purpose of estimating Russia's intentions. What matters for that is to form an estimate of *how much* the compulsive character of the Soviet Government's mission to spread communism has cooled and waned. And when we enter this quantitative field we enter a field of speculation indeed. Lenin's revolutionary internationalism envisaged, as Trotsky wrote, 'the territory of the earth . . . as a coherent field of combat,' on which the class war could and must be fought out to a finish. Mr Khruschev, as we have seen, sometimes at least envisages the world as a Noah's Ark of refuge into which all sensible peoples will come in order, precisely, to avoid nuclear war to the finish, not of one, but of both, sides (see p. 9 above). The question is how much of the distance between these two standpoints has the Soviet Government in fact traversed?

Again, how much is it simply the dread of nuclear war, and how much a general maturing and civilizing process, which has made the Soviet Government travel in the direction, at any rate, of the acceptance of the possibility of co-existence? Both factors have, in my view, been at work. But the effect of a realization of the consequences of nuclear war should not be underestimated. It may well be that Lenin himself, in the nuclear age, would have endorsed Kruschev's Noah's Ark speech. But would Lenin have endorsed it at its face value, or would he have merely regarded it as a shrewd tactical move? In other words to what extent does the Soviet Government now sincerely agree that the world-wide struggle, which incontestably exists, both can, and must, be conducted without resort to all-out war?

Leninist Doctrine on War and Violence

It can hardly be contested that the main strand in Lenin's thinking was to the effect that a further bout of wars, in part at least between the Soviet Union and some or all of the remaining Capitalist states, was inevitable. He would have smiled his shrewd smile at any comrade who thought otherwise.[1] Moreover, his relentless antagonism would have been vented upon anyone who tried to deflect Russian policy from the necessity of preparing for such conflicts. Lenin was representative of the communist thought of his day in this respect. There is no doubt about what was the real attitude of the Soviet Government to the matter right up to 1941. It can be conveniently summed up in two antithetical propositions. First, war between the Soviet Union and at least some parts of the rest of the world was inevitable. But, second, this war must be postponed for as long as possible and by every conceivable means, including if necessary great caution and restraint, and even, if unavoidable, by serious sacrifices upon the part of the Soviet Government.

[1] I am reminded of the anecdote of Lenin's reaction when he was shown a pamphlet by Eden and Cedar Paul, two elderly English pacifists (and translators of the first volume of *Capital*) who were expressing their admiration for the Soviet Union. After reading a few pages on the wholly pacific character of communism, Lenin enquired: 'These be very young comrades?'

The explanation of why the Soviet Government should have gone to such lengths in order to postpone a conflict which they were convinced was inevitable sooner or later is simple. They were sure that Soviet strength was on a rapidly rising curve. If only the war could be put off long enough it would take place after the curves had intersected. Then Soviet strength would prove the greater and the capitalists would be defeated. It would be foolish to suggest that this Leninist prognosis of world development, and the policy which was built upon it, had proved entirely mistaken. After all, war between Russia and a part of the capitalist world did in fact break out in 1941. The Soviet Government, at least, is no doubt convinced that it was only postponed until the twenty-fourth year after the Revolution by caution and deft manoeuvring on their own part. And when war did come Russia, and her allies, were in fact victorious.

In the pre-nuclear age the Leninist prognosis did not, then, prove far wrong in one sense. Nor, it is certain, would Lenin have flinched from the view that it was only by means of world war—and very likely a series of world wars—that the goal of world communism could be reached. He was entirely convinced that until and unless that goal was reached, violence was the inevitable means of social progress. It was not, to be sure, that the revolutionists deliberately *chose* violence. There was no such choice open to them. Every decisive encounter in which the vital interests of social classes were involved had invariably been decided by violence. True, secondary and indecisive advantages might be won by non-violent means and these should not be neglected. But, equally, it was cowardice and treachery of the worst sort when the leaders of the workers flinched from violent means when these, as they always would, at the point of crisis, became inevitable. Lenin wrote one of his most forceful passages defining exactly this attitude to violence. He does so mainly in the context of internal, revolutionary violence. But he adopted exactly the same attitude to international violence, which was in the last resort for him always an expression, however indirect, of the conflict of social classes:

Today there is no revolutionary situation apparent; there are no such conditions as would cause a ferment among the masses or heighten their activities; today you are given an election ballot— take it. Understand how to organize for it, to hit your enemies with it, and not to place men in soft parliamentary berths who cling to their seat in fear of prison. Tomorrow you are deprived of the election ballot, you are given a rifle and a splendid machine-gun equipped according to the last word of machine technique—take this weapon of death and destruction, do not listen to the sentimental whiners who are afraid of war. Much has been left in the world that *must* be destroyed by fire and iron for the liberation of the working class. (Lenin, *Collected Works*, Vol. XVIII, p. 316.)

Here we have the communist view of the matter expressed with matchless vigour. Nor is there any proof that Lenin would have taken the view that the development of nuclear weapons was, in itself, a reason for revising this basic doctrine as to the nature of human society and its methods of development. The question is, however, not so much whether in the nuclear age Lenin would or would not have modified this orthodox communist attitude to violence in general, and in particular to the question of the inevitability of further general war; the question is rather whether the present Soviet leaders have in fact done so. If they have, we may be sure that they have only done so gradually, reluctantly, and, probably, only half consciously. We may be sure that for a long time, even after the Second World War, they still adhered to the two Leninist propositions (*a*) that further general war between Russia and 'the Imperialists' was inevitable, and (*b*) that it should be postponed, by every possible means, for as long as possible.

Russian Policy in Practice

Let us notice at once, however, that the practical policies of a Government that believes that general war is inevitable, but must be postponed by every possible means, will probably be very similar to those of a Government which supposes that war may be averted altogether. This is especially true if one of the main hypotheses on which the prognosis of inevitability is

based begins to prove more and more doubtful. That hypothesis was that, as the curve of communist strength ascended,
the curve of the strength of the rest of the world, hopelessly
bedevilled by the 'inner contradictions' of capitalism, would
equally descend. For it was upon the basis of this hypothesis
that the communists concluded that the despairing capitalists
would be certain sooner or later to attack, foreseeing that if they
delayed too long their position would become hopeless.

In the real development of events over the last quarter
century, one part of this prognosis has been fulfilled. Communist strength has grown greatly. But the other part of the
prognosis has gone hopelessly astray. The non-communist
world is unquestionably in a far healthier, and far stronger
state than it was in, say, 1932. The advanced, industrialized,
capitalisms are thriving instead of sinking into intolerable
stagnation. Consequently, as every Marxist ought (but refuses)
to accept, their wage-earners have largely ceased to be open to
revolutionary propaganda. Their empires, which turn out to
have been a source of weakness, not of strength, to them, have
become 'the underdeveloped world', which, with varying but
appreciable success, is at least striving to progress. The curve
of the strength of the non-communist world, instead of descend-
ing, to intersect the rising curve of communist strength, is
running upwards somewhere roughly parallel to it.

To what extent have the rulers of Russia noticed all this? Of
course it would never do for them to acknowledge any of it.
We cannot expect that. Until very recently they stuck with
unshakeable dogmatism to the theory of the ever-increasing
misery of the wage-earners of the non-communist world,
reiterating it more and more passionately as it became more
and more preposterously at variance with the facts. That was
only to be expected. (As this chapter is being drafted, however,
signs are at last appearing that the dogma of ever-increasing
misery has been shaken. An admission of the existence of the
affluent society is implicit in some of Mr Khruschev's speeches.
And an explicit denial that such a thing is impossible is beginning to appear in some of the work of the most knowledgeable

Soviet economists.) Nevertheless the new Russian thesis that a further general war is no longer inevitable is still usually based in public precisely upon the view that 'the Imperialists' (i.e. non-communists) are getting weaker so quickly that, with careful handling, they may miss their moment, and be induced, in effect, to surrender peacefully. Any other explanation of the idea that further general war is no longer inevitable would be too un-Leninist. It would involve too unorthodox assumptions about the character of the real development in the non-communist world, about the intentions of the rulers of that world, and about the general uncertainty of future social development, to be publicly presentable inside the communist world.

But what do Mr Khruschev and his fellow-members of the Praesidium really think? They are beginning to go about the world. Do the wage earners of the United States *look* to them as if they were sinking into ever-increasing misery? Do the wage earners of Britain, West Germany, the Netherlands, Belgium, Scandinavia, Japan, Australasia, and now even of much of France and Northern Italy, seem to be promising material for revolutionary propaganda? As 'the affluent society' (with all its faults and vulgarity and ugliness) spreads itself across the Western world, does it not occur to them, in the privacy of their studies at least, that something queer and unforeseen is happening?

If once the thought that the real development of events in the West is diverging from the Leninist prognosis enters their minds, they will surely find it hard to avoid noting other divergencies. For even with them events have not really followed the Leninist forecast. True, the 'Socialist Camp' has grown right enough, in geographical extent as well as in armed power. But it has not grown in the simple, Leninist, internationalist form of the adhesion on the part of each new state, as it comes under communist rule, to the Soviet Union. On the contrary with the single exception of the Baltic States (and can the members of the Praesidium persuade even themselves that there was anything voluntary in that?) all the new states of the communist world have become, nominally at least, fully sovereign independent states. True, most of them are effectively dominated by Russian power, including in some cases Russian occupation. But that is a very different thing from voluntary inclusion in the U.S.S.R. How different a thing it is became apparent when movements of revolt took place in East Germany and Poland and actual revolt broke out in Hungary.

And then there is the painful spectacle of Yugoslavia. What would Lenin have said to a state which has been through a thorough-going communist revolution, in which 'the power of the bourgeoisie has been liquidated' quite as effectively as elsewhere in the communist world, but which, far from federating itself within the Soviet Union, obstinately goes its own way, and often has much worse relations with Russia than with 'the Imperialists' themselves; 'De heretico comburendo', was what Stalin did say!

But far more important than all this is the fact of China. Here is the second great nation—potentially at least another super-power—to go communist. And no one has ever (to my knowledge) even suggested that she should become a member of the Soviet Union. It is taken for granted that she has become a totally independent, communist *nation*. What would Lenin have said to that? Would he have pointed out that a communist *nation*, in that full sense, was a contradiction in terms? That communism was a concept expressly and from the outset designed to transcend nationalism? How could he have denied that the emergence of completely separate and completely sovereign communist nations was an anomaly which gave further disturbing evidence that world development was by no means proceeding according to plan? I daresay that in practice Lenin would have merely closed his eyes to narrower slits and repeated his favourite maxim that 'History is more cunning than any of us'. But if so that would have been because he was an extremely shrewd man, as well as a devoted Marxist.

Chinese Intentions

It may be possible rightly to gauge both the extent and the limits of the change in Russian intentions and attitudes to war by a study of the controversy which developed during 1960 and 1961 between the Russian and Chinese Governments and communist parties. That controversy is far too complex and too obscure for it to be possible to give any adequate account of it here. But even its more obvious features reveal the fact that the Chinese Government has intentions of a different character from those of the Russian Government.

One of the best accounts of this controversy is to be found in a book by Mr Kardelj, the scholarly Prime Minister of Yugoslavia, entitled *Socialism and War* (Jugoslavija Publishing House). Mr Kardelj is intent to answer not only Chinese but also Russian charges against Yugoslavia. For the Yugoslavs were in a sense the whipping-boys of both sides in this affair. The Chinese would accuse the Russians of being almost as bad deviationists as those abominable heretics the Yugoslavs. The Russians would answer back indignantly pointing out the wide differences between their own attitudes, which they said, were still strictly Leninist, and the, admittedly, inexcusable heresies of the Yugoslavs. So Mr Kardelj had plenty to answer!

The controversy largely turned in fact if not in form precisely upon this issue of whether or not a third world war with 'the Imperialists' was or was not inevitable. But the issue was blurred by the fact that the Chinese would never say flat out that it was. On the whole they took up the position that (*a*) the Imperialists would never surrender without a fight; (*b*) that it was of course indispensable to rid the world of Imperialism and (*c*) that anyhow a third world war wouldn't be so bad after all, for the damage it would do to the Socialist countries could be quickly repaired: and then a Socialist world could go rapidly ahead in conditions of permanent and assured peace. Mr Kardelj sums up the Chinese attitude as follows:

Only incurable petty-bourgeois pacifists could believe that war is not inevitable, say the Chinese critics of Yugoslavia. Only men whose heads are full of illusions or who deliberately aim at putting a good face on imperialism could assert that imperialism will renounce war, and only revisionists who have no faith in the vital strength and mind of man could assert that military technique can influence the course of social development, these same critics continue.

We must allow for the fact that Mr Kardelj is writing a a highly polemical work: I repeat that so far as I know the Chinese have never in public said that a third world war is inevitable. Nevertheless Mr Kardelj is able to substantiate that the above is not very different from the Chinese attitude, especially on the point that there is nothing particularly disastrous about nuclear war, by quotations from the Chinese Press. For example *Red Flag* (Peking, April 19th, 1960) is quoted as writing:

. . . were the imperialists to insist on imposing such sacrifices on the nations, we are convinced that those sacrifices would soon be redeemed, as the experience of the Russian and the Chinese revolutions has shown. On the ruins of dead imperialism the victorious peoples will soon build up a civilization a thousand times higher in level than the capitalist system, and a future for themselves which would be really glorious.

Moreover, we now have a good deal of evidence, of varying degrees of reliability it is true, but which in sum establishes pretty conclusively that the Chinese attitude to war is approximately this. If so, it is approximately what the Russian attitude was a quarter of a century ago. Since then the Russians, but not the Chinese, have appreciated the character of nuclear war. They are aware, for both Mr Khruschev and General Talensky have told them so, that a third world war, since it would almost certainly be nuclear, would cause damage to their part of the world which, far from being quickly reparable, would be likely to set back human civilization, of whatever sort—bourgeois, proletarian, socialist, imperialist alike, for an indefinite period.

Who Can Make the Chinese Listen?

When will the Russians or anyone else succeed in telling the Chinese about all this? Probably the Russians have been endeavouring to do so for some time now. What success they have had in making the Chinese listen—never an easy task—is unknown. But no task could, surely, be more urgent than to

educate Chinese ruling opinion on the realities of nuclear war:
on what might perhaps be called 'the facts of death'. For
whether they know it or not the facts of nuclear death now apply
just as much to China as to the rest of us. Indeed it might have
been supposed that a country, possessing neither means of
nuclear retaliation nor remotely effective means of stopping
the nuclear weapons of its potential opponents, would show
some signs of a consciousness of the consequences for it of
nuclear war.

It is often said that the Chinese leaders do not fear nuclear
attack because of the large size of their country and because it
contains over 600 million inhabitants. Even if, they are reported as arguing, 100 million Chinese were killed, that would
still leave 500 million to carry on. But what, we may enquire,
makes the Chinese leaders suppose that only 100 million
Chinese would be likely to be killed in a full-scale nuclear
attack upon China? If they do in fact suppose anything of this
sort they are horribly misinformed. They must be still thinking
in terms of fission weapons of the order of magnitude of the
bombs which fell upon Japan nearly twenty years ago. For it is
true that such weapons as these, of which the main effects were
by fire and blast, would be relatively ineffective against a
vast peasant population scattered over millions of square miles.
But none of this is true of the thermonuclear weapons in the
megaton range of the nineteen-sixties. For one of the main
effects of these is, as we have noted, their lethal 'fall-out' which,
though local in the sense that it does not spread throughout the
world, covers areas of millions of square miles down wind from
the point of explosion. Peasant populations living in insub-
stantial houses of brick, mud or straw might be appallingly
vulnerable to such a fall-out. It is nauseating even to have to
write the words but it is difficult to see why, not 100 million
out of the 600 million, but say 500 out of the 600 million
Chinese would not be annihilated by the dropping of no very
fantastic number of the more 'dirty' types of nuclear weapons
in the megaton range. And if so what chance would the remaining (circa) 100 million have of survival, at any rate as any kind

of organized society, in their horribly polluted habitat, bereft of all cities, of all control of the great rivers and confronted with a catastrophe far greater than humanity has ever yet experienced?

It is, surely, exceedingly important that the Chinese communist leaders should come to realize the dreadful facts of the nuclear age. It is important that they should realize all this, not in order that they should be menaced or attacked (and this they may rely on, for after all they have Russian retaliatory power behind them so long as they maintain their alliance), but in order that a realization of their own fearful vulnerability should restrain them from pressing down upon their neighbours, as in the case of India they have actually done. For the present they seem both to act and to speak out of a mood of wholly illusory serenity, which they suppose the size and character of their population to give them. If and when the Chinese leaders come to realize the extreme jeopardy in which they, like all the rest of us, stand today, may they not revise at least this one of their dogmas?

'Making People Happy by Force'

However the Sino-Russian controversy is a much deeper one than a dispute as to the consequences of nuclear war. It involves the whole question of the attitude of communists to war and aggression in general. In this wider field the controversy is largely carried on by means of swopping quotations from Marx, Engels and Lenin. In this form of warfare it is not certain that the Chinese would, on the whole, be worsted in the exchanges. Mr Kardelj is able to produce some fairly effective remarks by Lenin: but an equally erudite Chinese Leninist might be able to show that the main weight of Lenin's thought was on his side. It is not till Mr Kardelj widens the argument at any rate to the extent of quoting Marx and Engels as well as Lenin that he is really able to score. But then he does. For he recalls to us that statement of Engels, in his mature and mellow old age, to the effect that he and Marx had always been against 'trying to make people happy by force'. They had, Engels claims, always opposed 'exporting' the Revolution forcibly by means of conquering some neighbouring country, the people of which might or might not be ready for it, and imposing socialism on them by military power.

It can hardly be claimed that the young Marx and Engels had in fact always lived up to this eminently wise view. This was not because they would have dissented from it consciously but because they had dogmatically believed that the workers everywhere and always were 'really' passionately anxious to revolt and throw off the chains of their oppressors. Thus, in practice, it might be quite legitimate to liberate them with an invading army, if they could not do the job for themselves. It may be surmised that this is the present (1962) standpoint of the Chinese Communists. No doubt they too would say that they do not believe in exporting revolution or 'making other people happy by force'. Nevertheless their view of the world is as one-sided as was that of Marx and Engels in the eighteen-forties and with, on the whole, less justification. They are sure that all peoples everywhere in the non-communist world, are desperately seeking for the opportunity to revolt. Therefore, any and every form of armed assistance which can be given them is fully justified. The Chinese make little distinction between movements of colonial revolt, such as those of Angola and Algeria, which not only they, but also the Russians, and for that matter many people in the West (including myself) consider justified, and non-existent movements of revolt which they affect to see in the highly developed non-communist societies. It is the extreme lack of any discriminating and objective appreciation of contemporary social reality which distinguishes the Chinese from the Russian Communists in 1962.

Not that the Russian Communists are free from distortions of reality, especially when what they suppose to be their own vital interests are concerned. We may be sure that many Russian communists were able to persuade themselves that the Hungarian workers were 'really' on the Russian side in 1956. The fact that *phenomenally* the workers were fighting upon the other side and had to be trampled under the tank tracks of several Soviet armoured divisions was a mere appearance, unconnected with the essence of things. For the word 'really' has come to mean its opposite, namely 'ideally', in the philosophical, metaphysical or transcendental sense. Such are the uses of philosophy.[1]

We unphilosophic British can only reflect upon how much better, safer and longer lived this world might be if only communists, Russians as well as Chinese, would take seriously the words of Engels in his maturity. For Engels at the end of his life had begun to mean them seriously himself. He had noticed that the world was a different sort of place from what it had been in 1848. True, he was still, on the whole, a revolutionary because he, correctly, foresaw that the European powers were driving or drifting towards internecine war, and might well therefore present the workers with both the necessity and the opportunity of a violent seizure of power. But he had come to see that general war was likely to prove the one remaining revolutionary occasion. Moreover, and in spite of this, Engels was quite clear that it was highly advantageous for the European workers to postpone war indefinitely if possible, for the power to influence society by democratic means was steadily gaining and must, if uninterrupted by war and revolution, become in the end predominant.

The Lessons of the Controversy

In any event one of the main impressions which the Sino-Russian controversy must make upon the Western observer is that it is impossible to deny that the Russians have in fact revised their views on war and aggression. It is fully open to them to point out that they have only done so because the 'objective circumstances' of the world situation have dramatically changed. Indeed it is just for their failure to adapt their

[1] For instance: 'Trained by the Communist Party, the armed forces of the U.S.S.R. live up to their international duty. This was demonstrated by the aid they gave to the working people of Hungary. . . .' (Colonel G. Federor writing in Krasnaia Zvezda, March 22nd, 1957) (quoted in the Soviet Design for a World State).

attitudes to objective changes which stare them in the face that we must blame the Chinese. But revised their attitudes the Russians undoubtedly have. If they had not there could not be any such thing as the Sino-Russian dispute.

On the other hand the existence of the dispute must continually remind us that there is now another communist great power, which, if by no means as strong as Russia, will no doubt grow in strength, and which retains much of the older and unmodified communist attitudes and intentions to war and aggression. Communist China is not indeed a society built on the model of the original Leninist concept of the abolition of the nation-state and the substitution for it of a federation of Socialist Republics. If she were she would presumably have become a federal republic of the Soviet Union. China is, then, a nation-state, and in that respect her very existence flouts the fully internationalist communist vision. But she is obviously very much of a nation-state-with-a-mission. She still takes the spread of communism in at least her part of the world very seriously. No such cooling and tempering process, by means of which Russia has, we appreciate, begun at least to approximate to a run-of-the-mill-nation-state, has taken place in her case. For the Chinese the communist parties of the world are, or at any rate ought to be, a church militant. Thus we must face the fact that Chinese communist militancy and intransigence will be a destabilizing factor in the world situation for some time to come.

China is firmly allied to the Soviet Union and that alliance is not likely to break down while the obvious necessity for it exists. But is not every year bringing further evidence that the Soviet-Chinese alliance is remarkably like other alliances? That the relations of the allies are by no means always harmonious? That both allies sometimes feel irked and provoked by the very necessity which forces them to *be* allies? That the Soviet-Chinese relationship is at least as uneasy, though perhaps also as firm, as the Western alliance? And does not all this amount to a very strong suggestion at least that 'the socialist camp' is not and cannot be a monolithic, fully unified, structure, any more than can the rest of the world? The fact is that this almost incredibly hardy social phenomenon, '*the nation*' (whatever a nation may be), has persisted into the post-revolutionary epoch: that nations do not after all disappear, or even tend to whither away, after they have organized their economies on the communist pattern.

But if nation-states survive the revolution: if nationalism proves to be a social force just as likely to transcend the communist faith as to be transcended by it—then indeed we are in a different and much more loosely-conditioned world than Lenin ever foresaw. We are in a world in which, indeed, the outbreak of all sorts of conflicts becomes only too plausible, but in which the 'inevitable' set-piece of a world-wide communist-capitalist war is by no means the ineluctable denouement.

The Apparition of Nuclear Weapons

On top of all these unforeseen developments has come the astounding phenomenon of nuclear weapons. It is true that, as not only the Chinese but also every Marxist-Leninist is quick to point out, nuclear weapons do not in themselves alter social relations. If these relations really were, predictably, driving to a further bout of world war before the apparition of the new weapons, they would presumably continue to do so. All that the new weapons would do would be to make that denouement far more terrible. But here their dialectical training should come to the assistance of the communist leaders and preserve them from being impaled upon the simple logic of their own social philosophy. True, nuclear weapons are only a quantitative stepping-up of the destructiveness of war. But a quantitative stepping-up of this magnitude may be expected to make a qualitative change in the situation. Nuclear war is a different thing, with different consequences, from conventional war. As and when the present generation of mankind comes to realize this fact, profound changes in their attitudes to war and to violence in general may become apparent.

Do we not catch the dawning of a realization of this profound change in social reality in the Russian Government's new attitude to nuclear war, which, as we have seen, has, after a false start by Malenkov, been adopted by Mr Khruschev, and has now been reiterated and given the stamp of orthodoxy in the controversy with the Chinese? That new attitude is based upon two different but related realizations. First, that full-scale nuclear war may be expected to spare neither communist nor 'imperialist'; that both will be engulfed in that 'common ruin' of which the Communist Manifesto speaks as the only possible alternative to the successful emergence to power of new classes. And second, that the development of new social relations, which is so evidently and undeniably going on in the world, may not after all involve a further bout of world war, now that we know that it would be nuclear war. How far the change of attitude is due to the apparition of nuclear weapons, and how far to the divergencies which world development has made from the Leninist prognosis I do not know. But that there has been a real change of attitude on the part of the Russians is undeniable: how otherwise can we account for the scandalization of the Chinese 'Old Believers'?

In any event it is clear that, for whatever reasons, the dogma of the inevitability of further world war has been dropped by the Russian Government. This is a major event. The old dogma did not indeed necessarily involve any immediate Russian aggression, for it was always modified by the caveat that the inevitable must be postponed as long as possible. Still, the dogma of the inevitability of a further world war was a profoundly vicious influence on Russian thinking, making any approach towards more genuine co-existence almost impossible. If we ask *why* the dogma has been abandoned we can only guess at an answer. Perhaps the realization of the impartiality of nuclear weapons was only the last straw, which broke the back of the old dogmatists. It is forty-three years since the volcano of the October Revolution erupted. The lava has cooled.[1]

[1] Mr Gomulka, the head of the Polish Government, speaking at Katowice on July 6th, 1960, and reported in full in *Polish Perspectives* for August–September 1960 gave an indication of the various factors at work. (As often, the Polish communists prove to be the most articulate.)

The policy of peaceful co-existence pursued by the Socialist states now has greater chances of victory than ever before. In the military domain

Summary

We may perhaps summarize our conclusions as to communist intentions as follows. First, Russian intentions: Soviet Russia has for some time now definitely ceased to be the mere base for an international movement, or secular faith, transcending all national loyalties. She has become a nation-state, but a nation-state-with-a-mission. She thinks, that is to say, not only of her national interests but also of the interests of communism as a faith, of which she is the guardian and protagonist—just as Philip II of Spain thought of the Catholic Church or the earlier French Revolutionary leaders of the principles of 1789. But

such highly destructive weapons have been created that their use in the event of war would produce catastrophic results. The total destructive power of modern warfare constitutes a factor mobilizing the masses for the struggle against imperialism and intensifying the struggle of the peoples for peaceful co-existence. The generally known military superiority of the defensive power of the Soviet Union, demonstrated by the weight of its Sputniks and the precise functioning of its interplanetary and ballistic rockets, has caused even part of the imperialist bourgeoisie to reject war, although it realizes the growing possibilities of the triumph of Socialism in peaceful competition with capitalism. They see that the victory of Socialism in the future is a lesser evil for them than war, that war puts them and the entire capitalist system in danger of annihilation and all mankind in danger of incalculable consequences. The revolution in the realm of military weapons has created a new historical factor which must not be omitted in any evaluation of present day reality and the possibility of the triumph of the idea of peaceful co-existence.

But, lest this should sound too complacent, Mr Gomulka hastens to make it clear that he considers that war can only be avoided by, first, agitation against it in the non-communist world and second by continually strengthening the communist world.

Peace cannot be obtained by pleading with the imperialists. Peace and peaceful co-existence can only be fought out. . . . If the Socialist countries were weak, if the Soviet peoples had not built the might they possess today, the possibility of preventing a new world war would be slender; in fact there would be no such possibility at all.

Just how we are to 'fight out' peace and peaceful co-existence is not explained. But Mr Gomulka's general sense is clear enough. This is merely the communists' way of saying that they must 'negotiate from strength'. And small blame to them for believing that! The attitude of the rest of the world has left them in no doubt as to what would have happened to them if they had not. Only it all makes their endless denunciations of us, when we too say that strength is a desirable basis for negotiations, inexpressibly tedious.

noted, but also and perhaps above all owing to the dread of
nuclear war, Soviet Russia is beginning to regard her mission
as the protagonist of world communism with increasing caution. She is showing the preliminary signs of changing again
from a nation-state-with-a-mission into an ordinary, common
or garden, nation-state. We should devoutly welcome every
sign of this transformation. Anything more perilous than a
nation-state-with-a-mission in the nuclear age is hard to
imagine.

What then should be our own reactions to this development
of Russian intentions? First, we should have done once and for
all with the pernicious nonsense that it is impossible to deal
with Russia because she is 'determined to attack us'. But on the
other hand we should delude ourselves if we supposed that
Russia's transformation into an ordinary nation-state, even if
it were completed (and it is far from complete), would solve the
problem of the prevention of war in the nuclear age.

Even run-of-the-mill-nation-states are profoundly self-
regarding organisms. They do not, usually, actually want war.
But they usually want things which prove unattainable without
war. It is said that, when Bismarck was asked whether he
wanted war, he replied 'Certainly not. What I want is victory.'
It may be surmised that, as a first very rough approximation,
some such attitude as this has underlain many of the recent
activities of the rulers of Soviet Russia. In this respect they have
not differed very markedly from most rulers of most other
states at most times. The rulers of states who, like Hitler, have
welcomed the prospect of war almost for its own sake, have been
comparatively rare. What nearly all rulers of strong states
have wanted was not war. What they have wanted was their
way. And like everybody else they would have preferred to have
their way with the minimum of trouble, risk and expense.
They sincerely regretted it when, as so frequently happened,
attempting to get their way did in fact involve them in war.
But only the more sophisticated of them have been inclined to
notice that as what they wanted usually contradicted flatly

what some other state wanted, war was sooner or later bound to break out.

In so far as the Russia of the nineteen-sixties is becoming a nation-state like another it is inherently probable that the intentions of her rulers do not diverge very much from this familiar pattern. Russia, in my view, gives little evidence of being one of those exceptionally aggressive, predator, states of which Nazi Germany, Napoleonic France (in a milder way), or Assyria in the ancient world are examples. Equally, however, she gives no evidence of being an exceptionally pacific state. (Examples of such exceptionally pacific states, at any rate amongst major powers, are much more difficult to find. Perhaps Asoka's India could be cited.) Russia gives the impression of being determined to have her way whenever she can, and of being not in the least averse to using force to get it, if she thinks she can do so without undue risk. On the other hand she gives evidence of taking the risks of nuclear war most seriously into account and of being loath indeed to incur them.

We may conclude that, again in so far as Russia is an ordinary nation-state, she must be dealt with, in default of the evolution of at least some rudimentary world authority, in the familiar way. Other states, that is to say, will be faced with the alternative of bowing to her will, or of developing sufficient military strength to deter her from actions to which they particularly object. This is all painfully familiar. But what is still more painful, and not at all familiar, is that the force involved on both sides is now nuclear force, which, if used, may be expected to have the consequences described in Chapter 1. True, a realization of what those consequences would be is growing and provides, by its dread, a certain barrier to war. But who can suppose that that barrier would in itself prove permanently adequate? The relationships of all nation-states, of whatever kind, have always been punctuated by war, merely, it seems, because they were nation-states. There would, therefore, be little assurance of peace even on the assumption (and it would be today a premature assumption) that Russia was another nation-state like the rest, neither especially bellicose nor especially pacific. On the contrary a world of such 'normal' nation-states, if they remain sovereign, must, unless all historical experience can be set aside, go to war sooner or later. Such a situation of primal international anarchy has always proved inherently unstable. For the world to remain indefinitely organized into completely sovereign nation-states in the nuclear age must prove fatal.

Second, Chinese intentions: the intentions of the Government of China are manifestly more belligerent than those of the Russian Government. That is what the dispute is about. We may gauge the extent, and the limits, of the change in the world-attitudes of the Russian Government by contrasting them with the present world-attitudes of the Chinese Government. For the Chinese stand today approximately where the Russians stood a quarter of a century ago.

It might be expected that in the circumstances the Chinese would be especially sensitive to even the slightest sign of Soviet-American rapprochement. And that is in fact what we do find. For example the publication of the interview which President Kennedy gave to its editor in *Izvestia* at the close of 1961 provoked the most extreme symptoms of alarm and displeasure in China. The *People's Daily Observer* published a lengthy diatribe devoted entirely to asserting that President Kennedy's interview far from giving any evidence of moderation on the part of the American Government 'unmasked his unbridled aggression' etc., etc. From which we may deduce that, naturally enough, anything like an American-Russian agreement on a test ban, or for that matter on anything else, would be regarded by the Chinese with extreme alarm and disfavour.

15

Western Intentions

American Intentions

IT is more difficult to say anything definite about western intentions than about the intentions of the two major communist régimes. For they are less definite.

We may consider American intentions first. Does, then, the American Government regard a third world war as inevitable? No doubt it does not. But at one time or another during the past seventeen years important individual American statesmen and military leaders, including, it may be surmised, Mr John Foster Dulles, at any rate in the early years of his period of office, may well have done so. Again, as we noted in Part One (see p. 41 above) the commanders of S.A.C. at one time accepted a doctrine of the necessity of pre-emption and prepared a force suitable for this purpose.

Nor, as it is sometimes alleged, is the American abstention from using her nuclear monopoly, and later nuclear predominance, while these existed, proof that a belief in the inevitability of a third world war was always held by a negligible minority of American leaders alone. For it is doubtful if there was ever, quite, a period in which *net* American predominance, taking nuclear and conventional forces together, as they equated at the given time, was so great as to offer the American Government much temptation to make war. Nevertheless, I may offer my own subjective opinion that even if its net predominance had been much greater than it was the American Government would not have struck. To suppose that it would have done so is to fall into the Russian error of discounting almost completely non-material—or moral and psychological— factors, factors such as the prevailing national climate of opinion, with all the diversities which exist within contemporary Western democracies. These criss-cross currents of opinion would always make it unlikely that such a society as the American would be sufficiently decisive—if you will—to embark upon the daunting adventure of a nuclear preventive war, even if the logical arguments in favour of so doing were overwhelming. (As Bertrand Russell, probably erroneously, at one time supposed them to be.) This may be regarded as either a terrible weakness, or as a saving grace, of multi-centred societies such as we have evolved in the West. I certainly regard it as the latter. In any case, with the achievement of effective nuclear parity on the part of the Russians, all question of any one sane in America regarding nuclear war as inevitable, with the implication that it should be consciously undertaken at a favourable moment, has (naturally) disappeared. (Nevertheless, there may be an increasing number of Americans who see, as is argued in these pages, that nuclear war *is* inevitable in the long run in the sense that an 'unintended war', as defined in Chapter 4, will ultimately take place, unless the world is reorganized; and there may be despairing pessimists who believe, as I do not, that such reorganization is inherently impracticable.)

America a Nation-State-With-A-Mission?

There remains the question of the general character of the American nation-state. Is she a 'nation-state-with-a-mission' or a 'run of the mill nation-state', though of exceptional size and strength? In my opinion she is now predominantly the latter. Nevertheless, it is often overlooked by British and European opinion (and still more of course by communist opinion) that America is in origin 'a nation-state-with-a-mission', and that this sense of her mission lingers on to an appreciable extent. Like all nation-states with a revolutionary origin the American

Union was founded with a conscious purpose. She was to incarnate certain values. Her national purposes, her mission, are nobly set out in the Declaration of Independence. That was all nearly two hundred years ago, it may be objected. Nevertheless the American revolutionary tradition is not quite dead yet. American leaders who in their internal social and economic policies seem to us extremely conservative still feel, to a varying degree, that they must lead the world in 'a Crusade' for a certain set of values, or as they often put it, for 'a way of life'—the American way of life.

What are these values? They are of course the values or ideas of the eighteenth century enlightenment, predominantly French in their *provenance*, but with an admixture of English 'Left Whig' thought. They are the ideas which accompanied the birth of the capitalist, free enterprise, bourgeois—call it what you will—type of society. Whatever the rest of the world may think of them these ideas still vibrate in the American heart and head. Many American statesmen most genuinely suppose that, in leading 'a Crusade' against communism, they are also and at the same time leading a crusade *for* something— something which they would probably sum up in the word 'liberty'.

I, for one, accept the view that the assertion of the traditional concepts, and of some of the institutions suggested by this word, is of undiminished importance. But it seems impossible for many American leaders to understand that this is by no means how a very large part of the contemporary world looks upon them and their purposes. Rightly or wrongly—to put the point in a single sentence—a large part of the rest of the world—and not only that part which lies under communist domination—regards the American crusade for liberty as a crusade for the liberty to exploit. Until this fact is far better appreciated by American opinion than it is today, American intervention in the world will lead to a series of ironic rebuffs and disillusionments. And this is perilous for peace. For when one of these rebuffs occur—when the Chinese people support the communists (as they undoubtedly did in 1949—however much they may have regretted it since): when the Cuban people do *not* rise against Castro: when even reactionary Latin American governments show that they do *not* consider it part of the American mission to 'liberate' Cuba—the American reaction is all too often simply to sulk!

This international sulking, this refusal to recognize facts which contradict the American vision, has taken the disastrous form of a refusal, over fourteen years now, to recognize the existence of one of the main facts of the world situation, namely that China has a communist government. It is this dogmatic deviation from reality, and not any intense aggressiveness, which is the main defect of the contemporary American attitude to the world. For the communist allegation that the American Government has shown itself intensely aggressive is quite false. On the contrary, America, in her sphere of influence, has been far less 'firm' than Russia has been in her sphere. (Cf. Hungary and Cuba.) The real criticism is that the American leadership shows little sign of understanding how America is regarded by a great part of the rest of the world, and what therefore are the real limits and opportunities before American policy today.

America's True Mission

On the whole it would greatly improve matters if America could realize that she had better relinquish her traditional revolutionary claim to be 'a nation-state-with-a-mission' and take her place as a normal nation-state looking after her own interests in the world. That would be well understood. Her pretention to a revolutionary mission seems to many people in the rest of the world incomprehensible or hypocritical. Moreover in looking after her own interests as a normal nation-state, America would, in my opinion, discover her true contemporary mission. For she, and the West as a whole, have such a mission. But it is defensive rather than positive: it is to prevent something, not to do something. It is to prevent the involuntary inclusion by force of arms of unwilling peoples into the communist system. It is, to return to Engels' words, to prevent the communists from the trying 'to make people happy by force'.

O.P.W.–R

That may seem too negative and limited a purpose for ardent American spirits. Nevertheless such an attitude would have its advantages: for that matter it would prove, if it could be successfully applied, much more far-reaching in its consequences than appears at first sight: and it is, nevertheless, compatible with peace.

To take the second issue first: the imposition of liberty, in the American comprehension of that word, upon large parts of the world which are not in that sense free, is not compatible with peace. It is usually as mistaken to try to make people free, as to make them happy, by force. The successful prevention of the communist powers from indulging in their undoubted propensity 'to make people happy by force' is all that can be accomplished without nuclear war. Moreover, it is also all that we are ourselves fit to attempt. The fact is that we in the West do not know how either our own national societies, or human society as a whole, will, can, or should, be organized over, say, the next hundred years. We only make ourselves ridiculous when we pretend that we do. What we have a right to insist upon to the limits of our powers is that the maximum practicable degree of variety and diversity in development shall remain open to the people of the world. Moreover, so to insist is an effective and severe challenge to the communists. For they suppose, far more dogmatically than does the most crusading American, that they *do* know how human development should proceed. Experience, however, has now shown conclusively that they do not. That is why they have to be resolutely and firmly opposed by the West. For if they were unopposed, they could not restrain themselves from clamping down their rigid system upon the whole world, although it is now clear that it is grossly inappropriate to a large part of it. The results would be likely to be hideous.

Therefore, the mission of America in particular, and of the West in general, though, if you will, negative and defensive, is of supreme importance. It is to preserve the right, the freedom, of two-thirds of the human race to develop empirically and experimentally. We believe that we possess in the democratic process, with representative government and the other political

institutions of the more advanced Western nations, a device
which will enable peoples broadly to control their own development; to point that development at least in the direction which
they really want to go, rather than in the direction that other
people think that they ought to want to go. And we believe that
these evolving political institutions may spread, as they appear
to have done in the crucially important case of India for
example, to the less economically advanced parts of the non-
communist world. To keep open this experimental, empirical,
evolutionary path of development for mankind, is properly
understood, one of the most inspiring missions to which an
individual, or a whole society, can devote itself. For the sake of
this the peoples of the West are, rightly, unwilling to surrender
to the communist powers, even though that surrender can be
represented as the one way in which all risk of nuclear war
could be avoided.

If it cannot be claimed that the prosecution of even this
preventative mission is free from all risk of nuclear war, yet it is
at least compatible with peace. 'Crusading' for this or that conception of liberty, or happiness—for conceptions which are
certain to prove one-sided and inadequate—is far too dangerous
a national propensity to be indulged during the nuclear age. Mr
Hedley Bull (op. cit., p. 180) has well defined the illusory
element involved in pushing the present world struggle between
the West and Russia beyond a certain point. He writes of 'a
failure to appreciate the triviality, *sub specie aeternitatis*, of a conflict between two ways of life each of which resembles the other
more than it does any other that exists, or has ever existed, and
both of which are bound to be superseded'. Such coolness of
judgement makes it all the more remarkable that Mr Bull
refuses to consider any of the more far-reaching methods for
reconciling the interests of the protagonists by means of an
attempt to modify the traditional state of nature of a world of
sovereign states.

The World Role of Democratic Socialism

It is in this connexion that those political attitudes—that

whole point of view—to which we in Britain at least usually affix the label 'democratic socialism' is relevant to the enquiry undertaken in this volume. The pursuit of international peace is indeed one of the basic traditions of the socialist movement and no explanation of why one volume in a series devoted to a discussion of the principles of democratic socialism should deal with this issue is necessary. But it is precisely when we come to discuss the *intentions* of our respective nation-states that we see why nation-states which are strongly influenced by the attitudes and policies of democratic socialism really will tend to be more pacific than nation-states which are not so influenced. For the truth is that, to put the matter in a phrase, warfare or welfare are the alternative ideals or goals to which contemporary nation-states can devote themselves. The predominant aspirations and energies of any vigorous nation may be caught up, on the whole, in either the effort to dominate other peoples, or in the effort to increase its own welfare. It is true that in practice most nation-states have been actuated by a mixture of these motives. It is also true that in the past the domination and exploitation of other peoples seemed, and at one time no doubt actually was, the most natural way of increasing one's own welfare. But that—the imperialist road to welfare—is today as foolish and misconceived as it is dangerous and criminal. Today the augmentation of their own annual production of wealth and its just distribution amongst their citizens are incomparably the most effective means by which a nation-state can increase its own welfare.

Moreover if once a people is inspired by this vision of its own welfare it will be ready to appreciate the basic economic fact of the contemporary world. That basic economic fact is that the welfare of all other peoples is not merely compatible with its own welfare, but is actually a condition for its maximum growth. These are the attitudes which in Britain and over much of Western Europe, and in many other parts of the world are called, for short, the attitudes of democratic socialism. They are attitudes of mind which give the world the opportunity, and indeed the propensity, for peace: for they strive to realize the brotherhood of man. Nevertheless, it is important to add that it is these attitudes of mind themselves and not the label which we put upon them that are important. Thus, if—as an American liberal for example might well do—anyone objects that these are merely the attitudes of all reasonable and well disposed men, and have nothing to do with any form of socialism, which is an economic theory with which he can by no means agree, and the protagonists of which he distrusts, we should feel no need to argue with him. For no argument could be more barrenly semantic than would be a dispute as to whether or not the adoption of the ideal of human welfare and of the brotherhood of man should or should not be labelled 'democratic socialism'. It is the contents of the bottle, not the label, that matter.

Other Western Intentions

It would take too long to discuss the national intentions of the other members of the Western Alliance—of Britain, France, West Germany, Australia, Canada, Italy, etc.—although they are not without importance. On the whole the powers of the second rank accept the, if you will, defensive mission defined above. For they have had their wings clipped. Whatever they may have been in the past they are certainly today run-of-the-mill nation-states without particular 'missions'. It is often supposed that West Germany is an exception, since she is a divided nation with the elementary mission to reunite herself. To some extent no doubt this is true. But even in her case it is doubtful if there is much crusading zeal left in the West German national climate of opinion. Upon the whole we may, I think, rely upon the secondary powers to adopt what is in fact the correct attitude for the short run purpose of avoiding nuclear war without surrender.

National Intentions in the Rest of the World

There remains the question of the national intentions of the new or reborn nations of the rest of the world; of India, Brazil, Japan, Nigeria, Indonesia, Argentina, Yugoslavia, Egypt,

Pakistan, to name one or two of the most important amongst a various host. Naturally their national intentions vary as widely as their traditions and other characteristics. But perhaps just one common feature can be discovered. They are extremely nationalistic. Their real purpose is to exist as nations. They have set themselves to be, or to become, effective, organized developing nation-states. In most cases that in itself is a tremendous task, absorbing most of their energies and enthusiasms. What they want from the rest of the world is help without interference. (And it is not easy to get.)

This passionate nationalism on the part of the new or reborn nations of the world must be taken into account both for the short-run purpose of avoiding nuclear war without surrender and for the long-run purpose of creating a world sufficiently organized to render nuclear war indefinitely avoidable. For the short-run purpose the passionate nationalisms of the new states will put a high premium upon extreme moderation and non-interference upon the part of the super-powers and their allies. The continuing instances of residual imperialism—the French in North Africa, the Portuguese in their African colonies, and, if we are not very careful, the British in Central Africa and in the Persian Gulf, or of the United States in Central America— may do grave injury to the Western cause. On the other hand the neo-imperialism of China in Tibet, and along the Indian frontier, and of Russia in Eastern Europe may do just as much injury to the communist cause. On the whole the new nationalisms, if we know how to respect them, are a potential asset of high value to the West. For this sudden upsurge of national consciousness throughout the whole undeveloped world runs contrary to the communist world vision. It reveals that Marx's major oversight was his underestimation of nationalism. Far from the workers of the world having 'no fatherland', as he supposed, they are now determined to organize themselves into nation-states: and this determination usually transcends their class purposes as workers in their struggles with their own possessing classes.

On the other hand the new nationalisms obviously constitute an obstacle in the path of modifying the state of nature in which the sovereign states of the world at present exist. Nor shall we accomplish anything, except the alienation of the new states by lecturing them on the pitfalls of nationalism. It may be all very well for a British writer, in particular, with ten centuries of continuous national existence behind him, to express his belief in the necessity of transcending the exclusive sovereignty of nation-states. He is completely confident in the national integration of his own society and is for that very reason willing to contemplate its closer and closer association with other such societies. It is a very different—indeed an impossible—thing to ask a spokesman of one of the new nations to do any such thing. We should be asking him to oppose the sentiment which is proving itself the one effective unifying bond with which to cement the still fragile structures of new nations.

Have we not here, it may be asked, discovered one more insurmountable obstacle in the path of any attempt to create even that minimum degree of world organization which is indispensable for nuclear peace? Before, however, assenting to so despairing a conclusion, let us enquire whether there may not be ways of establishing just enough world authority to prevent nuclear war without challenging head-on the national passions of the new-born nations.

Summary

These two chapters have provided the merest sketch of what may be the national intentions of the various categories of the nation-states of the contemporary world. Their sole purpose is to recall to the reader's mind that we cannot study the question of the prevention of war without having some concept, whether explicit or implicit, in our heads as to the intentions, as well as the capabilities, of the nation-states of the contemporary world. For those hundred and more states are the *dramatis personae* of a drama which we wish to prevent from reaching that *finale*, so habitual in the English Elizabethan theatre, in which the stage during the third act is littered with corpses.

PART FOUR

Possibilities of Survival

16

The Knock-out Tournament Solution

Two Analogies

How can it be conceived that out of the existing turmoil of contrasting economic and political systems, conflicting ideologies, national passions, fears and rivalries, any sort of world authority can ever emerge? Curiously enough, the answer is that in one sense we can conceive it only too easily. History provides two precedents, or analogies, which indicate the way in which 'states of nature' have been ended when they became intolerable. But unfortunately this well-established method of producing unity and peace out of a chaos of warring elements will be found to be prohibitively destructive for a world in the nuclear epoch. Nevertheless we must realize that it exists, if only to see what is likely to be attempted if we do not find a better way.

There is first the analogy provided by the way in which the quasi-sovereign local powers of the nobles within feudal societies have been, frequently enough, brought under a sufficient degree of central authority to prevent them making war on each other. Second, there is the analogy of the way in which groups of warring states, which often comprised the whole of the world as known at the given time, have been subjected to a central authority sufficiently strong to still their conflicts.

Castles and Countries

The first analogy is apposite in one respect. The extinction of the quasi-sovereign local powers of the feudal nobles was to a considerable extent effected by means of an invention in military technique. It was gunpowder which blew up feudalism. Of course there were many more profound causes for the destruction of the feudal system in, for example, Western Europe at the close of the Middle Ages. The new proto-capitalist forces of the merchants needed many other and varied instruments with which to reconstruct society in their own image. They needed a new version of the Christian religion: they needed an immensely strengthened royal power as their centralizing instrument: they needed the inventions of the compass, the ocean-going ship, the discovery of the New World, the opening of effective communications with Asia. They needed and found all these things, and many more. But they also needed and found the crude, physical, instrument of gunpowder with which to pound down the once impregnable castles of the barons. Once war was conducted with artillery, *local* sovereign power became as vulnerable as it had become intolerable. The castle walls were broken down, and Richelieu had himself carried through the breaches in his litter in a stately progress deliberately intended to symbolize the triumph of the pacifying power of those central governments which were becoming the governments of the modern nations. The analogy for us is this: gunpowder could destroy castles, nuclear explosives can destroy countries.

In other respects the feudal analogy may not be very illuminating for our purposes. The internally-pacified nation-states of the contemporary West usually evolved out of the intra-nation anarchy of the feudal period by means of the imposition of the power of the royal-burgher coalition upon still extant feudalists, rather than by the self-elimination of the barons in their internecine conflicts. In England, however, it is worth recollecting that the latter process played a significant part. The English feudal aristocracy did very largely eliminate itself in the course of the Wars of the Roses. At the end there were hardly any feudal lords left alive. This was undeniably convenient. It accounts in part perhaps for the relatively small degree of damage done to the English social fabric, as compared to the terrible experiences of France, Germany, Italy, and the Low Countries, during the transition to the new social system. At all events we here catch a glimpse of one way in which a multiplicity of local centres of power may turn into one central power: namely by means of self-elimination in a kind of 'knock-out tournament'.

Periods of Contending States

When we turn to the second analogy, that of a group of contending states, making up what we may call for short a 'known world', with more or less insignificant contacts with the rest of the contemporary human race, this element of self-elimination becomes predominant. The record is similar for each of the separate largely self-contained 'known worlds' of China, of Central America, of South America, of Egypt and of the Mediterranean Basin. In each case a century or so of what the Chinese actually called 'the period of the contending states', was succeeded by a more or less unified empire. And the process of unification, though of course very different in detail, was in essence the same. The contending states fought each other until all were prostrate and ready to submit to one surviving conqueror, which thus became an empire, universal in the sense that it extended over the whole of the known world in question.

The chief variation in the historical pattern is that in some cases the knock-out tournament of the contending states was fought out without interference from new powers appearing upon the scene from outside the particular known world. In other and perhaps more frequent cases some such 'outsider' intervened, usually in a late phase of the tournament, when all the contestants were more or less exhausted, and snatched the prize of empire for himself. For example this was the role of Cortés and his ship-load of Conquistadors, with their invincible armour and horses, when they intervened at the last moment in the tournament of the Central American contending states, and snatched the crown of empire from Montezuma.

Again there has sometimes been an intermediate type of development in which the intervening 'outsider' state has not appeared as if from Mars, as Cortés did, but from the periphery of the known world. This was the case in the example best known to us in the West, that of the knock-out tournament of the Greek city-states. In the end none of them won. They were all swallowed up by the semi-Greek, semi-barbarian Macedon. But in the evolution of the centralized '*imperium*' of the Mediterranean known world, from which our modern Western civilization derives, two knock-out tournaments were superimposed upon each other. For Macedon, though she succeeded in establishing her hegemony over Hellas itself, just failed to establish her empire over the Mediterranean basin as a whole. A new period of contending states immediately arose.

In the end their knock-out tournament, as sometimes happens in such events, was decided in the semi-finals rather than in the finals. Towards the end of the pre-Christian period there were only three considerable powers left in the Hellenic World. Rome, Carthage and, someway behind, Macedon. Rome and Carthage fought it out in the appallingly well contested semi-final of the three Punic Wars. Carthage was eliminated. The final round between Rome and the now not very powerful Macedon was 'a push-over' for Rome. Rome duly established her *imperium* over the Mediterranean basin.

This pattern has continued into modern history. At the Renaissance the contending city states of Italy were busily engaged in the eliminating rounds[1] of their knock-out tournament. Left to itself the 'Italian-zone tournament' would no doubt have resulted in the unification of Italy under one of them had not two super-powers, France and Spain, loomed up from over the horizon and, almost disregarding the petty contests of

[1] It is true that with Italian good sense the tournament was largely conducted by the comparatively painless method of employing Condottieri (some of them English and German) to do the actual fighting—what there was of it. What a pity so admirable an arrangement could not have been left to work itself out in the unification of Italy under Venice, or Florence, or Genoa, or the Papal States sometime in the sixteenth century! But in that event a united Italy would have had to raise a real army to defend herself. Very likely she could have done so.

the city states, chosen Italy as their battleground for an early round of the succeeding knock-out tournament for the hegemony of Europe as a whole.

Neither of them won. On the contrary that tournament continued, with varying fortunes, with respites, pauses, and with periods of the qualified predominance of particular states (notably of Britain in the nineteenth century), to only five years short of the mid-point of our own century. The two 'World Wars' of our own experience were clearly in their origins attempts to fight out the final stages of the 'European-zone' tournament. And let us face the fact that on each occasion these attempted final rounds would in all likelihood have resulted, in the absence of extra-European interference, in the victory of Germany and the establishment of a German Pax Europa. By the twentieth century, however, Europe was far from being a self-contained known world, with insignificant contacts with the rest of the human race. When the European states tried to fight out their rivalry and establish a Pax Europa by the traditional method, they inevitably found that their contest was transcended. The twentieth century wars quickly became world wars: they were taken over, as it were, by the two super-powers of the periphery, America and Russia. In the result a new, and now for the first time in human history, genuinely world-wide, 'period of the contending states' supervened well before a Pax-Europa could be established.

For who can doubt that we have now entered a 'period of the contending states' upon a global scale? True, the contest has in its first seventeen years taken on the aspect of a duel between Russia and America, and their respective allies, rather than a knock-out tournament in which there are still, say, half-a-dozen contestants. We have noted, however, that there are already signs that this phase may pass: that unless the Russian-American duel is ended, in one way or another, within, at a hazard, ten to twenty years, new nuclear super-powers—China, a more or less unified Western Europe, India, Japan, Brazil?—are likely to enter the arena. Then the world will find itself back at an early stage of the tournament, instead of before the final round. We shall discuss the probable consequences for the chances of human survival of these alternative hypotheses.

Is There An Analogy?

Here the single point is being made that unless historical experience is quite misleading some such development of the world situation as this will, if things are left to themselves, occur. Unless something drastic is done, the same causes, namely the existence of two or more contending super-powers in a state of nature, will produce the same result, namely a series of wars tending to culminate in the hegemony of one of them.

All this assumes that there is something to be learnt about the probable future course of events from an acquaintance with past events. And this is a proposition hotly denied by most professional historians. They tell us that no 'regularities' are detectable in human history and so no grounds exist for supposing that one future development is more likely than another. Well, the 'regularity' here assumed is that sovereign states have hitherto regularly gone to war with each other. If this is denied then indeed the whole argument falls to the ground: there is no problem to discuss. The rest of this book, is, then, addressed solely to those who agree (i) that sovereign states in a state of nature have hitherto 'regularly' fought each other and (ii) that this fact gives an ominous degree of probability to the proposition that unless something is done about it, they will continue to do so.

Two Prospects Before Us

Let us then continue to examine the nature of what our future will probably be *unless* some unprecedented degree of conscious intervention in the historical process is achieved. There appear to be alternative prospects which we may examine in turn. First there is the possibility of early thermonuclear war between the existing nuclear powers and their allies. We have noted that just as gunpowder was able physically to eliminate castles, so thermonuclear weapons can physically eliminate countries, in the sense of killing almost all their inhabitants.

It is true that countries could, very exceptionally, be physically eliminated in the pre-nuclear age. The instance always
given is that of the destruction of Carthage by Rome at the end
of the Third Punic War. But this was exceptional. Typically,
defeated countries lived on (*vide* Clausewitz, p.75 above) to
fight another day, though often no longer with pretentions to
the mastery of their known world. Curiously enough nuclear
war promises to be, in a sense, still less decisive. If the Russian
and American coalitions set about each other with their thermonuclear weapons in the next few years, it is usually supposed
that both will cease to exist as organized societies. This indeed
is the most plausible, though not the certain, result. (See
Chapter 1 for reasons for supposing that we know very little
about what would be the real character and consequences of
nuclear war.) Thus neither America nor Russia would be there
to establish an *imperium*. It is this probability which gives
nuclear war its special aimlessness. It is not even likely to
provide the world with a conqueror.

But what would happen to the less directly involved parts of
the world? They would be appallingly damaged by the long
term fall-out which would be a by-product of the war. But
human life, it is thought, would not be likely to be extinguished.
Some even of the highly organized advanced societies would be
likely to continue to exist. Would one of them, or a group of
survivors acting together, and perhaps fusing their sovereignties, establish their hegemony over the ruined world? Or would
human life regress to a feudal, or perhaps a tribal, level with
only local centres of authority? It is not very profitable to
speculate about the consequences of a disaster of a different
order of magnitude to any known to historical experience. (As
we noted (Chapter 1, p. 20) disasters of a comparable magnitude have happened, but only locally, in particular known
worlds (as in the disintegration of the Roman *imperium* of the
Mediterranean basin) or in particular countries (such as in
Europe at the time of the Black Death).

Let us next assume the more comforting, and as it seems to
me, more probable hypothesis that by means of the traditional

methods of maintaining the balance of power, as discussed in Part One, the impending conflict of the Russian and American coalitions is continually avoided, or at least kept below the nuclear level. Then, after a given number of years—perhaps ten or even twenty—new super-powers equipped with full-scale thermonuclear armaments are likely to appear. The world situation would then somewhat resemble the European situation as it was in the first decade of the twentieth century. There would be, say, half-a-dozen nuclear superpowers of varying but significant importance. And there would also be, as in pre-1914 Europe, a 'Balkans' of much smaller but nuclearly armed, restless, and in some cases irresponsibly governed, nations, with intense local rivalries: a 'Balkans' of smaller nation-states, some attached willingly or unwillingly to one or other of the superpowers, some genuinely independent in the sense that they would throw their weight sometimes one way, sometimes another.

How long could we give the peace of the world in such conditions? Can anyone seriously suppose that the result would be any different from what it always has been in the past, namely recurrent wars between the super-powers, which could only be ended by the establishment of the hegemony of one survivor? There is only the difference that it is difficult to believe that there would *be* a survivor at the end of a series of thermonuclear wars.

Is the Balance of Power Enough?

Is all this a mere nightmare? Certainly most people behave as if it were. The immense majority of practical politicians, of diplomatists and officials, and of responsible leaders of opinion show by what they do and say that all that they consider either necessary or practicable is to maintain, and if possible improve, the stability of the balance of power by every possible means. To do so is, indeed, the condition of our survival for long enough to be able even to attempt anything else. But is it enough? Nearly all men of affairs evidently think so, for they stigmatize all consideration of the emergence of some world authority as at best unreal dreaming and at worst a positive hindrance to, and distraction from, the hard work of keeping the peace through each successive crisis—be it Berlin, Korea, Indo-China or Berlin again. We may quote as typical the opinion of Sir William Hayter, an ex-Ambassador to Moscow, and now Warden of New College in the University of Oxford. He wrote:

Aiming at world government is now in my opinion actually wrong. It distracts our attention from what we ought really to be doing, which is to search for ways of living safely in an inevitably divided world. (*The Observer*, February 12th, 1961.)

Sir William Hayter subsequently wrote (commenting upon extracts from this work published in *The Observer*, January 14th, 1962) that it 'is a mistake to take world government as an object of policy now . . .' for it was 'unattainable in present circumstances'. No one can contradict him in this latter view. But our aims will be short-term indeed if we never aim at anything the attainment of which requires changes in present circumstances.

It will be found that the whole of the concluding section of this book is devoted to this question of what should be our longer-term aim or ideal. No doubt some men feel no need to envisage any such distant objective, the attainment of which would necessitate drastic changes in present circumstances. They are content to devote themselves wholly to the immediate, urgent, problem of surviving from one crisis to another, in the world as it is. It would be foolish and ungrateful of us to quarrel with them on that account. For unless some people devoted themselves to these day-to-day tasks, our chances of even short-term survival would be minimal. It is partly at least a matter of temperament no doubt: but there are others of us who can hardly devote ourselves heart and soul to any cause— even to the cause of peace itself—unless they can envisage a longer term goal or ideal. To be satisfying to adult intelligence such an ideal must be free of self-contradictory features. And yet its attainment must accomplish, more or less permanently—

'seriously and for a long time' as the Russians often say—the sought-for objective, in this case world peace.

Those 'men of peace' who have striven so devotedly in our century for the general and complete disarmament of the nation-states of the present day world have all, like me, been people who have felt the need for a more or less ideal goal at which to aim. Part Two of this book was devoted to the ungrateful task of showing that the 'ideal', or longer-term goal of disarmament, as hitherto conceived, contained a self-contradiction which made it inherently unobtainable. This self-contradiction was that a world of completely disarmed, completely sovereign, states was a state of things impossible to realize. Those of us who need a long-term aim, towards which step-by-step measures can be seen to approximate, are therefore bound to turn to the concept of a unification of the world under some form of pacifying authority. We therefore claim, not that the creation of such an authority is 'attainable in present circumstances', but that this is precisely the proper *aim* at which our endeavours to change present circumstances should be directed.

For we do not consider it historically correct, as do the practical men, either consciously or unconsciously, to assume a world of sovereign states in a state of nature as the permanent condition of human existence, so that it is idle and frivolous to consider any other.[1] On the other hand, if the practical men are merely intent to assert that the continuance of the present 'period of contending states' on a world scale is by far the most *probable* prospect before us, we can have no quarrel with them. Of course it is: this is what will happen unless we do something

---

[1] They do so partly I think because of the quaint way in which history has usually been taught in the West. Neglecting the longer historical perspective, historians have habitually concentrated their attention on one or other period of contending states; often, in the case of modern historians, on the European eighteenth century, or, in the case of ancient historians, on the Greek city-states up to the end of the Peloponnesian War, or alternatively on Rome up to the final establishment of the *principiate* by Augustus. The tacit presumption is that this is history: that this is how nations live and always must live. The centuries in which they have lived, on the contrary, under a central *imperium* are largely ignored as uninteresting.

about it. But if they are asserting that the continuance of such a situation is ultimately compatible with the prevention of nuclear war, we must dissent. A highly probable, and in that sense reasonable, prospect, to be anticipated by all experienced men, may yet be a fatal prospect.

There exists, however, one important school of thought which does not take the view that the unification of the world is a more or less idle speculation. Communist leaders and spokesmen, as trained Marxists, do not imagine that the world either can or should continue to be a congeries of periodically warring states. We noted in Part Two above that, long before the advent of nuclear weapons, it had become an established part of communist doctrine that the world must be unified. We must now re-examine the communist view of how alone this can be done.

17

The Communist Solution

Are the Communists For or Against World Unification?

IN Chapter 14 we saw that a unification of the world, in the form of a federation of communist societies, of which the U.S.S.R. was to be the nucleus and prototype, has always formed part of the intentions of the Soviet Government.

Professor Goodman considered this *Soviet Design for a World State*, as he entitled his book, a dastardly conspiracy which it was his duty to expose. To many people, on the other hand, a recognition of the necessity to unify the world in the nuclear age will seem plain common sense. Indeed if it should become apparent over the next few decades that the communists are the only people to take the possibility of world unification seriously, their seriousness will stand them in increasingly good stead. As the consequences of nuclear devastation are appreciated, the demand that war shall somehow be prevented will become stronger and stronger.

Let us then look more particularly at the communist view of the matter. It will be objected at once that whatever they may say in their theorizing, the communists show themselves in practice to be implacable opponents of the development of even embryonic elements of a world authority. We have traced in these pages how bitterly they have opposed the slightest weakening of the veto in the Security Council of the United Nations, the development of an International Atomic Energy

Authority, or even the creation of a 'test ban' authority capable of inspecting a nation's nuclear activities against its will. Finally, in 1960 and 1961, the Soviet Government demanded that the very machinery of the United Nations be 'nationalized', in the sense that its officials were to be appointed not as international civil servants with their loyalty to the United Nations itself, but as representatives of the three-fold division of Western, communist and uncommitted nations. How then can it be denied that in practice the communists are determined opponents of even the slightest move towards world unification?

The resolution of this paradox is, of course, that the communists believe that world unification is as impossible as it would be undesirable *until* all considerable states have passed through the revolutionary process; until, that is to say, they have abolished capitalist 'relations of production' and established socialist relations of production under the rule of their wage-earning classes. After that, the unification of the world, in a Federation of Socialist Republics, would follow naturally, the communists believe. Indeed Professor Goodman quotes several passages in which Bukharin (often a somewhat *simpliste* exponent of Marxist theory), suggests that, after the revolution has become world-wide, world unification will take place automatically.

This view of the matter depends upon the basic communist insight that states are not just states: that they are states of a particular kind; in this case either bourgeois-capitalist states or proletarian-socialist states. Indeed in Marxist theory, post-revolutionary proletarian states are not really states at all: they are quasi-states, destined to wither away into societies which cohere and co-operate voluntarily and naturally, without need of any special institution for the coercion of their citizens. They further believe that these two kinds or categories of states are so different that they will behave in almost completely divergent ways: what is blankly impossible for the one kind will be natural and inevitable for the other.

There is, of course, a great deal of truth in the assertion that there are distinct kinds or categories of states. Western anticommunists would also emphasize the differences between the two kinds of nation-states. No one pretends that the Russian and American nations are organized in exactly the same way. (Nevertheless, are they in some respects so diametrically opposite as they mutually suppose? See p. 303 below.) But whatever may be the real degree of difference between the two main kinds of contemporary nation-states—and even accepting the usual view that they are polar opposites—must we accept the communist hypothesis that world unification is impossible as between bourgeois-capitalist states and almost automatic as between proletarian-socialist states? If we must, then the communists undoubtedly have a trump card in their hands. As the peoples of the world come to realize that some degree of world unification is the sole conceivable way of keeping the peace, they will examine attentively any claim that there is a way, however arduous, of achieving world unity. Moreover, the communists, as good propagandists, will naturally slur over the violent character of the road to eventual peace which they are in fact proposing; they will, and do, preach peace in its simplest, least sophisticated form. And they might be held to be justified in doing so if their original proposition that world unity could be achieved in this way, and in no other, were well founded.

Do Communist States Unite?

Unfortunately, or fortunately, it is becoming less and less easy to believe that this basic element in the communist world-view is valid. Evidence accumulates which makes it harder and harder to suppose either that proletarian, socialist states will automatically—or for that matter at all if they can help it—unite in a federal, or still less in a centralized, state. And further evidence, by no means so strong, but yet significant, is appearing that states in which capitalist relations of production still predominate may be capable of some forms of unification.

It will be unnecessary to do more than recapitulate in a few sentences the evidence noted in Chapter 14 that the nation-state as an institution has survived the revolution after all. No one cares even to speak of China becoming part of the U.S.S.R. Yugoslavia could only be brought to do so by conquest. The other East European communist nations are, it is clear, only held in the looser relations of satellites by physical force. Nor is there any sign that even the new generation of their citizens, brought up though they have been in fully communist educational institutions, would regard their countries becoming republics of the U.S.S.R. as anything else than Russian annexation. The revolution has come and gone, and lo and behold China is still China, Poland is still Poland, Hungary still Hungary—and even a new national entity, Yugoslavia, appears to have firmly established itself. Finally, the U.S.S.R. is still very much Russia.

In a word these new proletarian nations are still, for good and ill, real nations with all the prides, passions—and obsessions, if you will—of nation-states as we have known them in the last few centuries of history. They simply cannot be made into districts of the U.S.S.R., permitted to retain their own style of folk dancing, but not very much more. This awkward fact of the post-revolutionary persistence of nationality has caused an extreme distortion of the original and inspiring communist vision of the reign of peace upon earth by means of the free and voluntary federation of every post-revolutionary society. In the end the vision has become so distorted that it has largely degenerated into simple, old-fashioned, Russian and Chinese imperialism.

This tragic degeneration has occurred because the communists have been, as usual, sure that they knew best. The workers had no fatherlands—the Manifesto had said so. Therefore every apparent manifestation of post-revolutionary nationalism outside Russia must be the work of imperialist agents, provocateurs, 'bourgeois remnants' and the like, to be stamped out under the tank tracks with a good heart, secure in the knowledge that the workers must 'really' be on the side of the Russians, even if they had to be killed in order to have the point explained to them.

All this evidence strongly suggests that, whatever else the transcending of capitalist relation of production, together with the political dominance of the wage-earners, throughout the world[1] may do, it is unlikely to solve the problem of the prevention of war by means of world unification. At most it may prove easier for socialist societies to unite in a world federation. Thus we cannot regard the second proposition of the communist solution, namely that post-revolutionary, socialist societies, and they alone, will be able, willingly and naturally, to unify the world and so prevent the recurrence of nuclear war, as valid. But if this leg of the communist argument is undermined, much of the mustification for the present world policy of communist governments falls to the ground. We are being asked to reject with contempt all attempts towards the unification of the world as it is, and to pass through the fires of revolution (in practice in the form of a Russian or Chinese conquest) partly at least for the sake of what can increasingly be seen to be the illusory hope of thereby achieving permanent world unity and peace.

Can Non-communist States Unite?

But what of the first proposition of the communist solution, namely that bourgeois-capitalist societies are inherently incapable of creating a world sufficiently unified to avoid war? (Or that they are unable to do so, except by the traditional method of a knock-out tournament, as a result of which one such society subjects all the others to an exploitative empire.) Here no doubt the evidence is much less definite. The communist view has much historical experience on its side. In the world as it was up till the middle of the twentieth century, before the capitalist societies were very seriously challenged by communism, and before the apparition of nuclear weapons, the advanced capitalist nation-states showed only the slightest propensity to unify themselves and so avoid periodic war. Men of affairs recognized indeed that war was a terrible thing; but it had always occurred and perhaps always would: the duty of practical men was no doubt to avoid it if at all possible, mainly

---

[1] I for my part believe that, in the fullness of time, and in our part of the world by democratic and evolutionary means, both these things will and should come to pass.

by maintaining the balance of power. But it was also their duty to see to it by every means that their own society survived and was on the winning side, if and when war came.

But whether the practical men appreciate it or not, things really are rather different, in the second half of the twentieth century, from what they have ever been before in human history. The challenge of the new, militant communist super-powers and their allies is acute. And war has become nuclear. For these two reasons the question of whether or not it is possible to move towards the unification of the world is forcing itself upon our attention. The pressure of these two changes in the environment has already led to significant developments of two different kinds. On the one hand there has been the establishment of the United Nations. The world's yearning for unity and peace has become strong enough for it to be impossible for the leaders of either the Western or the Communist worlds to avoid, even if they had wished to do so, the re-establishment of this attempt at a world organism. For the United Nations is already the second avatar of the world's will to unity and peace. The League of Nations was formed in just the same way as a result of men's feelings of revulsion from the First World War. We shall discuss this development in the next chapter.

The other development is more recent. In recent years an undeniably significant current has flowed over Western Europe in favour of some form of regional unification. After several false starts, and amidst much scepticism, this movement is today (1962) making obvious progress in the form of the European Common Market or customs union. How fast or how far this attempt to begin at least the process of fusing the sovereignties of some of the oldest and most deeply established nation-states will go, it is as yet impossible to say. Moreover, as we have several times noted, even the fullest success for the movement for the unification of Western Europe would not unify the world or even, necessarily, lead in that direction. What it would do, to the extent that it succeeded, is to create a new super-power of the full stature of Russia, America and China. We shall discuss below the question of whether the appearance of new super-powers would render easier or more difficult the attainment of a sufficient degree of world unity to avoid the recurrence of nuclear war. Here we are concerned with this development merely for such evidence as it affords that the communists may prove to be in error in supposing that non-communist nation-states are in general incapable of uniting themselves into larger entities. It may turn out that, if the pressure upon them is sufficient, it is by no means impossible for societies, whose economies are on the whole founded upon the private ownership of the means of production and the market mechanism, to unite with each other. Certainly it is a difficult business: but then, so it seems, is the unification of communist societies.

The Deformation of the Communist Ideal

There is then evidence to show that both parts of the communist dogma, that the unification of the world is only possible by means of universal revolution, are invalid. Socialist relations of production may prove to be superior in productivity to capitalist relations of production.[1] But it appears less and less likely that they will provide the sole key to a unification of the world to a sufficient degree to prevent the recurrence of war.

What is left then of the original and imposing communist vision of world unification by means of the revolutionary establishment of proletarian socialist societies? It is to be feared that all that is left of it is the stark and forbidding prospect of Russian, or Chinese, world conquest. Well, it may be objected (as we noted in Chapter 9 above), is not even that road to world unity and peace far preferable to nuclear war? Once again there is no need even to try to answer this question, for there is

---

[1] We have nothing like enough experience as yet on which to decide this question. As a democratic socialist I, naturally, put my money upon relations of production, which, while originally capitalist, have been empirically modified out of all recognition, in what may be broadly called the socialist direction, by the pressure of the wage-earners using democratic political institutions. But we shall see: or rather we shall only see if we can solve the problem with which this volume is concerned, namely the prevention of nuclear war.

no such choice open to us. The non-communist world is no more likely to surrender to Russia and China than the communist world is likely to surrender to America and her allies. By deforming and debasing the communist vision of the free union of socialist societies, by subjecting that vision to the state interests of the two communist super-powers, the very possibility of the world accepting the communist solution to the problem of its unification has been ruled out by the communists themselves.

On the other hand, and paradoxically, this very deformation and debasement of the communist vision of world revolution, when looked at from the opposite point of view, gives us grounds for hope. For this is the same process, which we noted in Chapter 14, devoted to 'Communist Intentions', by which Russia has gradually passed from being the revolution incarnate, through the stage of being what we called 'a nation-state-with-a-mission' towards, at least, the stage of being a nation-state like another. And, as the path to world unification through world revolution is closed, it is only to the extent that Russia becomes 'a-nation-state-like-another' that we can hope to engage with her in the very difficult, but not inherently impossible, task of achieving the necessary degree of world unity by non-revolutionary means.

18

The United Nations Solution

Forum or Authority?

WE have already attempted (in Part Two) to appreciate the powerful peace movement which has resulted from the two world wars, and is now sustained by a well justified dread of nuclear weapons. We made this appreciation, however, in terms of the movement for disarmament and we came to the melancholy conclusion that not only had the successive disarmament conferences ended in frustration, but that this was due, not to series of mischances and mistakes, but to certain basic causes. These basic causes might be summed up by saying that general and complete disarmament between sovereign states existing in a state of nature was almost a contradiction in terms.

It would, however, be an injustice to the movement for peace to suggest that its serious supporters had seen the issue in the comparatively narrow terms of disarmament alone. On the contrary, from the inception of the peace movement in its present day form, during the closing years of the First World War, until today, the men of peace have realized that some new form of world organization was indispensable to the attainment of their aims, including disarmament itself. First the League of Nations and then the United Nations have been the practical results of this realization.

It is sometimes said that both the League and the U.N. have been mere international forums of debate. But this is an over-

simplified version of the records of the first two world organizations in human history. If we consider first the League of
Nations we shall find that there was a period, roughly corresponding to the nineteen-twenties, in which the League was a
rather effective body. This was in spite of—or perhaps actually
because of—the fact that neither America nor Russia, both
already looming up as the super-powers of the future, were
members of it. The League mainly consisted of the European
victors in the First World War, essentially Britain and France.
Its purpose, to put the point with brutal brevity, was at bottom
to maintain the European settlement arrived at Versailles. (And
to maintain 'a peace'—in this case the Versailles peace—is
after all to maintain there and then, 'the peace'. *That* peace,
that particular *status quo*, may be good or bad: but to maintain
it *is* to maintain a peace of some sort.) For this purpose the
League proved fairly efficacious. No doubt the job could have
been done by a simple Anglo-French alliance: but it was surely
better done, and not only for appearance's sake, by an international organization such as the League. For the League had
to allow at least the voices of other nations to be heard.

This example illustrates aptly the principal point which it is
desired to make in this chapter. Such world organizations as the
League or the U.N. can work well if they contain a core of
like-minded nations with some simple common purpose: but if
not, not. For when, for remarkable reasons (in fact their supposed class interests), the Governments of Britain and France
lost their determination to maintain the Versailles Settlement,
the League became ineffective and in the end impotent.

Why the U.N. Has Worked Hitherto

The history of the United Nations has been different. Both of
the then existing super-powers, America and Russia, were
founder members, and from the outset they had largely contradictory purposes. It may be wondered, then, how the U.N. has
ever been able to act at all or, at any rate, to accomplish anything. And yet it has undoubtedly been fairly effective on
several occasions. For instance it was able to condemn the

aggression of North against South Korea, and throw the mantle of its moral authority over the expeditionary forces with which America and her allies in the end repelled that aggression. Again the U.N., this time largely by its authority alone, put a stop to the Anglo-French-Israeli aggression upon Egypt. Finally after many vicissitudes it appears that it has been relatively successful in a major salvage operation in the Congo, by means of which the total breakdown of society has been averted in that huge area of Africa. How can these and other not inconsiderable successes have been achieved in the face of the implacable mutual hostility of the U.N.'s two main members, America and Russia, and of their determination to pursue contradictory purposes?

To some extent no doubt the true answer is simply luck! It was the sheer luck of the ill-judged Russian 'walk-out' which enabled the U.N. to condemn the North Korean aggression and to support the resistance to it. But this is only a small part of the story. The truth is that in those important, but after all secondary, situations in which the U.N. has been able to act effectively (nobody even suggests that it can settle such problems of direct conflict between the super-powers as for example Berlin), it has acted, on the whole, as the instrument of the Western Powers and of Western purposes. Suez is the one great exception to this rule. But it is an exception which is illustrative and revealing. What happened at Suez was that the conduct of the British and French Governments became so preposterous that they succeeded, momentarily, in uniting Russia and America in a common purpose. And when *that* was accomplished the U.N. became in a flash irresistible! Two of the most important secondary powers, Britain and France, had to bow to its will within twenty-four hours, break off their military operation, and accept a humiliating rebuff.

But in Korea, in the Congo, and in many other less dramatic situations, a neutral observer—if, *pace* Mr Khruschev, such a one exists—would probably report that by and large the U.N., both in what it has done and condemned, and also in what it has *not* done, and has condoned, has operated broadly in accordance with the purposes of the West in general, and of America in particular. For example the U.N. condemned the Russians in Hungary, but not the French in Algeria: the law and order which it has tried to re-establish in the Congo has been, on the whole, the kind of law and order familiar and acceptable to the West: of the two dictatorships of North and South Korea the Southern has been unhesitatingly preferred (even before the act of aggression by the North was committed): the American Government was not condemned for its attempt to overthrow the Castro regime in Cuba: America has been able to block for a whole decade the admission of the third emergent super-power itself, Communist China. Moreover, in the day-to-day workings of the U.N. and its agencies, the purposes pursued, and the methods used, have been essentially Western liberal, and therefore anti-communist (in the communists' interpretation at least): for the operating staffs have been predominantly Western. These actions and omissions may have been right or wrong but it can hardly be denied that they have been agreeable to the Western, rather than to the communist, block.

All this has been possible because the West has possessed an at first substantial, then a working, and now a sometimes precarious, majority throughout the organs of the U.N. The veto provisions of the Security Council have enabled Russia and her allies to stop the U.N. from endangering their vital interests: but they have had to tolerate, or at any rate have hitherto tolerated, the U.N. acting in the interests of the West in most secondary matters. All this of course is what Mr Khruschev, since the autumn of 1960, has become determined to stop. Apparently the U.N. 'settlement' of the Congo emergency in the broadly pro-Western sense of support for Mr Kasavubu instead of Mr Lumumba was the last straw for Mr Khruschev. He accordingly put forward his 'troika' proposals which were broadly designed to have the effect of giving the communist members of the organization an effective veto on U.N. action at every level, right down to the administrative application of Security Council and Assembly decisions.

O.P.W.–T

Two questions immediately arise: why did not the communist members make some such move as this earlier; and what will be the effect of their having done so at the beginning of the nineteen-sixties? The answer to the two questions is perhaps the same. The communists did not move earlier to block U.N. decisions unwelcome to themselves because they recognized, if only tacitly, that the U.N. was not *merely* an instrument of Western purposes, but was also an institution highly valued and esteemed by the potentially decisive uncommitted third of the world. If they had appeared too early or too obviously to hamstring the U.N. they would have incurred an unacceptable odium amongst the uncommitted. Similarly the genuinely pro-U.N. attitude of the new, weaker nations of the uncommitted world makes it, in 1962, increasingly uncertain whether Russia and her allies can afford to push their 'troika' and other similar proposals to the full. Many of the Afro-Asian, and some even of the South American states (those which are not firm American satellites), really do regard the U.N., not as an instrument of Western purposes, but as their refuge and protection—not very effective perhaps, but yet much better than nothing—against the bullying of the major powers. Thus, Mr Khruschev's troika proposals and his generally anti-U.N. policy have had a mixed reception amongst just those members to whose opinion the Russians must be sensitive. Moreover, these pro-U.N. uncommitted nations are able to point out to Mr Khruschev that his 'patience became exhausted' just at the moment when America and her allies were on the point of losing their automatic majority in the organs of the U.N.!

Evidence of the loss of Western hegemony within the U.N. accumulated during 1961. For if the Russians were profoundly dissatisfied with the U.N.'s policy in the Congo, so, though with much less reason, were the more extreme, and less reflective, proponents of 'Westernism'. It became clear that the predominant part of ruling opinion in continental Europe, much Conservative opinion in Britain, and some conservative opinion in America, was profoundly dissatisfied with the U.N. because it had become clear that Afro-Asian opinion could not now be over-ridden, even in secondary matters, in the way in which both it and communist opinion had been over-ridden in the 'forties and 'fifties. In the early months of 1962 it remains to be seen to what extent the newly important Afro-Asian nations, acting as they often do in general accord with some at least of the officials who staff the organization, will be able to give the U.N. a sufficient sense of common purpose to enable it to act. In secondary matters it may be that they will—I for one hope so. But it must be concluded, however regretfully, that in major matters, such as those which deeply affect the interests of either of the super-powers or their principal allies, they will not. It is true that President Kennedy's Administration, with great wisdom, is attempting to preserve the capacity to act of the U.N., even if that means that it must often flout the particular national interests of this or that Western state, such as the British investment interests in Katanga, or Portuguese or French colonialism. But such enlightenment is bound to arouse the most violent opposition in the more reactionary circles of the West, which are naïvely outraged at the very idea of the U.N. ceasing to be their instrument.

In the early months of 1962 it is impossible to say how all this will end. To a remarkable degree the enlightened self-interest of the present American Administration, combined with Russia's crass misunderstanding of the real attitudes and aspirations of the new Afro-Asian members, appear to be preserving, and even extending, the U.N. authority and ability to act in secondary matters. This is a wonderful gain for the possibility of peace—for of course even these secondary disputes, which do not directly involve the vital interests of the super-powers and their main allies, are acutely dangerous, since they may at any time spread and deepen into primary disputes between the world alliances. It will, therefore, be an immense gain if a working majority, consisting of a sort of coalition of the more intelligent and enlightened Western governments, and of most of the Afro-Asian members can be found for such U.N. operations as that of the Congo. It must be admitted, however, that this is a possibility rather than an assured prospect. Moreover, even if it is realized in full it will leave the U.N. as unable as it has always been to deal with primary disputes directly involving the vital interests of the main alliances. Neither amendments in the Charter, nor revisions of its constitution can alter this inevitable predicament of the U.N. in a world in which intentions and power-relationships are as they are. What *could* alter the situation would be the discovery on the part of the super-powers of a common interest.

A Core of Like-mindedness Essential

These reflections upon the situation in the League of Nations in the inter-war period, and in the United Nations in the early nineteen-sixties, are intended merely to illustrate the simple fact that these two first world-organizations in human history have been effective only to the extent that they have contained a core of essentially like-minded members. This core of member-nations has had to have certain basic common purposes, and to command a majority in the institutions of the organization. Moreover a further condition of effectiveness is that, at least in secondary matters, the minority submits to the will of this majority, which can and does act to enforce, or at least promote, its common purposes. For the first fifteen years of its existence the United Nations did to a certain extent contain such a core of like-mindedness in the form of America and her allies: it may or may not do so in the future.

The purpose of recalling all this is to illuminate the great gulf which is fixed between organizations such as the old League, or the present U.N. and even an embryonic world authority. It is legalistic and narrow-minded to think of this in terms of some defect in the original Charter in which, by a tragic mistake, the veto power was embodied. The veto on the actions of the U.N. is not written into the Charter; it is written into the world situation. It is inescapably present in the basic fact that one super-power cannot coerce another without full-scale nuclear war. (If it could, the coerced super-power would *ipso facto* have relinquished its claim to be a super-power.) In the same way there can be no such thing as a world authority with power to keep the peace unless that authority can, in the very last resort, coerce all existing nation-states, and can do so without war, or by means of a brief and certainly successful war. (This probably comes to the same thing, for in that case the threat of war should always suffice.)

The Question of Power

These crude considerations should be sufficient to bring home to our minds what a very different thing a world authority would be from the existing United Nations, even if, as is probable, it were still called by the same name. In the final chapters we shall discuss the question of whether or not there is any conceivable way—other than the now impossible way of a knock-out tournament fought to a finish—by which such an authority might come into existence during, say, the remainder of our century.

Here it may be well to reflect for a moment upon the illusory element which appears to have become commingled with the admirable and indispensable work of the peace movement. This illusory element developed because of a failure to face squarely the question of power.

The experiences in two world wars of the men and women who have been the backbone of the world-wide peace movement, together with, no doubt, their own innately humane and 'tender' cast of mind, have made them profoundly suspicious of the exercise of power. And no wonder! In our own lifetimes we have seen much of what is best and most civilized in the world trampled upon, not once but again and again, by the unbridled exercise of arbitrary power. It is hardly too much to say that all this has caused the men of peace to dream of a power-less world. But this is indeed a dream. (Curiously enough it is the same dream as that dreamt by the communists: for the communists, too, dream of a powerless, state-less, united world: the difference is only that the communists believe that this is a dream this side of the revolution: that it is only after the revolution that it will become a reality.)

The solution proposed by the more fervent protagonists of immediate, general and complete disarmament, and of the United Nations, is in fact a world power-vacuum. We can say this with confidence that upon any time-scale relevant to our present inquiry this cannot be. Somewhere, somehow, there will have to be a centre of power, wielded by somebody. And power must be read in this context as meaning nuclear power. Disarmament must play an indispensable part in the emergence of an organized world. But it must be the disarmament of everybody else before the armament of a single centre. After all, to recall our historical analogies, not otherwise than this was the disarmament of the barons effected before the royal power at the end of feudalism: not otherwise was the disarmament of, for example, the local states of the Mediterranean basin effected before, first, the phalanx of Macedon and then the legions of Rome. Not otherwise was the disarmament of the local states of China effected before the armies of the Ts'in. The United Nations must become the instrument of world-peace; but it must have a sword in its hand, and in our time at least that sword can be only the sword of one or more of the super-powers.

This is no doubt a brutal conclusion. But surely the evidence of the events of the first half of our century and, for that matter, of any serious reflection upon the human condition as it exists for our generation, must confirm it. Yet such a conclusion will be fiercely resisted. Throughout history any view which has sought to take into account the realities of power has always been fiercely resented. Why have Machiavelli, Hobbes, Clausewitz and Marx been the great scandalizers?[1] Mainly because each of them has dealt in terms of power. In this they have been exceptions amongst the theorists of public affairs. The question of what main group or class within a community: or of what nation-state, or coalition of nation-states within the known world of the period, is to hold power has often been felt to be too hot a matter for men to be able to contemplate calmly. People have felt outraged when a writer has dragged

[1] I am indebted to Mr Michael Howard for this observation.

the question of power out into the open. Practical men of affairs have, it is true, never had any illusions on the subject: they could not possibly have maintained their positions in public life if they had had. But they have preferred to act upon their usually acute insight into the location of power rather than to talk about it.

What then should be required of the men of peace? Of, that is to say, the supporters of disarmament and of the United Nations as the salvation of the world? It is not that they should abandon in any degree their enthusiasm for these causes. Disarmament, in the end general and complete (with one central exception): a United Nations Organization far more imposing than that which we now know, is an indispensable institution for a world which is to have any hope of the permanent prevention of nuclear war. What is required of the men of peace is that they should face squarely the issue of where ultimate power is to be located in such a world. For ultimate power, let them make no mistake about it, there has got to be. Nor is it any answer at all to say that that power must reside in the United Nations itself. The United Nations is largely and, it is to be feared, may become increasingly an arena in which the two great world coalitions meet and argue before an audience (which both must try to avoid offending) of the uncommitted nations. The world has need for such an arena. But it makes no sense to say that ultimate world power can be wielded by an arena: you might as well say that the Wimbledon tennis tournament ought not to be won by either of the finalists, but by the Centre Court!

The desperate tournament of the nations is, however, of a peculiar kind. It is at least conceivable that the finalists may, at any rate for some one limited purpose, drop their contention and begin to play on the same side of the net. At the cost of straining the analogy still further it might be said that they might start playing against the other competitors who had been knocked out in earlier rounds. We noted above that something of the sort actually, if momentarily, did happen during the Suez crisis of 1956. America and Russia both, though no doubt for different reasons, and with different calculations as to the consequences, wished to stop the Anglo-French-Israeli war on Egypt. And in twenty-four hours they stopped it. Moreover they used the United Nations as the obvious instrument of their common purpose. Indeed the United Nations was probably an indispensable instrument. It was much easier for the two bitterly antagonistic super-powers to act together with the other sixty member-nations than to issue a joint ultimatum; and it was much more possible for the British and French Governments to yield to the United Nations than to the naked will of the two super-powers. But, of course, it was their will that counted. If—and how great an if it is!—the super-powers could find any abiding and stable common purpose—be it only the elementary common purpose of their own survival—the United Nations would at once and automatically become an irresistible instrument of their will for the fulfilment of that purpose.

'A Power-of-last-Resort'

And this raises the issue of what the nuclear epoch demands of the practical men who manage the affairs of the nations. Let them not relax for one moment their efforts to increase the stability of the balance of power, for on that depends the possibility of gaining enough time for there to be any chance of finding a solution to the problem of the prevention of war in the nuclear age. (The whole of Part One of this volume is devoted to the problem of the balance, primarily in its military aspect. But of course it has an at least equally important political aspect.) But will not the men of power recognize that the men of peace have been right in asserting that in the nuclear age the pursuit of the balance of power is catastrophically inadequate? True the men of peace have gone to the other extreme and supposed that the cardinal issue of power and its location could be neglected. But if this error is avoided and the issue is faced of how a single 'power-of-last-resort' is to be developed and exercised, as the sole conceivable way of preserving the peace in the longer term, then some such organ as the United Nations is seen to be of the greatest importance.

It is true that to say that the U.N. ought to be equipped with its own predominant armed force is to beg the question which has to be answered. For if the super-powers were ready to do that it would mean that they had already united their wills for the achievement of a common purpose. The problem is to identify some very simple, very limited common purpose, for the realization of which the super-powers may be willing to unite their wills. The moment they did that, the United Nations would become irresistible for the achievement of this purpose, even without the creation of an international armed force—though no doubt the creation of such a force would follow. What we have a right to demand of the men of power is that they shall cease to regard this issue of the progressive development of a world authority as an academic, dreamy speculation, and see that it is indispensable to human survival in the nuclear age.

19

Two Possibilities

The Argument So Far

THE problem of the maintenance of peace for an indefinite period is clearly extremely difficult, even if it is not, as many men of affairs suppose, so remote of solution as to be not worth talking about.

True, the thing has been done before, over fairly long periods and fairly wide areas, but only by the unification of a 'known world' by means of a knock-out tournament; and that method is no longer available. The communist solution by way of universal revolution is also closed to us, not only because it would be, perhaps, as violent as wars of conquest themselves, but also because much recent evidence goes to show that it is an illusion to suppose that post-revolutionary nation-states are particularly likely to unite voluntarily. And finally the solution of the men of peace, by way of the United Nations and general and complete disarmament, is, partly, vitiated by the illusion that there can be, in our time at any rate, a powerless world.

What remains? There remains at any rate the conceptual possibility that two or more of the super-powers might pool their authority, for the one purpose of preventing the outbreak of full-scale nuclear war. Such a pooling of power might take place either in the fairly immediate future between the two existing super-powers, America and Russia (their respective allies consenting or 'influenced' to consent). Or it could take place one or two decades from now between a group of, say, half a dozen nuclear super-powers which may have come into existence by then. Before considering these two possibilities it is necessary to define more closely than has been attempted so far what we mean by the term 'a super-power'.

What is a Super-Power?

In 1962 it is not difficult to answer this question. America and Russia are super-powers. The gap between their strength and the next most powerful nation-state (which in 1962 is still Britain since she alone of the rest has some effective nuclear capability) is wider than the gap between the strengths of all other important nation-states relatively to each other. It is thus evident that when we use the term a super-power we do not merely mean a nuclear power: Britain is a nuclear power but not a super-power. In fact no exact definition of a super-power can be made—but we know them well enough when we see them!

Perhaps, however, we might say that a super-power is a power which is convincingly capable of deterring America or Russia from unwelcome acts by means of its own nuclear capability: in 1962 there is no such third power. What, however, is chiefly relevant to the present discussion is the question which we first raised in Chapter 11, namely are the two existing super-powers likely to maintain their predominance indefinitely or are they likely to be joined by several new super-powers, and if so in how long? We saw that the defence experts differed widely on this issue. Some supposed that if nothing were done in the next ten or twenty years a number of powers would emerge which, for practical purposes, would have a parity of nuclear capability with that of America and Russia. Others supposed, on the contrary, that the American-Russian lead could never be even shortened: that there might never be any new super-powers: that the real and, perhaps, no less alarming prospect was of the continued predominance of the existing nuclear super-powers, but surrounded by nuclearly-armed satellites, allies and neutrals, all capable of destroying each other, and themselves, but not of resisting the super-powers.

I do not know which of these prospects is the real one: and I suspect that no one else knows either. But if the time-scale is sufficiently extended—to say twenty or even fifty years—the first hypothesis, namely a world containing several nuclear super-powers, seems the more probable. There seems little reason to suppose that such major communities as China, India or a United Western Europe, if it comes into being, would not, *given time*, generate sufficient all-round nuclear capability to be, for practical purposes, the peers of America and Russia. For the fact that America and Russia in the meanwhile had pushed on to still greater heights of nuclear power might not have much practical significance. It would merely enable them to destroy their rivals ten times over while being destroyed only once themselves!

Thus the practical question is probably—though not certainly—one of *time*. How long will America and Russia remain in their present position as the world's only super-powers? On that issue estimates also vary widely, even amongst the experts who do not believe that their predominance will last for ever. I have used the term ' ten or twenty years' to express this period. No doubt it would be more scientific to write 'x years when x = more than ten and less than one hundred'.

On neither of these issues, namely the certainty of the eventual emergence of new super-powers (if they are not prevented) or the likely time period for their emergence, is there any need to be dogmatic. For the same principle of the maximum possible degree of the unification of nuclear power as the sole way of permanently averting nuclear war will apply whether America and Russia have ten or fifty years of natural predominance ahead of them, or even if they have an indefinite period. All that is necessary is that we should consider two possibilities for the unification of nuclear power: (i) as between two rival super-powers and (ii) as between a number.

American-Russian Predominance?

Let us in the first place then examine the possibility of America and Russia taking joint action to stabilize and perpetuate their present nuclear predominance, and in so doing discovering that they have a joint interest in the prevention of nuclear war.

At first sight the possibility of any such a getting together of America and Russia, even for this strictly limited purpose, is too remote to be worth discussing. Their stark mutual hostility, based upon what each supposes the other to be like, much exceeds even the normal degree of mutual hostility between rival nation-states. It stands like a brick wall in the way. It is hard to say which would prove the more intractable obstacle, the violent, largely instinctive American repugnance for communist Russia and all she stands for, or the rigidly thought-out, doctrinaire, repugnance of the communists for capitalist America and all she stands for. In much of recent American practice, and in communist theory and practice, each government has almost invariably and throughout the world supported those national and social forces which the other has opposed, and opposed those forces which the other has supported. How could they possibly combine their wills for even the most strictly limited purpose? If, then, the subject is worth discussing, as I evidently believe that it is, it must be because strong and pervasive forces can be descried which, given time, will tend to overcome this present impasse of extreme mutual hostility. I believe that it is not difficult to identify these forces.

The Indispensable Minimum

First, however, we must be clear about the nature and extent of the task. If nuclear war could only be prevented by a close alliance, or *a fortiori*, by some sort of federation, between America and Russia, the world's situation might indeed be judged to be hopeless. Fortunately far less than this is needed, at any rate, initially. What is indispensable is some form of workable, effective agreement between America and Russia (while they maintain their nuclear predominance):

(*a*) to prevent any other state acquiring or using nuclear arms;

(*b*) to abstain from resorting to their use between themselves.

If they could do that they could pursue their national rivalries as heretofore without destroying themselves, and us. Let us see if there is any method by which this limited goal might be reached during, say, the remaining ten or twenty years in which America and Russia may retain, between them, overwhelming nuclear power as against the rest of the world.

Mr Herman Kahn, who is often, though wholly unjustly, accused of being a nuclear warmonger rather than a pacifist idealist, has actually proposed that the Russian and American Governments should sign a one-clause treaty binding themselves never to use their nuclear weapons except for the coercion of any state which itself used such weapons. This is indeed the essence of the matter. Nevertheless, the signing of such a treaty might mean little in itself: it would only be significant if it gave formal approval to a world policy which the two super-powers were visually pursuing. Moreover there is, surely, a much more practicable and politically acceptable method of approach to this goal? And that is, I repeat, the successful conclusion of a test ban treaty.

Chapter 11 was devoted to showing that the conclusion of a test ban treaty was at once a far more difficult and a far more important thing than is usually realized. For such a treaty would either quickly break down or would commit the American and Russian Governments to a policy of denying nuclear weapons to all other countries in the world. (To begin with, Britain and France might no doubt retain their present small nuclear capacities, but if China, and other potential super-powers, were to be excluded, Britain and France would surely before long have to be 'induced' to give up theirs.) Once the Governments of the two super-powers were embarked upon such a policy as that (acting no doubt through the United Nations) they would find themselves collaborating in one of the most important of all international purposes, namely the prevention of the spread of nuclear weapons.

Moreover this purpose is in effect identical with the concentration of ultimate power in the hands of the two existing super-powers. It is not, in my view, impossible to envisage the

American and Russian Governments, influenced by the developing social forces enumerated below and, in spite of their intense mutual hostility and suspicion, engaging in a policy so naturally attractive to their own self regard and interests. For the two 'top dogs' in any situation, even if they fear each other, may yet combine to prevent any of the other dogs from challenging their joint hegemony. But of course that would only take them part of the way. As well as effectively forbidding everyone else from making nuclear war they would have to show effectively, and by their actions, that they would in no circumstance make nuclear war upon each other. That is a goal still more difficult of attainment, and one towards which an effective test ban treaty would be only a short step. Such a treaty might be completely successful in preventing the spread of the nuclear arms race to the rest of the world, while making only a small contribution to abating the arms race between Russia and America. For those very considerations which would, probably, make it safe enough to sign such a treaty, even with only partially effective inspection provisions, depend for their validity (see Chapter 11 above) upon the fact that the further perfection of the nuclear warheads themselves is not now the main theme of the arms race. What really matters is the perfection and rendering invulnerable of the means of delivery. Therefore, the nuclear arms race might, in principle, continue almost unabated between America and Russia even when they had signed a test ban treaty.

Nevertheless, the conclusion of such a treaty would be a step, at least, towards a truce even between the super-powers themselves. As they learned to co-operate in suppressing the nuclear capabilities of everyone else, they would almost certainly learn a certain toleration for each other. No doubt their world-rivalry would continue for many years; it could be fought out by economic, political, and even, if needs be, by local wars fought by allies and by conventional forces—as has happened already. But the mere fact that a *common purpose*, namely the prevention of anyone else from waging nuclear war, had been recognized would surely have a considerable mitigating effect. It is extraordinary to realize that such an epoch-making event as the conclusion of a test ban treaty came far nearer, at any rate, to consummation than any other recent proposal in the field of disarmament. That is what gives it its quite exceptional importance. A test ban treaty is at one and the same time by far the most important and by far the most practicable disarmament proposal before the world today.

What Sort of a Peace?

Two objections may at once be raised against the better prospects of survival which a test ban treaty would open up before the world. Even if, it may be objected, a test ban treaty might prove the 'growth point' out of which a joint American-Russian world hegemony for the prevention of nuclear war developed, would a world peace so achieved prove either stable or just? The answer is, of course not. What planet do such objectors suppose that they inhabit? This is the earth; if they want perfectly stable and perfectly just solutions to the problem of achieving a long-term peace in the nuclear age they had better try Mars or Venus. They are not likely to find them on earth. What can be said is that the conclusion of a test ban treaty would lead the American and Russian Governments towards the indefinite maintenance of a joint world nuclear hegemony; and this would be a far more stable state of things than either a multi-nuclear world or than the present 'delicate balance of terror'.

A Point of No Return?

Perhaps, however, I should have written 'would have been' rather than 'would be' in the previous sentence. For the attempt to achieve a test ban treaty made at the Geneva Conference, which extended from 1958 to 1962, failed. Russia's fanatical desire to preserve intact the asymmetrical advantage given her by the far greater security possibilities available to her type of 'closed' social system, and her general dissatisfaction with Western predominance in the United Nations, together with Western inability to evaluate sufficiently modestly the whole issue of the inspection of tests, have made the conclusion of a treaty impossible. Accordingly, there are those who, now that Russia's dependence upon the inviolable security of her rather small number of I.C.B.M. sites has been revealed, regard a test ban treaty as an unpromising 'growth point'. But this is, surely, to disregard two possibilities. First there is the possibility of the American authorities being made to realize the relatively 'vacuous' character (to use Brennan's and Halperin's phrase) of the demand for rigorous on-site inspection: and second there is the possibility, indeed probability, that the Russians will supplement and to some extent replace their existing I.C.B.M. sites with inherently invulnerable weapons—of, say, the Polaris-carrying submarine type—and so free themselves from their present extreme dependence upon freedom from inspection.

It would therefore be quite premature to say that the breakdown of the Geneva test ban talks foredoomed to failure all attempts on the part of America and Russia to preserve their effective joint nuclear hegemony. (For that, I repeat, would be the essential effect of a test ban treaty.) At any time during the next few years the American and Russian Governments will be able to come back to the attempt if they wish to do so. And I for one believe that the successful conclusion of such a treaty would do far more to set the feet of the world on to the road which leads towards salvation than any other visible eventuality.

Nevertheless, it must be admitted that the odds may be against the American and Russian Governments signing a test ban treaty before their nuclear hegemony slips away from them. It will be difficult for either Government to recede from the final positions which they have taken up at the Geneva Conference. It is doubtful if either Government appreciates the momentous consequences which the signing of such a treaty would involve. (Perhaps the last consideration is an asset: it may be that they would not have come even as near to success as they did if they had realized that such a treaty would involve them in a long period of collaboration, in this one sphere of nuclear armaments at least!) But the real reason why unfortunately the stabilization of a joint American-Russian nuclear hegemony seems doubtful is the time factor. Those positive forces driving the world towards some sort of unity, in order to escape destruction, will hardly have had time to make a decisive impact, before the American-Russian hegemony has evaporated. For these forces, though very powerful, are slow moving.

The Nuclear World of the Nineteen-seventies

We must therefore face the alternative hypothesis that by, say, the nineteen-seventies or eighties the Russian and American nuclear predominance has slipped, or is slipping, away: that half-a-dozen or so nuclear super-powers occupy the centre of the world stage, and that effective and cheap nuclear capacity threatens to spread to many smaller, poorer and less responsible nation-states (see Chapter 11 above).

The dangers of such a world situation need no emphasis. (Unless the idea of such a world frightens the reader, this is not the book for him.) Clearly the creation of a unique centre of nuclear power would in such conditions be a more complex business than it is today, while only two super-powers are involved. Nevertheless it would be premature to give way to resignation and despair even if things come to this pass. *Given the will*—and by the nineteen-seventies, for reasons to be stated, such a will really may have come into existence—there will still be a way by which a single centre of world nuclear authority might be evolved.

A 'Concert of the World'

Here too, after all, we are not without historical precedents and analogies. Just as there have been 'periods of contending states', in which the maintenance of a balance of power has been the only way to keep, for a while, a precarious peace; and just as there have been knock-out tournaments which have been fought to a finish, so also there have been periods in which peace has been maintained, though not indefinitely, by 'a concert of powers'. The 'concert of Europe' in the nineteenth century is the obvious example. What can be envisaged for the

nineteen-seventies is 'a concert of the world' in which the
nuclear super-powers arrange humanity's affairs amongst themselves (and no doubt to suit themselves) and for that purpose
keep the rest of the world in order, using the United Nations
as their instrument.

There is nothing in itself particularly far-fetched about such
a conception. But we must remember that such a concert of
nuclear super-powers would inevitably have to contain, as
well as America and Russia, Communist China with her at
present really very crude and aggressive set of intentions (see
Chapter 14 above) towards the non-communist world. America
therefore would have had to abandon her fantasy that, somehow, the communist regime in China will disappear if she goes
on pretending that it isn't there. However, we know very little
about what the intentions, attitudes and policies of the American, the Russian or the Chinese Governments, or of the
Governments of the future nuclear super-powers, are likely to
be in the nineteen-seventies. Only too much will no doubt have
happened. But if we are still there we shall all perhaps have
learnt some lessons about what is indispensable to survival in
the nuclear age.

For these reasons it is not even certain that it would be more
difficult for half-a-dozen super-powers in the nineteen-seventies
to form between them some sort of nuclear world authority
than it is for the American and Russian Governments to do so
today. Perhaps such a 'concert', or committee, of nuclear super-
powers would begin to assert its authority in the same way that
America and Russia thought at least of beginning to assert
theirs in the early nineteen-sixties, namely by seeking to prevent
anyone else from acquiring nuclear capacity. And perhaps they
would actually try to do it by a test ban treaty or a 'cut-off' in
nuclear production or both. No doubt the conclusion of such a
treaty between five or six roughly equal nuclear powers would
be in itself more difficult even than the conclusion of such a
treaty between the two super-powers of the 'sixties (and Britain)
proved to be. On the other hand the second part of the requirement for long-term survival might actually be easier to achieve

by six or more such powers than by two. For a treaty (written or established by usage, and no doubt in either case operated through the United Nations) between five or six super-powers must contain at least two provisions. First that the contracting parties bind themselves to prevent any further nation-states from acquiring nuclear capacity. Second that they would set upon, with all their nuclear forces, and so extinguish, anyone of themselves who, for any cause whatsoever and however just that cause might be held to be, resorted to the use of nuclear weapons.

Once again all claims that peace so procured would necessarily be stable or just must be repudiated. These speculations are not travel-bookings for Utopia; they are attempts to descry a gleam of light which might guide us towards the possibility of survival in the nuclear age.

What chances are there of an oligarchy of super-states arising to perform the indispensable function of the creation of a single nuclear authority in the nineteen-seventies, or in some later decade before nuclear wars recur? On the whole, and in spite of the decidedly more complex problem presented by the establishment of such a 'concert of the world', I am inclined to think that the chances of some such development are a little the better of the two possibilities canvassed. And that entirely because of the time factor. Perhaps as many decades will prove to be available—if we set ourselves with iron determination to improve the stability of the balance meanwhile—for such a development to come to pass as there are years available for the establishment of the alternative American-Russian joint nuclear hegemony. And it is time above all that we need.

The Nature of World Power

At this point in the argument it is indispensable to spell out the conception of world power as it is used in these pages. Otherwise it may be said that when it comes to the point all that is being suggested is some sort of functional world authority engaged in enforcing a test ban treaty, or a nuclear cut-off, relying upon the authority of either the two existing super-powers or of a concert of five or six future super-powers. This *is* indeed what is suggested in the first instance; but only as the growth point out of which a real, political, world authority may develop. And this not merely because without a real, political, authority the prevention of nuclear war could not be accomplished but also because there can be, in the supreme, nuclear, sphere at any rate, no such thing, in the long run, as a limited functional authority.

The truth is that there can be, *in principle*, no limitation upon power. If, that is to say, America and Russia, or five or six super-powers jointly, were able, and did in fact, prevent the rest of the world from acquiring nuclear capability then they would be able, in theory at least, to prevent it from doing anything else either. There is no way, no paper constitution, no safeguard, by means of which, if once nuclear authority is being exercised over the world, that authority can be circumscribed. Power, much more than peace, is *in principle* indivisible. Nevertheless, this alarming conclusion would be much mitigated *in practice* by the size and complexity of the world. In practice our super-powers would be hard put to it indeed to do more than enforce that one indispensable commandment of our epoch— 'thou shalt not make nuclear war'. They would *have* to leave a great deal of freedom to the local governments of the world. We may rely on this not because we should trust their good intentions, but because those local governments would be so many, so different and, we may be sure, so 'difficult'.

Moreover, initially of course America and Russia, or the concert of five or six super-powers, would have differing and conflicting purposes, so that the rest of the world could, and no doubt would, retain a great deal of freedom by playing off one against another, as indeed they do now. But this sort of freedom would be highly dangerous, since it would inevitably tend towards the break-up of the emergent world authority. The fact is that either the super-powers would have to resist those divisive pressures and by so doing grow into a firmer and firmer authority, or the world would break down again into its present state of nature.

The Credibility of World Power

And this brings us back again to the question of whether or not
it is credible that such a world authority or world power—call
it what you will—can ever exist. To many people it is blankly
incredible. Sir William Hayter has been instanced as a per-
suasive, though regretful, spokesman of this scepticism. And in
fact no serious man supposes that out of the world as it is today,
in 1962, any effective world authority can suddenly be created.
But what is being obstinately maintained in these pages is that
the conditions out of which such an authority might gradually
emerge both could and should be created. Or as we have put it
above, that our present and immediate policies should *aim* at
this ideal rather than at the more familiar ideal of 'a totally
disarmed world of totally sovereign states'. This is the real
issue. No one can prove that we can reach the goal of a world
authority. All that can be shown is that this is a possible goal,
or ideal, at which to aim, free of those self contradictions which
experience has shown to inhere in the goal of the general and
complete disarmament of completely sovereign states.

In conclusion it may be worth observing that all such major
changes in human organization as an ending of the state of
nature in which sovereign nation-states must live seem incredible and impossible, until they happen. For example there
have been several fundamental changes in the social relations
within which the productive process by which men live has been
carried on. And each such change seemed inconceivable till it
occurred. Thus a Roman patrician could not conceive of a
world without slavery. But slavery was in the end abolished. A
feudal lord could not conceive of the mercantile world, governed
by contract, of the nineteenth century, yet it came into existence. The theorists of the nineteenth and early twentieth
centuries could not conceive of a world of planned economic
activity depending hardly at all on market forces; yet nearly
one-third of the human race now lives in such a world. (And
the verdict of history upon this last change may prove to be that
both the advantages and disadvantages of the new relations of

production as compared to a market world are limited! Yet Professor von Mises, by no means a stupid man, wrote learned works to prove the inherent impossibility of a fully planned economy some years after the Russians had established one.)

In the same way we may suppose that difficult as it is for us to conceive of it, yet a world-wide authority strong enough to prevent the outbreak of recurrent nuclear war may yet be set up before human civilization has destroyed itself. Perhaps one of the obstacles to conceiving of such a development lies in the habit of Western thought of looking at things in their being or not being, rather than in their becoming. This somewhat static way of looking at things predisposes us to believe that because the reality which we have always known is that of sovereign states living in a state of nature, this is reality itself, with which it is foolish to quarrel. But things do change. Human society has already taken on very various forms: it may be possible that it will change again, or can be made to change, in this vital respect. *How* such major social changes occur we do not exactly know. The historical record seems to show that they usually happen by a combination of relatively slow development, punctuated by brief periods of much faster and more disconcerting change. Of one thing we may be certain however. Such changes do not happen of themselves. Unless there are real and powerful social forces at work making in the direction of the change in question, it will indeed be a waste of time to discuss it, however clearly it can be shown that existing society is doomed unless the change takes place. Are any powerful forces, then, making towards that unification of the world which has, so suddenly but so obviously, become a condition of our survival? I believe that there are. The last task of this book is to identify these social forces.

20

Three Forces of Hope

The Three Forces

THE reflections contained in the last chapter are intended to illustrate the kind of way in which the recurrence of nuclear war might be avoided. As such there is little point in elaborating them. For in practice no doubt the real development of events, if it be toward world unification, by either of the routes suggested, will be different, and probably much more subtle. For example one can imagine a mixture between the two possibilities, in which America and Russia retained some of their nuclear predominance, but four or five new nuclear super-powers formed a 'concert' of power for the preservation of world peace, under their joint presidency as it were.

What is essential is not the form which the single authority might take, or even the number and character of the nuclear super-powers on which it must initially be based. What is essential is that the super-powers, be they two or several, should, either *de facto* or *de jure*, progressively sink that aspect of their sovereignty which enables them to wage nuclear war independently. In practice no written treaty and no international institution could in themselves accomplish this. The fact of world unification would have to emerge out of the practice of the states concerned, while no doubt embodying and supporting itself in treaties and supra-national institutions.

Be all that as it may, the function of these remaining pages

is not to continue such speculations but to identify social forces
which may in due course make possible some such 'world-unity-
for-the-limited-purpose-of-survival'. For unless such forces
exist, and can be counted upon to push and press us in this
direction, then, it must be conceded, it would be a waste of
breath to consider the matter further. I believe that there are
in fact three kinds of social forces at work in the contemporary
world which, *given time*, may be relied upon to erode or to over-
ride the immense obstacles which today stand in the way of
the establishment of even the most limited degree of world
authority. Whether they will have *time* to do so is another
matter: but the speed and efficacy with which existing social
forces can be brought to bear is precisely the kind of issue which
we can ourselves effect, perhaps decisively, by taking thought.
The three social forces which can be relied upon to push the
world in the direction of collaboration under the authority of
some nucleus (in both senses of that word) of world power are
these. First, there is a tendency for the economic and social
systems of the advanced, industrialized nation-states to approximate to each other, whether they are organized in the communist or the capitalist way. Secondly, there is the sheer dread
of nuclear war. And thirdly, and in the long run most important, a new attitude of mind is emerging, an attitude transcending both national and ideological loyalties; an attitude of mind
essentially concerned to find a way in which the human race
may hope to continue to inhabit its narrow planet. Let us very
briefly consider these three forces in turn.

The Convergence of Contemporary Societies

Many of the rulers, spokesmen and prophets, and many of the
people also, of the Western and the communist nation-states
respectively, believe that they inhabit societies of an antithetical
kind. It is supposed that alike in respect of their ideologies, of
their political arrangements and of their economic foundations, America and Russia—to take the representative societies
of the two kinds—are antithetical in principle. Most Americans
profess, though not usually with great precision, a creed of

competitive free enterprise and suppose that they inhabit a society exemplifying such a creed. Communists, on the other hand, profess, usually only too precisely, a creed under the tenets of which competition, the price mechanism, and above all any private or 'free' economic enterprise, involving the individual ownership of the means of production, are anathema. They suppose that they live in a society which is in the process of extirpating the last traces of these abominations, and which is about to enter a Utopia of moneyless, priceless, classless communism, in which the distribution of goods and services will be effected upon the principle of 'to each according to their needs, from each according to their abilities'.

To an observer of these great societies, their real situation and probable course of development must seem very different. It would be far outside the scope of this volume to attempt to analyse either the Russian or the American economies and societies. But it is becoming something of an open secret amongst the more sophisticated economists and sociologists, on both sides of the curtain, who engage in this task, that, deep and real as their differences still are, the two economies are by no means antithetical. Above all, they appreciate that the differences between them though still wide are tending to decrease. Thus the American economy is a long way from the freely competitive 'model' of the classical economists, and would immediately collapse if it attempted to approximate to that model. On the other hand the growing success of the Russian economy in the *production* of goods and services is forcing it increasingly towards the introduction of some kind of price mechanism and competitive process. Nor will this process be much affected if the Russian Government decides, as it now proposes, to distribute some particular good or service, say bread or urban transport, free. For 'free' in this context means merely 'paid for out of taxation'. After all we in Britain have done the same thing already in the case of medical attention. And there is much to be said, in my opinion, for doing so in respect of certain commodities in certain social circumstances. Yet by and large, *and increasingly as the affluence and complexity of a society grows*, the advantages of the price mechanism (duly supervised and controlled) will appear compelling. Moreover, paradoxically, these advantages will be greatest in societies like Russia in which, for the present at least, relatively little inherited, unearned income exists.

Still more strikingly the type of 'executives' who must be found to manage the huge corporations or enterprises of both systems, and of the technicians and scientists who staff them, however owned, are seen to be approximating. Naturally so, for not only their conditions of work, their administrative and technical problems, but also the actual motives which actuate them are becoming similar. It is true that the motives of a representative capitalist, such as Engels used to meet in the hunting fields of Cheshire one hundred years ago (see *Marx-Engels Correspondence*, p. 86, Martin Lawrence, 1934), were very different from those of a present-day manager of a great Soviet enterprise. The Lancashire magnate then really did obey the dictates of sheer self-enrichment under the profit motive pretty faithfully. He owned his mill: what he paid his hands he could not pay himself: what he paid himself he could not pay his hands. Marx drew a lifelike and not wholly unflattering portrait of him in the first volume of *Capital*. Contrast the motives of the typical salaried executive of a present-day American, or British, major enterprise—a McNamara, a Paul Chambers, a Beeching, a Robert Shone—moving back and forth between commercial and governmental employment, with often unimportant holdings in the corporation he is at the moment managing, trying to decide upon the division of his gross proceeds between the claims of the organized workers, the pension fund, the salariat, re-investment for expansion, and the shareholders; his own salary wholly unaffected by the decision at which he arrives (or more realistically by the decision which is forced upon him and his board by the balance of the pressures exercised upon them).

We are less familiar with the habits of life and motivations of the Russian 'manager' of the second half of the twentieth century. No doubt some of his preoccupations and anxieties are

different. He will have much less trouble with his trade unions:
he has no shareholders to consider. But on the other hand there
is his Government! It taxes him, just as other Governments do—
and no worse perhaps. But then there are the planners, for
ever setting him unattainable targets, badgering, hectoring,
coercing him. They are for him what catering to the whims of
the consumer are to his Western brother under the skin. And
the planners, we may be sure, have their whims too: Mr
Khruschev loses his majority in the Praesidium—and everyone
is all for heavy industry again: he regains his majority in the
Central Committee—and light industry is restored to favour;
and so on. Worry for worry there may not be much in it.
Then again as to security of tenure—well, the Western manager
has the take-over bidder breathing down his neck. But the
Russian may have betted on the wrong man in the latest party
struggle. Either may lose his job—neither is particularly likely
to. But at any rate is it not obvious that both have far more in
common with each other than with their respective nineteenth
century 'individual' capitalist forebears? Both are well-paid,
overworked, *officials*—with precious little to do with the
entrepreneur of the textbooks. The development of the two
economies is seen to be convergent not divergent. Their respective priests and prophets may be confronted before long with
disconcerting similarities.

In good Marxist theory, of course, this convergence in the
development of the economic bases of the two societies ought
automatically to produce a convergence in their respective
political and ideological superstructures. Unfortunately there
is growing evidence to show that this Marxist Law of social
development works more slowly and uncertainly than was fore-
seen by its author. It is to be feared that very different political
systems, and above all ideologies, may be sustained for long
periods upon rather similar economic foundations. So far at
any rate there is little convergence in the political systems of
these two leading societies of their respective types. The main
differences between Russia and America today are not in the
way their economies are managed but in the existence of what

we call democracy, and the communists call a dictatorship of
the capitalists, in America, and of what they call 'a people's
democracy', and we call a dictatorship of the communist party,
in Russia. However, *given time*, we should feel some confidence
that there will be convergence in this intermediate, political
layer of the social structure also; that some form of effective,
competitive popular representation, with the civil liberties
associated with it, will one day develop in Russia and that
a growing predominance of the popular, political forces over
big business will develop in America. It is at the top, or ideological, layer of the social structure that convergence is likely
to be most difficult and most delayed. The capacity of men to
believe what they are told about both their own and other
people's societies, without looking at either to see what they
are really like, is very great. One can imagine only too easily
weary decades of mutual abuse between American and
Russian protagonists of systems which, to the outside observer,
were becoming increasingly similar.

Indeed the immediate prospect in America seems, in 1962, to
be an intensification of what may perhaps be called professional anti-communism. The hard facts of the world balance of
power in the nuclear age will inevitably deflect and on occasion frustrate the policies and purposes of the American Government. A section at least of American public opinion tends to
react by showing signs of hysteria. As it becomes clear that it
will be less and less possible to use the United Nations to promote what are, largely, Western purposes, even when those
purposes seem, to us at least, undoubtedly beneficent: when it
becomes impossible any longer to keep communist China out:
when Russia and her allies begin to attempt to use the United
Nations for *their* purposes, instead of as at present, merely to
attempt to prevent it from being used for *our* purposes, a strong
American reaction against both the United Nations and international action generally is likely. In such circumstances some
American opinion tends to 'take out' its frustrations upon the
by now nearly non-existent scapegoat of the American Communist Party and its associates. This might be a fairly harmless

practice were it not for the never-neglected opportunity which it gives for the most reactionary forces in the Union to attempt to destroy all native American liberalism at the same time. If this proves difficult, then the disastrous demand for a world anti-communist crusade, which either means little or early nuclear war, is raised. We must probably contrive to live through, during the nineteen-sixties, as best we may, a good deal of this sort of thing on the part of exceedingly vocal elements in American society. The sole anti-communist crusade which is needed, or which can possibly succeed, is of course the converse of all this. It consists above all in so steadily and continuously improving and reforming our societies that the communist regimes make no appeal to Western wage-earners, while taking care that the military balance of power is held even and stable. And in fact the West has been, on the whole, very successful so far in doing these two things. But we have done so, and must continue to do so, by methods which, in respect of the economic foundations of our societies, involve an important degree of convergence between the systems.

All this does not mean that the convergence of the systems has even come into sight of the point at which a communist regime would be tolerable to the wage-earners of the West. (We have just (1961) had striking evidence of this from the people of East Germany.) And conversely it may be that our type of society would be unsuitable for present-day Russians. But it does mean that an intention, on the part of either side, forcibly to impose the one society, or 'way of life', upon the other, at the almost certain cost of the destruction of both, will be increasingly seen by everyone who retains his sanity as a paranoiac's nightmare.

Thus if Russia and America were alone in question we might feel some confidence in a long-run erosion of the mutual hostility and suspicion which today stands squarely in the way of that degree of collaboration which is their, and our, prerequisite of survival. The question is, will the convergence reach *in time* a point at which, for example, both can see a plain common interest, such as the preservation of their present joint nuclear hegemony, when it stares them in the face. Unless it proceeds a good deal faster than it looks like doing, the convergence will be too late to preserve that hegemony. From then on it will be a question of the character and development of the Chinese, the West European, the Indian, the Japanese and perhaps some other, societies, as well as the American and the Russian. Once again, taking the long view, we may feel confidence in a process of convergence. These industrialized or industrializing societies cannot help themselves from showing ever-growing similarities. But it must be admitted that for a decade or so, and for practical political purposes, the attitudes and policies of the Chinese communist Government, in particular, are likely to present a most intractable problem for the rest of the world, including as we have seen already, her own ally Russia. The Chinese communists seem very much in the frame of mind exhibited by the Russian communists in the early nineteen-thirties. Their mental development may be a longer process, even, than the physical development of their vast territory.

Thus it would be folly to rely upon the process of convergence in the character of the industrialized or industrializing societies *automatically* to remove, in time, the formidable obstacles which stand in the way of human survival in the nuclear age. In itself such convergence would be likely to act too slowly to save us. And even if convergent social development had eroded altogether the special causes of antagonism between Russia and America, or between the new super-powers, it would still leave them normal, rival nation-states. Between such nation-states recurrent war has been habitual.

The Dread of Nuclear War

A much more powerful and immediate force makes the matter of world unification worthy, at least, of discussion. And that is simply the dread of nuclear war. For this dread provides the main immediate motive for all the attempts which are being made to find some way of preventing, or at least postponing, the outbreak of nuclear war.

Yet as a matter of fact how much *do* people dread the

outbreak of nuclear war? How much do I dread it? How much does the reader of these lines dread it? How much do we dread it in the sense of being moved *to act* in some way, as for example, to modify some of our fixed opinions and prejudices, or to sacrifice some of our interests, in order to avoid it? (The supporters of unilateral nuclear disarmament are undoubtedly so moved to act. But unfortunately their actions are doomed, as we have noted, to be barren (see Chapter 9 above).) It is very difficult to answer such questions. No doubt there is a general dread of nuclear war, common to both peoples and governments, which makes them markedly cautious in their international conduct. On the whole, probably, the governments are more alive to the real nature of the human predicament in the nuclear age than are the people: for men in public life, officials, commanders of the armed forces and diplomatists have had to make some acquaintance with the probable consequences of nuclear war. The popular reaction seems to fluctuate between passive horror and indifference. This may be because, except at moments of crises, this is too painful a subject to hold in the mind.

These are reasons against relying, as some even informed observers rely, almost exclusively upon the dread of nuclear war as an automatic and adequate assurance that the catastrophe will not come upon us. But of course this dread is a very real and a very valuable factor in the situation. It is to be hoped that it will grow symmetrically on both sides. It should do so, in all conscience. For the world during the first seventeen years of the nuclear age has passed from one crisis to another; and it is bound to continue to do so as long as it is composed of wholly sovereign nation-states. When moreover, as now, these states are, as to the most powerful of them, marshalled into two intensely hostile coalitions, what other results can we expect than what we get, namely recurrent crises?

These words are being written in early 1962 amidst the renewed Berlin crisis. The book was begun towards the end of 1959 during a relatively stable and peaceful interlude between crises. Thus the very simple prophecy (p. 5 above), that even while the book was being written the world would swing between a complacent belief that nuclear war was too remote a contingency to take seriously, and a panic view that it was likely within a few weeks or months has been fulfilled. There is little to be gained by trying to assess the degree of danger to which each particular crisis subjects the world. What is important to realize is that in the world as it is, periodic crises, such as we have experienced since 1948—Berlin, Korea, Indo-China, Suez, Hungary, the U2 incident, Berlin again—to list a few, are normal and must be expected to recur indefinitely. They are the predictable results of the international anarchy in general and of the rivalry of the two super-powers and their attendant allies in particular.

The writer of such a book as this must perforce assume that each of these crises will continue for some time to be solved without resort to full-scale nuclear war: for on any other assumption his book will never be read. But can the world really continue to live like this? It is no answer to say that the world always has. In the first place, as we have noted, it has not. The recurrent wars which the international anarchy in this or that 'known world' has invariably produced have usually in the end ruined all but one of the states which engaged in them and so raised one of them, by process of elimination, to an *imperium*. (And these were the relatively harmless, by comparison almost playful, wars of the pre-nuclear age! And even they had serious consequences on the quality of each civilization as it fought its way towards unification.) In the second place this is the nuclear age and the fact the world survived hitherto in spite of the recurrence of war is irrelevant to our situation.

International Fusion at High Temperatures

It may indeed be argued that the recurrence of crises, each of which, on the above necessary assumption, will have been 'solved' somehow or other without the outbreak of full-scale nuclear war, far from mobilizing the general dread, may dull the apprehensions of people and governments by causing them to assume that such crises always will be solved. If so, the outlook is dark. We can only hope that men will realize that the historical evidence (think of the twenty years before 1939 and the twenty years before 1914 for instance) suggests that the fact that a dozen, or a score, of crises have been solved peacefully is no reason to suppose that the thirteenth or the twenty-first will not result in general war. Perhaps men's reactions will largely depend upon *the way* in which the crises are resolved. Paradoxically the possibility of international action sufficiently drastic to break continuity and create a new frame of reference for the world, may depend on some of the crises taking us to the edge itself of nuclear war—or even half over it. Nothing less than an extreme shock, or series of shocks, may prove enough to shake the world into a new pattern.

In this connexion we may perhaps borrow an analogy from thermonuclear physics itself. It takes a temperature of many millions of degrees to cause the atoms of hydrogen to fuse, and in so doing, give off energies of a different order of magnitude from which we have previously known how to create. In the same way it may be that the international temperature will have to rise, even repeatedly, to agonizing heights, in which the danger of human destruction will be immediate, explicit and for all to see, before even that first, very incomplete, stage of international fusion which has been postulated above will become practicable. But at thermonuclear international temperatures those intractable atoms, the major nation-states, whether communist or Western, may begin to melt and fuse sufficiently to enable the core of a world authority to be established within the United Nations.

The Exercise of World Power

The above considerations press us towards the agonizing view that some such unforgettable experience as the destruction of a city or a country, in a nuclear war which was then, somehow, arrested, may, though heaven forbid it, have to be endured before men will face the necessities of survival in the nuclear age. If our folly and complacency proves otherwise ineradicable, some such ghastly lesson may prove necessary.

For the sole way of avoiding such disaster is, precisely, to foresee it imaginatively and then take the indispensable action necessary to forestall it. And men are not very imaginative. That is why it is the reverse of helpful to criticize those defence experts whose duty it is to foresee disaster and then propose an attempt to develop some form of world unity in order to prevent it. It is unhelpful to criticize them first for being un-realistic dreamers who suppose that a world authority is a possibility, and then for being cynical monsters because, in their pessimistic moments, they concede that it may prove only too true that it may take the shock of catastrophe to make it an actuality.

The shock of catastrophe may, alas, prove to be necessary, not only because of the immense difficulties which have been discussed but because of a simple, but very harsh, necessity as to the way in which such an authority would have to act once it had come into being. How, it is sometimes asked, would any such authority even if it could be evolved enforce its will and so prevent the outbreak of nuclear war? There can be only one answer. It has been given, curiously enough, by Bertrand Russell. In his recent book *Has Man a Future?* Russell writes:

. . . it seems indubitable that scientific man cannot long survive unless all the major weapons of war, and all the means of mass determination [destruction? J.S.] are in the hands of a single authority which, in consequence of its monopoly, would have irresistible power and, if challenged to war, could wipe out any rebellion within a few days without much danger except to the rebels. This, it seems plain, is an absolutely indispensable condition of the continued existence of a world possessed of scientific skill.

In other words a world authority, founded initially on the nuclear capability of the super-powers of the day, could only, in the last resort, enforce its authority by the threat, which it must be seen to be ready to execute, of wiping out rebellion by nuclear means. This is a stiff dose to swallow. It may be that only the shock of the beginning of a nuclear war will bring mankind to swallow it. In any case the sole way of avoiding the necessity of such desperate—and desperately dangerous—

shock treatment is for us to realize Russell's necessity imaginatively, in advance, so that we do not have to learn our lesson
the hard way. But is mankind capable of this kind of creative
imagination?

And yet if we could face the facts of our situation it is plain
that Russell is indisputably right in believing that a world
authority, however it developed, could not function unless it
was able and willing in the last resort to use nuclear weapons
against anyone who rebelled against it. Equally, however, it
would never in fact have to use such means if it were known to
be willing to do so. As was pointed out on page 167 above such
an authority, calling itself no doubt the United Nations, but in
fact constituted by the nuclear super-powers of the day, would
have at its disposal a long series of sanctions of ever-growing
severity which it would and could employ against a recalcitrant
nation-state long before the subject of nuclear punishment was
ever mentioned. Compliance would almost certainly come
before there was any need to use what the old diplomatists
used to call 'the language of menace'. Or rather, early and
prompt compliance would come if there were no doubt in
anyone's mind that the ultimate sanction of nuclear punishment could and would be applied if necessary. If the separate,
and no doubt still often-conflicting, purposes of the super-
powers, or a misplaced shrinking from the use of nuclear
weapons even for the purpose of enforcing the pacification of
the world, were to leave any doubt in anyone's mind of the
consequences of defiance, then alone would the possibility or
actually having to use them, arise.

There is another reason why this issue of *how* the will of a
world authority should be enforced cannot be slurred over. The
issue would arise at the earliest stage of the development of such
an authority. Let us suppose that matters had gone no further
than the signature of a test ban treaty by the existing nuclear
powers. As we saw in Chapter 11 such a treaty would quickly
become meaningless unless it was adhered to by all the *non-*
nuclear powers as well, so that in fact it arrested the diffusion of
nuclear weapons. But what if a particular state refused to

adhere and thus proclaimed its intention of producing its own nuclear capability? In the last resort its adherence would have to be imposed by means of progressively severe sanctions leading towards—though no doubt in practice never needing to reach— the threat of nuclear punishment. Unless and until the nuclear powers are willing to enforce, in the last resort, nuclear dis- armament on the rest of the world, even this first stage of the development of a world authority is impossible. But granted such a willingness the actual process of enforcement would be relatively easy. It is the establishment of the common will that is difficult, not its exercise.

These possibilities depend upon the second of the forces of hope which we have identified, namely, the dread of nuclear war. The problem is to convert that dread from maintaining at best a mere balance of terror between the nuclear powers, into the dread of condign punishment by a pacifying authority.

The Growth of a World Loyalty

An attempt to identify a positive urge to world unity must take us back to historical precedent and analogy.

Long before the various 'known worlds' were unified politi- cally, they had become single 'societies', or 'civilizations'—call them what you will—in the sense that the citizens of the still- contending nation-states were in intercourse with each other, knew about each other pretty well, had important trading relations, had to a greater or lesser extent common ideas, even sometimes a common literature, often a common religion. Moreover they had usually a common basis for their economies, in the sense of a prevailing 'relation of production', such as slavery in the Hellenic world, various types of feudalism in medieval Christendom, or the capitalistic relation of owners and wage-earners in the European-Atlantic nation-states during recent centuries. The fact of having so much in common has never prevented the national units of such civilizations from fighting each other: but it has often, as time went on, given their struggles an internecine or 'civil war' aspect, which has become more and more shocking to the more discerning spirits among their peoples. One cannot fail to notice the growth of this attitude of mind in, for instance, the later stage of the inter-Hellenic struggles—in Thucydides for instance—or amongst the ablest men in the fourteenth and fifteenth-century Italian contending city-states, of whom Machiavelli is the type; or in the first half of the twentieth century in the European-Atlantic world. Or again it appears that horror at the consequences of the wars of the local Indian nation-states was one at least of the inspirations of the Buddha, as it was certainly one of the inspirations of his great pacifying disciple the Emperor Asoka.

Who can doubt that as we enter the second half of the twentieth century, a world-wide society, or world civilization, in this sense, is now appearing for the first time in human history? Already the traveller of the nineteen-sixties, using hours upon his journeys where even his father used months, may on the whole be more surprised at the similarities which he will discover between the parts of the contemporary world than with their diversities. If he goes to New Delhi, to Moscow, to New York, to London, Rome, Frankfurt or Paris, to Cairo or to Lagos, to Sydney, to Rio de Janeiro, or even to Peking, he will find, at the upper directing end of society, not very different kinds of men engaged on not very different kinds of work. He will find them reading the news of the same events in their newspapers (though presented with very different biases); moved by decreasingly dissimilar forms of art and literature, reading, wherever they are allowed to, many of the same books, learning almost exactly the same scientific laws for the control of natural forces, and beginning to be aware that the various religions which some of them continue to profess are parallel attempts to give an insight into the nature of ultimate reality. What can all this mean but a startlingly rapid coming into being of a single world civilization?

Of course the differences between one part of the world and another are still very great. Above all the degree to which man's suddenly achieved command over natural forces has been applied differs vastly between say the Congo and the Ruhr. Over vast areas the majority of mankind, still peasant, is only now stirring from neolithic methods of production (nevertheless they are stirring): in other areas whole communities have lifted themselves above the level of primary poverty. Thus it is true that for the time being the differences of economic level are growing rather than diminishing. This is not, however, because the undeveloped countries are becoming still more undeveloped, but because the speed of their development cannot keep pace with what is, by all previous standards, the headlong further development of the already well developed countries. In every other respect the common features of a world society are obviously, rapidly and undeniably increasing. To test that assertion one has only to cast the mind back a mere two hundred years. We may compare the degree of familiarity between different parts of the world now and in the eighteenth century. It may be recalled that the great civilizations of Asia were then still largely ignorant of the very existence of the European-Atlantic civilization. Orme recounts that the Nawab of Bengal, Surajah Dowlah, could say that he did not believe that the whole of Europe contained as many as ten thousand inhabitants; and the Emperor of China could reply to Lord Macartney's embassy with the exquisite condescension of the Lord of the world hearing, with interest, of the praiseworthy efforts of remote barbarians to put themselves into touch with urbanity. Or again, if we go back less than another three centuries we may compare the world's present knowledge of itself with the apparition of the horsemen of Cortés amidst the well-established Aztec civilization of Central America, as if they had been men from Mars riding their flying saucers.

The Schism

The now rapid growth of a world society, or civilization, is obvious. But what, it will be immediately objected, of the great schism which has divided the world into communist and non-communist nations? which threatens to destroy the world in a nuclear war of ideology? that schism with which the pages of this book have been, perforce, so largely concerned? Has not this schism arrested the growth of a world society? Are the communists and the more extreme ideologists of the West not right in supposing that it has to be ended by the conversion of the one side to the faith of the other, or by the extirpation of the schismatics at the hands of the orthodox (whichever they may be considered to be), before a world society can come into being?

The readers will be aware by now that it is a main thesis of this book that the communists, and those who may, perhaps, be called 'the counter-communists' of the West, who concur in this judgement, have turned out to be wrong. The development of events *might* no doubt have gone this way. Capitalism, as it certainly seemed to be doing in the nineteen-thirties, might have gone into ever-steeper decline, leading to the intolerable excesses of Fascist regimes, and thus demonstrating that there was no way out until it had been got rid of. Or again the night-mare elements in the Stalinist regime—now officially recog-nized to have existed by the Soviet leaders themselves—might have led to a breakdown of communism in Russia, thus demonstrating that men simply could not live in that way. Neither event happened. Both systems have to a considerable degree pulled themselves together: neither, it may be guessed, is now intolerable to its inhabitants. Neither to be sure is by any means ideal; indeed, as has just been emphasized, both are beginning to exhibit interestingly similar advantages and defects. But for this very reason it seems more and more un-likely that the inhabitants of either system (except in some marginal areas where each is working particularly badly: for instance East Germany and to some extent Eastern Europe as a whole on the communist side, South Korea and some parts of South America perhaps, on the non-communist side) would be willing to make major sacrifices in order to substitute the one for the other. If the systems fight, as they easily may, destroying themselves and us with them, they will be largely fighting for the familiar, age-old, reasons which have always caused, and always must cause, fully sovereign nation-states to fight, rather than because either is engaging in a genuine crusade to extir-pate the other's heresy.

Such considerations will incline us to the view that the schism between the communist and non-communist worlds will not after all prove a decisive barrier to the growth of a world society. It will be transcended by the growing similarities between the advanced industrialized societies, whether communist or not, by the emergence of hitherto undeveloped major nation-states, such as India, with intermediate or original social and economic systems of their own, and by, above all, a growing realization that the promotion of neither communism nor counter-communism by physical force is permissible in the nuclear world.[1] This is the supreme lesson to be learnt both by ourselves in the West and by the communists. Neither side has learnt it yet. It may be mere Western prejudice but it seems probable that the lesson will be even more difficult for the communists to learn than for us, if only because of the explicit, written, precise character of their doctrine. For of course this view of the *relative* insignificance of the forcible promotion of the communist or anti-communist creeds, as compared to the prevention of full-scale nuclear war, is something extremely difficult for a communist theoretician to entertain. It flatly contradicts the central communist thesis of the absolute primacy of the class struggle: of the necessity of reaching a decision in that struggle before anything else can be done.

It is true that the present Soviet leaders have reached the point of enunciating the doctrine that the issue need not be fought out on a world scale by means of war. How great an advance this is can be seen by comparing it with the still traditionalist-communist attitude of the Chinese authorities (see Chapter 14 above). Nevertheless, this advance will not suffice. The communist leaders, and their Western 'counter-communist' equivalents, must go further.

Communists have hitherto unshakeably believed that a

---

[1] Is not this, it may be objected, almost identical with what the unilateralists sometimes say? Yes, it is. But they suppose that this realization can be unilateral on the part of the West. To be effective the realization must be not only bi-lateral but multilateral throughout the world.

fanatical, stop-at-nothing-hatred on the part of the possessing classes for the rising pretensions to power of the wage-earning masses, made it impossible to move an inch forward towards the unification of the world, and so to peace (or of course towards social justice within the nation-states) until 'all capitalist resistance has been crushed'. No one who has had practical experience of contemporary politics is likely to suppose that fear and dislike of the wage-earners on the part of the rich is a figment of the communists' imagination. But equally to any cool observer the experience of the last two decades in particular offers weighty evidence that at least in the favoured West (and apparently, by a sort of miracle, in India also) it is not after all necessary to fight out the class war to a finish in order to move forward both within and between the nations of the world. And this alters everything. Together with the increasingly similar results of the communist and non-communist ways of running industrialized societies, it reduces communism to simply one way, and not necessarily the most attractive way, of managing contemporary societies. This is a hard saying for a communist even to consider. Mr Khruschev recently (summer 1961) told a visiting delegation of Arab notables that 'Communism is sacred'. He and his colleagues will have to discover that this is just what it is not—in the same way as angry senators or officers of the U.S. Air Force, or West German, or British, big business-men, or French generals, will have to discover that it is not infamous either. Communism is just a very large fact of the twentieth century which has to be dealt with and lived with like all the other facts.

A Witness

What hope is there for nuclear man unless this cool, empirical attitude to the main contemporary schism in our emergent world society is somehow achieved? No doubt it will not be achieved tomorrow or next day: nevertheless it is beginning to develop. A remarkable example of this development came during 1961 from an unlikely source. In most cases those usually un-fortunate men and women who 'defect'—as the technical term has it—from the communist to the non-communist world, or vice versa, have little to tell us about the world they leave, except the bare fact that they did not like it. Exceptionally, however, one recent Russian defector, a Mr Lenchevsky, did have something to tell us of very great value. It concerned not only the Russia which he most reluctantly left, but the world's predicament. The political paragraphs of a letter which he addressed to Mr Khruschev, ran as follows:

> I am unable any longer to continue to subscribe to the doctrine of a merciless and irreconcilable class and anti-religious struggle, carried to holocaustic lengths, which forms a foundation-stone of communist teaching, both theoretical and political.
>
> I am possessed by the conviction that every kind of intolerance towards any kind of person, be it even for the sake of the loftiest ideals, is nothing but a tremendous anachronism in our atomic and space age, which has come upon us so suddenly—an anachronism which can only be explained by the existence of a certain time-gap between human thinking and reality.
>
> I am profoundly convinced, Nikita Sergeyevich, that only the greatest tolerance towards all heterodox individuals, including even those whose thought is hostile, is the only means of salvation for humanity from mass fratricide and degeneration—both physical and moral—and that no alternative exists in our age.
>
> I have for you very great respect, as a person who sincerely loves our people and strives in such an energetic manner to achieve a better life for them, as well as for the populations of the rest of the world, but, alas, by the use of completely non-contemporary conceptions and methods, as it seems to me.
>
> I believe, Nikita Sergeyevich, that in the course of time you will agree with me on many points!
>
> Forgive me!
>
> O. Lenchevsky.

Mr Lenchevsky has hit the nail upon the head, to use our English colloquialism, with a blow that should resound throughout the world. It is not that the communist doctrine of the necessity of fighting out the class war to a finish is wicked, foolish or falcaious: all that is after all a matter of opinion: it is simply that it is 'a tremendous anachronism in our atomic and space age which has come upon us so suddenly'. 'The

greatest tolerance' even to 'those whose thought is hostile' is
now not only a virtue as it always has been: it is a simple prerequisite for survival. To all the crusaders and the counter-
crusaders we must never cease to say what Mr Lenchevsky has
said in effect to Mr Khruschev—'you are no doubt fine fellows
—your intentions are admirable—but alas, you are going about
the job "by the use of completely non-contemporary conceptions and methods"!'

An orthodox communist would no doubt reply that he was
very ready to be tolerant, as soon as 'the Imperialists' showed
any sign of being tolerant too: but that that could never be. No
balanced view of the history of the past half century could deny
that this argument has had force. The major capitalist societies
have repeatedly shown themselves intolerant of the existence
of the Soviet Union and have not hesitated to use violent
methods in the attempt to get rid of it. But what the communists of China completely, and those of Russia partially, are
unable as yet to comprehend is that this period is over. Very
largely of course because of the sheer strength and size of the
communist societies, but also because of the above described
convergence in the results obtained from the two social systems,
and finally because of a dawning realization that force on the
great scale simply must not be used in the nuclear age, it is
already clear that there will be no more 'wars of intervention'
such as the Western allies in the nineteen-twenties, and Hitler
in the nineteen-forties, waged against communism. Moreover
it is no longer true that the ruling circles of the major capitalist
societies will go to any lengths—though they will go quite a
long way!—to prevent the steady rise of the political influence,
and in the end power, of the wage-earning majority. Thus the
necessity of intolerance is disappearing at the same time as the
use of violence is becoming unacceptably dangerous.

All this gives us a legitimate expectation that the great
schism will be transcended—if only we give ourselves time.
There is nothing left in either the communist or the anti-
communist crusades which would remotely justify nuclear war.
That does not mean that we can allow those who still suppose

that there is to trample on us. But it does mean that the world can find its pacification while still divided as to the way in which it organizes its economic life.

The Unity of the Contemporary World

If the great schism is no longer a decisive obstacle, how importunate become the forces driving us towards the pacification of the world! It is not only, nor even primarily perhaps, a question of the negative force of our fear of nuclear war. That will not be enough. There must also be a sustained growth of loyalty to the world society or civilization which is coming into being. There is nothing unprecedented in men coming to feel an intense love for their civilization, even while it is still rent by the wars of its contending states. We have all felt the agony of the damage to European civilization done by the two wars in which we, nevertheless, had to engage. It may already be possible for some men to feel that their primary allegiance is to the nascent world society and its civilization. It will be no good, of course if they merely feel that they *ought* to feel like this. But is not a genuine and spontaneous world-feeling becoming a natural response to the age in which we live? Is it not legitimate to believe that more and more people will come to feel that what mankind has already achieved, with its staggering diversity of expression and its staggering convergence of aspiration—that all the art, the science, the music, the religion of all the world—really is theirs, to be saved from destruction? The human achievement with which the world is already freighted is so immense—though perhaps so small compared to what man may yet achieve—that the mind reels at the thought of the destruction, not so much of the particular stones or canvases or books or scores in which these achievements are recorded, as of the species which has proved capable of such creation.

For these reasons it is difficult to feel much sympathy for those who object to proposals for the pacification of the world on the grounds that it would produce a dull uniformity repugnant to free spirits. I do not pretend to know whether a world at peace would be dull. I should have thought that a kind of elementary world authority, with its functions perforce confined to the prevention of full-scale nuclear war, would leave plenty of variety, of experiment, of difference—even of disorder—in the world. And then again would the alternative, which is a radio-active poison-desert, enduring for the next 10,000 years (see Mr Kahn's estimate, p. 15 above) be conducive to gay variety? Would the brutalized, malformed, desperate, struggling survivors of the rounds of nuclear warfare be superior to men who had acknowledged that they must give up *some* degree of national freedom for the sake of peace? And these really are the alternatives. Not even the most dedicated pacifist can perhaps envisage the full consequences of a series of nuclear wars. In the same way none of us can *feel*, however much we can convince ourselves of it intellectually, that such a catastrophe is the predictable alternative to a measure of world unification during the coming decades. But yet it is. It is this lag in our imaginative powers which makes it only too possible that nothing but the shock of extreme peril—or even, though heaven forbid it, of some degree of actual nuclear catastrophe— will drive mankind to save itself.

All this is not to deny that even a modest degree of world unification like everything else has a price. It is true that the historical evidence indicates that the most creative periods of past civilizations, in this or that 'known world', have been during their 'periods of contending states', before their unification under an *imperium*. Why this has been so is a matter of opinion. It may be that the relative sterility of the imperial periods has been the result of the terrible battering to which the civilizations in question were subjected during the process of their pacification by knock-out tournament. If that were the way in which world unification were to be achieved, then no one would deny that the resultant world empire (in the unlikely event of there being enough effective power left anywhere to establish it) would be brutal and sterile in the extreme. Whether a limited unification achieved, partly at least by agreement, need have oppressive and sterilizing consequences is another question. The fact must be faced that it might. To the degree that it did, that would be the price that would have to be paid for the prevention of recurrent nuclear war. We seldom get anything for nothing in this world.

What Is To Be Done?

It may be asked: what should we all *do* in order to prevent the destruction of human civilizations in nuclear war?

First of all, let us get a grasp of the nature of the problem. We are all helpless till we do that.

Second, let us not despise on any account the short term, staving-off, measures on behalf of the stability of the balance discussed in Part One of this book; for without them we stand precious little chance of surviving long enough to do anything else. In particular do not let us disdain the military issues, such as the invulnerability of the deterrents, or the true role of conventional forces, as too wicked or at least too unpleasant, for the attention of idealists: for unless we do attend to such things idealists and militarists will mix their particles in one fall-out.

Third, let us pay the most careful and detailed attention to every measure of mutual disarmament, and of *détente*, between the communist and Western worlds which is being discussed. Let us distinguish, in the light of the record, between those measures which are, perhaps inevitably, being put forward by both sides as move and countermove in the game of political warfare, and those measures, such as the I.A.D.A. proposal, the Test Ban Treaty, or, in the coming negotiations perhaps, the 'cut-off' of nuclear production, which are being seriously discussed with a view to their possible implementation.

Fourth, let us notice that all disarmament proposals involve more or less strict measures of international inspection and control, and that this in turn involves an inspector and controller: and that it is just on this issue that all these 'serious' proposals have so far foundered. For when it came to the point it was found impossible to get the existing super-powers to surrender sufficient authority over themselves to any body which they did not control. Disarmament without unification has proved impossible.

We shall conclude then that the view that United Nations is, in one sense, the true hope of the world is right enough. The United Nations, even as it exists, is an invaluable arena in which the jostling nation-states can plead their cases; in which, in particular, the weak can force a hearing out of the strong; and it has even proved surprisingly capable of handling secondary issues. For all these reasons its authority must be passionately upheld, even when—indeed *especially* when—it conflicts with the interests, or prejudices, of the Government of our own nation-state. Yet the United Nations is today an islet of internationalism in a world of sovereign states existing in a state of nature. As such it is something quite different from the sought-for authority which could permanently avert nuclear war. How can a genuine world authority even begin to grow up within it? How can this deadlock be resolved?

No one can prove that it *can* be resolved. However, it seems rash loudly and proudly to proclaim that the position is hopeless and to deride all those who even seek a remedy as woolly idealists. Of course the human situation is today more desperate than ever before: it does not require much perspicacity to see that. Nevertheless, it would be a poor spirit that gave up at this stage when, after all, no major nuclear catastrophe has yet occurred. If there is a way out it must lie in the evolution of an authority capable of preventing the waging of nuclear war and based upon the continued power of the nuclear super-powers existing at the time. And surely far the most likely 'growth point' out of which such an authority might evolve would be the joint resolve of the existing super-powers to see to it that no one else but themselves ever acquires a nuclear capability?

Therefore, we should push and press to the utmost along this line of the stabilization of the collective nuclear monopoly of the existing super-powers (be they two or several). For out of such a stabilized hegemony we can imagine the evolution of a world authority capable of keeping the peace. There are solid

forces making in that direction. Moreover, this goal of unifica-
tion-under-authority, rather than the more familiar goal of 'a
totally disarmed world of totally sovereign states', is alone free
from inner self-contradiction. (No doubt those of a more purely
empirical temperament will feel no need of any long-term goal
or ideal: for them 'one step enough for me': no matter, we who
do feel this need to know where we are going can certainly
collaborate wholeheartedly with them, secure in our conviction
that every step of pacification which proves practical will, in
fact, lead in our direction.)

This is what we can 'do'. Some readers may be disappointed
that it is not suggested that we should found societies for this or
demonstrate for that. Let them be reassured. Occasions will
arise when it will be vitally important to exercise every possibility of pressure, by voting, by talking, by writing, by 'joining',
by demonstrating, for or against particular courses of action
on the part of the Governments of our respective nation-states.
(I have been doing that sort of thing all my life so I should be
the last man to denigrate its importance.) Only, none of this
kind of activity is likely to be useful or effective unless it is
founded upon a comprehension of what is at issue and of the
general direction in which a solution may be found.

After all, what is in question is nothing less than the progressive eradication from human society of one of its fundamental
characteristics, namely war. We should hardly be surprised
when the enterprise proves, on examination, to be immensely
complex, likely to occupy a whole historical epoch and not to
be accomplished, like, say, a change in the gaming laws, by
the promotion of a society dedicated to this particular purpose.
The evolution of a world authority is no patent cure-all for the
peril of the nuclear age: such an evolution is simply the one
way in which—now that the atoms are loose—the survival of
scientific man may become at least possible.

Peace Itself

It will be objected, by pacifists amongst others, that the main
proposals of this book are not proposals for the establishment of
genuine world peace at all.

In a sense that is so. The attitudes of mind and consequent policies herein proposed are designed to secure results which are in essence modest, conservative, prosaic and above all merely provisional. The above degree of world unification would be itself merely a stop-gap measure for the relatively short term. It is perfectly true that a nuclear world authority constituted on either of the two bases canvassed above would be unlikely to last for ever. There would be large elements of instability in it. Unless it was in the end succeeded by some much more complete form of world unity it would cease in time to serve its purpose. Upon what could such a more complete, and therefore stable, form of world unity be founded? Not clearly upon an *imperium* established by one of the nuclear super-powers; for such a knock-out tournament would still be excluded by the conditions of the nuclear age.

Permanent peace—peace itself—could be founded upon nothing else than a universal realization that our true motherland was now the terrestrial globe. Upon such a consciousness could be founded not merely a world-wide society, or civilization, such as is unmistakably coming into existence, but an actual world government. Then alone would it be possible for some central organization truly to represent the whole living generations of mankind—whatever were the mechanics of its evolution—and to invoke that indispensable devotion without which its writ could not run throughout the globe. Then there would be no problem to discuss. Men would give it their assent as readily, or sometimes as grudgingly perhaps, but in any case as effectively, as they give their assent today to the necessary apparatus of law and its enforcement within their own societies.

We are still far from such a situation. Passionate divergencies of class, nation, and race still divide mankind; they are only beginning to grow less. Hence the necessity for the two stop-gap proposals with which the first, and then the subsequent, parts of this book have been respectively concerned. Nevertheless, we must never lose sight of the goal of peace itself. To establish peace on earth men would have to change not only their basic political allegiances, but also to carry much further that slow, uncertain process of the civilization of their attitudes to their fellow-men which has, in spite of everything, been going on since first we became something a little more than our hominid ancestors. The poet Isaiah, in perhaps his greatest and best known passage, expressed the vision of peace itself: the vision of the Holy Mountain into which 'all nations shall flow'.

We must believe that one day our descendants will scale and possess the Holy Mountain of peace. For us it is too distant and too high. Yet we can see its peak. If we were to lose sight of it we should wander for ever in the wilderness.

Index